We the People
and
Our Freedom Charters

John K. Pitkethly, MA

EABooks Publishing
Your Partner In Publishing

ISBN: 978-1-963611-98-4
LCCN: 2025901796

Edited by Dan Brownell and Eric Tarmy

Cover design: Robin Black

Cover illustration: Dave O'Connell
www.soevad.com
https://www.behance.net/soevadcrea5ed9

Published by EA Books Publishing, a division of Living Parables of Central Florida, Inc. a 501c3
EABooksPublishing.com

This book is written for, and dedicated to,
my little buddy, my baby girl,
and to their entire generation of Americans
(*Gen Z/Homeland Generation,* born A.D. 2005–2024)
for whom it may serve to inform, inspire, and sustain.

"May the Lord bless you and keep you,
the Lord make his face shine on you,
and be gracious to you; the Lord
turn His face toward you and give you peace."
Numbers 6:24–26

"All these people were still living by faith when they died. They did not receive the things promised; they only saw them and welcomed them from a distance, admitting that they were foreigners and strangers on earth. People who say such things show that they are looking for a country of their own. If they had been thinking of the country they had left, they would have had the opportunity to return. Instead, they were longing for a better country— a heavenly one. Therefore, God is not ashamed to be called their God, for he has prepared a city for them."
Hebrews 11:13–16

Table of Contents

Introduction

Who are "We the People?" We come from every human inhabited terrain on earth. We represent every human language and culture in the world. We are members of a single nation, a nation of federated states exclusively founded on the belief that there is a Creator God, and this Creator has bestowed upon each of us certain natural rights. These rights do not exist based upon human works. They simply exist as a gift of "Nature and Nature's God." We are citizens of the United States of America.

July 4, 1776, was the first time in the history of humanity that a nation was founded on such principles and beliefs, and it was established in a document entitled, *The unanimous Declaration of the thirteen united States of America*. Today, it is simply referred to as the Declaration of Independence, and our nation is referred to as the United States of America, the United States, or simply America.

We declared independence from being British colonies but had to fight a war against the strongest empire on earth at the time, against every odd and likelihood. Our Declaration was profound, but we needed to use a document called the *Articles of Confederation* during the war with Great Britain to run our fledgling government. After the war ended, those articles proved unworkable and needed to be replaced with something more stable and sustainable.

There were great debates, but it was decided to return to the principles of the Declaration of Independence for inspiration and guidance. Our Declaration of Independence is arguably one of the most significant documents ever constructed by the human mind and stated much more than the American reasons for separation from England. It was a statement about the rights of the individual person and was far more profound than many of the founders of our country understood at the time.

Our founders understood history and how various systems of government have come and gone. They took this knowledge and created a constitutional republic with a written constitution that establishes the rule of law over the rule of individuals, organizations, societies, and governments.

With our justification for existence at the ready, our founders put together a group of representatives who worked out a United States Constitution and Bill of Rights to establish a newly structured society of representative government. These framers of the Constitution were brilliant in their construction of a basis for government that has endured almost 250 years.

Even so, there were already in existence many cultural problems that our new country inherited from colonization. A central problem was that only white, Anglo, Protestant males were recognized as having the inherent substance to be free with full constitutional rights and responsibilities. All others were seen as much less, ranging from subservient (women, children and ethnic minorities) to slaves (Native Africans and African Americans).

Over eighty years later, it took a civil war that claimed hundreds of thousands of lives and the destruction of countless properties and resources, to rectify one of many flaws inherited by our society. It has also taken many more years to fully realize the ideals of the American constitutional system, with an ongoing process to make it inclusive for all people within our borders, sharing in its protections.

These writings refer to the United States Declaration of Independence, U.S. Constitution, Bill of Rights, and subsequent amendments as our

Freedom Charters, and they belong to everyone. These documents were far more advanced than the people who forged them knew at the time. Only now in the twenty-first century after Christ, have we come to realize the full extent that our Freedom Charters have to offer.

While they have been instrumental in the justification, establishment, and continuation of the United States of America as a free and prosperous constitutional republic, their influence and impact has far more reaching consequences on the human condition, individually, collectively, and globally. This is due to their unique significance in elevating the rights and powers of the individual person while limiting the powers of government entities.

Since 1945, the United States has been a world superpower with a global effect, and while its creation only dates to 1776, its development can be traced much further back in time to the beginnings of human civilization. This connection with the past is rarely recognized but it is essential to fully understand the immense undertaking that was, is, and will be required for its present existence and future preservation.

Today, the United States of America is considered a distinctly modern, Western nation geographically and culturally but, in reality, is much more complicated. This single nation of separate states is pieced together from thousands of years of human experience in countless societies throughout human history. Understanding the efforts and intents that have produced this extraordinary country is also instrumental to its current greatness and future success.

To fully appreciate the founding philosophy and internal workings of our Freedom Charters, one must understand their original source, fundamental premises, and systematic processes. Most essential is the belief that people possess inherent natural rights, and these rights are not derived from other human beings or government entities, but from a conscious creator of nature and humanity.

For the previous two millennia, Western civilization has conceptualized nature's God as the God of Abraham, known in Judaism as *The LORD God*, in Christianity as *God the Father*, and in Islam as *The God*. The God of Abraham is the "first sovereign" and the architect of eternal and divine laws. These laws give substance to the laws of nature, natural law, which in turn should be emulated by human-made laws, human law. Following this model, human law should be specifically designed to safeguard the inherent rights of people through an established system of legal protections and due process.

While the laws of nature are inherent from creation, natural laws alone do not grant human beings the best chance for self-preservation (life), self-determination (liberty), and the pursuit of one's desires (happiness). Therefore, the establishment and enforcement of a system of human laws, applied equally through a system of due process, becomes essential.

Decisions made by "We the People," an informed citizenry, must be responsible for the direction of our cities/townships, counties/parishes, states, and country. Collectively, we sovereign individuals form a popular sovereign entity, American society, and consolidate into sovereign legal entities such as private and public organizations. We decide who will lead certain aspects of our sovereign governing entities through a series of free and transparent elections.

Another premise of our Freedom Charters is that human beings are created with free will. Free will is the power to think and act independently of fate, destiny, and the will of others. Humans specifically possess rational minds, and the ability to reason. Each human being also has a duty to use reason to make independent choices that respect the general life, liberty, and happiness of themselves and others.

Free will is fundamental for our informed people to follow their conscience and is essential for the most basic natural right, self-preservation. From this starting point, free will and the desire for self-preservation control many human actions and inactions, as self-determination blooms in the process of making personal choices for the pursuit of one's desires.

Natural rights also provide every person with personal responsibilities to themselves and to others because, as choices are presented and decided upon, those actions produce consequences, positive and/or negative. Consequences can be immediate or occur over time, but these consequences can affect the life, liberty, and pursuit of happiness of the decision maker and others. Therefore, every American has some level of personal responsibility to themselves, their community, society, their state, and the nation.

Furthermore, having been created in God's image, every individual person can exercise his or her free will as an individual sovereign. While the concept of sovereignty is ancient and historically rooted in religion or a political/social class of people, our Freedom Charters are the first documents to illustrate that sovereignty begins with our Creator God and is gifted to each individual person through nature. So, unlike other societies in history, individual Americans have a right to individual freedoms, which are rooted in being children of our Creator God and citizens of the constitutional republic created by our Freedom Charters. They are not granted, limited, or owed by a birth status, such as servant or subject from a lord, king, pope, or other potentate.

While individual sovereignty is vital to these American ideals, other sovereign entities provide a counterbalance to abuses that can be perpetrated by the individual person. These entities are private and public organizations, society at large, and government entities, each of which has certain rights and responsibilities addressed in our Freedom Charters and work as balances and counterbalances to each other. If any of the four fall out of balance, abuses and crimes against the other(s) can occur. Because human experience has demonstrated that this is a likely occurrence and extremely undesirable, our Freedom Charters assign certain rights, responsibilities, and limits to all entities.

This means there must also be great care toward the inherent rights of individuals, private and public organizations, society, and government entities if human laws are going to promote justice and provide all entities with a humane and prosperous environment in which to exist and thrive.

⟞⟝

Civilization can be defined in various ways; thus, I will not attempt to impose my own views here. That said, there is one thing that I believe serves as the dividing line between civilized and uncivilized living. That line is not physical, but psychological and behavioral.

First is an awareness of oneself, one's own dignity, and one's own behaviors, which are not solely based on instinct. Second is a general awareness, concern, and respect for the dignity and well-being of others. Anyone can live in civilization, but civilized living is somewhat different. Civilized living has less to do with physical lifestyle and much more to do with how we view and treat ourselves and each other.

Currently on earth, only human beings can create civilization. A cat, for instance, cannot create civilization because it lacks the mental capacity to separate itself from the natural world. Humans keep domesticated cats as pets but, without humans, a cat would simply return to living in the wild.

Domesticated animals like dogs, cats, chickens, pigs, cows, horses, camels, etc., think and behave exactly like their ancestors and there is nothing that can be done to change that reality in their current state. Put simply, they just exist. These animals are born, grow, reproduce, and die, while not advancing beyond that reality.

Humans are different from every other animal on earth. We have the capacity to remove ourselves from the natural order both mentally and physically. Humans use our primary skills and imagination to develop our inherited resources to make progress.

Humans are not bound by simple instincts. We have the ability to reason and choose whether to follow our instincts or use imagination to create new options. This is the core of free will in humanity. Free will allows us to use our imagination and all mental capabilities to remove ourselves from the natural world. This creates an abstract and physically artificial world based on our own vision and will.

Through human reasoning, our thoughts can turn into ideas, and ideas into actions. Our physical bodies are extremely well endowed to turn our mental and emotional desires into physical realities, and with these special gifts, humans can create and maintain the physical and abstract elements of civilization.

Part I

CHAPTER 1

Prehistoric and Ancient Times (The Far and Near East)

Before civilization, humans were engaged in basic survival. The acquisition of fresh water and food, as well as protection from the elements and other organisms was most imperative. Early people were too susceptible to the biological dangers of dehydration, starvation, injury, infection, and disease, as well as the environmental dangers of drought, famine, fires, floods, predators, and infestations.

Humanity had no user manual for civilization. People simply learned through successes and failures. While success might have helped them survive and progress for a year or so, failure was often costly and even fatal. Humans learned through trial and error but began making greater progress by making physical and intellectual adaptations to their lives and lifestyles, as well as teaching developed ideas and skills to their offspring.

Before written languages, people could only pass on learned information through art, physical demonstration, and/or oral communication. This means that we do not know the specific thoughts, attitudes, and beliefs of people who lived in prehistory, and we can only speculate about those thoughts, personalities, and cultures from artifacts they have left behind.

Even so, I cannot help but believe that these people had individual desires, and whether expressed or not, must have been aware that there were things they liked and disliked, with the innate free will to act based upon their own sensibilities and from the choices available.

Humans may have created civilization, but they were not free in the modern sense, mainly because humans have an instinctual order that usually begins with a dominant person, a leader who uses persuasion or force to impose their will on others. Enforcers are allies of the leader who recognize the dominant person as leader. The leader then projects his will in a convincing manner through persuasion, force, or threat of force with their allies at the ready to assist.

This exists at every level from family and friendship circles to tribal hierarchies and intertribal levels. Leaders and enforcers of prehistoric societies certainly noticed their own wills and the ability to impose them onto others.

Leaders and enforcers are important to understand because these people establish the basis and environment in which individual free will is exercised. Like furnishing a home, our expressions of free will are limited by the foundation and framing of the structure in which we occupy, and the foundation and framing of societies, for better or worse, are determined by leaders and their enforcers and followers/supporters.

Our Freedom Charters establish how leaders are chosen or appointed. They also establish legal limits on those leaders and the enforcers to eliminate arbitrary rule. Laws, not whimsical decisions, are the final authorities in our constitutional structure. Rights, responsibilities, and limits established by law for the individual, organizations, the population, and government entities are the foundation of the American republic and the keys to its genius, but what are they exactly, and where do they come from?

———

Settled living likely occurred because it was more comfortable and secure than wandering with the migrating herds and the seasons. Permanent shelters meant greater protection from the elements, predators, and other humans. Early attempts at settled living required certain necessities, two of which required construction or modification of the land for food, housing, and defense and second, access to fresh water and grazing land. Hunting and gathering likely continued at some level, but for a settlement to be self-sustaining, food needed to be somewhat reliable.

While some early settlements were certainly successful and long-lasting, many more were likely shorter lived for various reasons, such as poor terrain, harsh or changing climate, limited access to food and fresh water, as well as other groups of humans who might have migrated into their territory and incorporated or subjugated them.

Societies that dotted the Nile, Euphrates, Tigris, Indus, and the Yalu Rivers were some of the earliest settlements that had long-lasting effects on human civilization and culture. For our purposes, the early permanent settlements on the Indus River are the most important, as the belief structures that were created in prehistory are still with us today in the tenets of Hinduism.

Hinduism is the oldest human religion. It has no original written foundation and can be divided into many sects. The Hindu belief systems were later documented in writings collectively called "The Vedas" and the book "Bhagavad Gita." Hindu people believe in reincarnation of the spirit into physical bodies, and that each person makes choices that are "good" or "bad," determining the individual state of following lives.

The greatest aspects and advancement of free will in Hinduism were the concepts of responsibility and consequences. A person was free to make choices based upon his or her assigned duties in life, and they would receive just rewards/punishments because of the choices made.

Although ancient Hindu people valued free will, they were still subject to the traditional expectations of family members, neighbors, and tribal officials. The social strata were very rigid compared to today, and their spirituality was much more entrenched in mysticism. Thus, the modern concept of free will and personal freedom was still very far ahead in humanity's future.

One universal belief throughout Hinduism is the concepts of Dharma and Karma. Dharma are the duties one has in this life, i.e., responsibility. Karma is the far-reaching sum of the person's choices, which reflects his or her behaviors from past lives, i.e., consequences. Each person in society had the responsibility to fulfill their role in that society, which was not determined by them and not always aligned with their own benefit. Even so, they had the free will to choose their own path along with the consequences those paths provided over several lifetimes.

Hinduism eventually spread its influence out of what we now call India into other settled areas, primarily east into what would become China and northwest into what would become Persia and Mesopotamia. Mesopotamian and Persian religions also benefited from contact with Hinduism and developed their own concepts of civilization and free will.

Even so, many of these ancient religions held the idea that our destinies were predetermined by a fate outside of our control. Interpretations of these fates could range from observing the formation of bird flocks, to the positions of celestial objects, to the health of organs in sacrificed animals. Most religions at the time taught that people were created to be slaves of various gods, and human lives were nothing more than pawns to be manipulated for the personal political games of these divine beings.

⚊⚉⚊

As civilized societies became more successful and prosperous with the domestication of crops and animals, something new occurred: surplus. Surplus is the act of creating and having more than what is required to survive. As these surpluses grew and became more bountiful, certain challenges arose, two of which were storage and ownership.

Storage occurred through the construction of sturdy buildings, furnishings, or subterranean catacombs, and through the watchful eyes of armed and unarmed guards. The question of ownership was answered with humanity's next great invention: writing. Writing was first invented to establish ownership, count inventories, and record business transactions. Tiny wedge shapes on clay tablets began in Mesopotamia, the land between the Tigris and Euphrates Rivers.

At first, these wedge shapes were pictures, but later evolved into symbols called cuneiform, which represented a concept or object. An important aspect of human imagination is symbolism. Symbolism is important in writing, and of the human mind and culture in general. Symbols inform but also motivate and inspire people.

The invention of writing also changed the way humans organized societies. Societal planning became more sophisticated, and the specialization of skills became more pronounced. Construction, pottery, weaving, art, farming, and ranching became the sole work of certain individuals and their families who excelled in these areas, and written symbols became the identifying marks of objects and for ownership.

Societal administration also grew as organizations became more complex. One reason for this was the development of large-scale pasturing of grazing animals, fishing, forestry, and mining practices. As humans began to use the natural environment and resources in new and innovative ways, these human- and animal-powered industries projected human civilization to entirely new levels of sophistication and intricacy.

While the Mesopotamian societies (Sumerian, Akkadian, Assyrian, Babylonian) were not the only civilizations to invent writing, the structure and form of their early writings were of the utmost importance to human civilization in the long term. Mesopotamian writings not only established an early alphabet, but also established a base ten and a base six number system, which was essential for the tracking of time through the sundial (clocks) and planting and harvesting seasons (calendars).

Mesopotamian literature also had an impact on the human understanding of civilized living. Histories and stories, which had been transmitted through oral traditions, were tangibly recorded so they could be preserved for persons living in other areas and in future times. One of the most insightful works of Mesopotamian literature was a story entitled *The Epic of Gilgamesh*. This story suggested and pronounced the continuation of civilization itself as the key to "human immortality."

The Mesopotamian system of writing was so successful that other settlements around the Fertile Crescent started using this method when it was brought to them through trade. Trade occurs when people and organizations exchange certain surpluses for other things they lack. With trade came even more surplus and diversity in goods, which led to writing becoming ever more important and sophisticated.

16

It also was discovered in those early settlements that individual free will is a double-edged sword. While free will was essential in the creation and enhancement of civilization, it also can pose a threat to it. Unbridled free will means that if someone want something, he can take it regardless of to whom it belongs, usually by intimidation, deception, or force. While each person is endowed with free will, the dynamic interactions between these individual wills create a dilemma for civilization. Societies cannot sustain themselves if people are simply behaving by any means desired; so there needed to be the establishment of written laws along with the means to enforce them.

Laws needed to be established to settle disputes and to protect lives, properties, families, and resources. It is important to mention, however, that laws in ancient times were more like what we call "principles" today. Ancient law codes set the ideals of what the laws were meant to achieve; they were not the steadfast statutes that we experience through governmental approval today. Ancient laws set the viewpoints and the expectations that the leaders of societies wanted to achieve.

Chaos occurred often in ancient Mesopotamia, so order became the primary concern of the leaders and enforcers as communities became larger and more prosperous. For this to be accomplished on larger scales, systems of administration needed to be established.

Administrative systems were established to effectively manage the enforcement of laws and the will of the leaders. As societies grew, and the first cities were established, the administrative structures became so necessary that they became part of the self-preservation of the society itself.

Thus, government systems with established law enforcement and militaries became necessary entities unto themselves for the sustainability of civilized society.

Leaders, enforcers, and administrators formed large organizations called bureaucracies that are necessary for administrating laws that the people must follow and for providing public services that people might require and may not be able to obtain by themselves. Laws also needed to be enforceable so people felt intimidated and protected by them, while the leaders, enforcers, and administrators worked to preserve society through "justice" as well as secure their places of authority by fulfilling the will of their gods.

<hr/>

Ancient founders and framers developed various solutions for securing their authority, two of which were brute force and the concept of sovereignty. Brute force is physical, and the final authority to enforce any situation, and the enforcers of these laws would deliver with superior might through the backing of police and military entities. Once the leaders demonstrated their ability and willingness to use force, usually against other aspiring leaders and their families, they usually did not often need to use violence again for some time. Leaders required the loyalty of the enforcers to intimidate or inflict violence on others who might or did challenge their authority, while administrators managed the necessary bureaucracy that kept the enforcers supplied, sustained, and in place.

Sovereignty is psychological, and essentially the perceived rightfulness of power and authority. Sovereignty is a necessary perception for most in society to support and sustain the integrity and components of the government entities and structures. People will not follow those they do not deem to be rightfully in charge, or they will follow reluctantly, as they do not want to be targeted by the leaders, enforcers, or administrators for persecution. Convincing others that one was superior and worthy to be in charge became a psychological and sociological construct, which shaped the nature of ancient human societies and continues in various forms to this day.

Although easier to wield, brute force requires much effort, can be very costly on surpluses, and breeds resentment in people. So, leaders also invented a concept called divine sovereignty. Divine sovereignty was the idea that the laws and lawmakers were favored by the gods. The power and peaceful existence of the leadership often relied upon the belief by the populace that the administrative state was supported by a divine origin.

The Mesopotamian religion established why the leaders, enforcers, and administrators were ordained with sacred missions. The leaders presented themselves as servants of the gods by "establishing justice" among the population through the creation and enforcement of their laws. Finally, it also was discovered that these written languages could be much more useful than just establishing ownership and sacred laws. Written words themselves could in fact be seen as divine and sacred.

⚜

Laws and the threat of force were always available to the leaders to protect everything within Mesopotamian societies, but laws themselves are also a double-edged sword when it comes to human freedom. While the administrative state was needed to protect the society from foreign invaders and domestic strife, they may not have always been seen that way by the populace, who could resent the perceived over-stepping of laws and authority. Especially when the populace were expected to yield portions of their free will and limited freedoms, while paying for it with their hard-earned surplus.

Leaders needed to take surpluses to maintain their administrative states, but people were not always willing to give up what they had worked for and owned. Thus, the will of the leaders and that of the people became a point of possible contention.

Laws were established not only to protect people from each other, but also to protect and sustain the administrative state. Part of this concept was the enforceable collections of taxes. Taxes can take on various forms, but until money had been invented, taxes were paid directly from surplus. This, of course, was a problem when the surplus was small or nonexistent.

━━⊶⊷━━

In addition to the contributions made by the societies in the Mesopotamian regions, the Lydians and the Phoenicians were two later civilizations that existed in the western part of the Near East, now modern Turkey, Syria, and Lebanon.

In Lydia, a system of weights and measures was developed that standardized the value of metals. They also invented retail sales and coinage to improve the ease and continuity of transactions. Their invention of money was a pivotal point in human history. Instead of a barter system, an established financial system standardized the prices of goods and labor.

An important aspect here is the market value of money and labor. Money is essentially quantified labor that can be carried or stored for later use. Money can be used to acquire almost anything labor can produce and is the primary tool for the utilization of one's free will in almost every human society. That is why money has been one of the single greatest motivators of people in all of human history and continues to be acquired for the prestige and power of individuals, organizations, societies, and governments throughout the world.

Due to the importance and scarcity of certain skills, the value of work can be generally determined by an abstract entity called the market or market demand. Money can then be exchanged for various forms of labor at market prices. Unfortunately, markets can also be artificially manipulated; therefore, a system of written commercial laws must also be established to regulate commerce and reduce fraud, embezzlement, bribes/payoffs, and other deviant behaviors that usually cheat people, organizations, and governments of what they are supposedly due.

Furthermore, money is not the final goal of attainment. It's what money can buy. It buys control. For scrupulous people, it can buy more control over one's life, and for unscrupulous people, it can buy more control over the lives of others. This kind of control is ultimately an illusion because there are many things in life that money cannot buy, but with more money comes more control over one's own will. Compared to those who don't have money, this control appears very real. This makes the basic existence of governmental laws and regulations for people and property essential.

The Phoenicians were great mariners who established colonies and trade across the Mediterranean Sea. The Phoenicians invented an alphabet that was later adapted by the Greeks, whose writings became the intellectual standard for thousands of years.

Trade became a vast and intercontinental system crossing many territories and cultures, and in turn helped to reshape all of them. The trade of the Phoenicians was important for its establishment of the Mediterranean Sea basin as a central powerhouse of developing colonial societies and eventual great empires over the next several thousand years.

Finally, both the Lydians and Phoenicians were instrumental in shaping the developing ancient world through their very practical technologies, which had been borrowed and shared with and by other societies. Thus, these often-ignored societies were a significant influence on the developing societies and growing civilization rising around the Mediterranean basin.

—◦—

One final ancient Mediterranean culture that is important to our Freedom Charters is the little-known Lycian Confederacy. Lycia was a confederacy of city-states in the southern part of Anatolia (modern Turkey.) First referenced in modern times by the French political philosopher Montesquieu and later studied as a viable option for a larger federal entity in republican style by James Madison, this ancient alliance of city-states had representation based upon population size and material contributions.

Our House of Representatives in Article I of the U.S. Constitution, an integral part of the American legislative branch was one form of representation adopted from the Lycians. Each state is given a certain number of representatives based on its population size.

—◦—

All these historical factors influenced civilization and, inevitably, our Freedom Charters because a very large aspect of a free society is economic prosperity. Without it, people become desperate for survival and will look to any person and any means for self-preservation. They will inevitably attempt to liberate themselves from the depths of economic despair or depression through extreme people using extreme measures. This makes economic prosperity a central component of stability and sustainability in a free society.

Private property rights also became a central tenet of our Freedom Charters due to its tangible ability to exercise and display the free will and sovereignty of the individual person. The more property a person possesses, the more they can use their own willpower to fulfill their needs, satisfy their desires, and affect their destiny.

With money, available choices become much broader and higher in sophistication and quality, and the more spending of money in a society, the greater the productivity to meet demands for goods and labor. Laws governing trade and the value of goods and labor are also addressed in our Freedom Charters, as government entities are charged with their taxation and regulation. The creation of money and regulating interstate and international trade is a power given to the American federal government in our constitutional system. Individual states also have the power to tax goods and labor but do not have the authority to print their own money.

The ability of government entities to tax income has been a particular point of contention in American society, since the original Constitution forbade it. While those changes came many years after the original framers were long gone, the paying of income taxes by the American population is often seen in a negative light and resented by many who labor for meager and not-so meager incomes.

—◦◦◦◦◦◦◦—

Work requires effort, and some efforts are less desirable than others. Slavery, the treatment of people as property, became a resulting system by many societies throughout the ancient world to defer the efforts and costs of harsh and difficult labor. With slaves, "free men" could afford to live comparatively comfortable lifestyles, but this comes at great costs. Ironically and hypocritically, our Freedom Charters did not immediately remove slavery as a legal institution. It protected it for many decades, and it was only after the costliest war in all American history that slavery was forbidden by our Freedom Charters through the Thirteenth Amendment to the U.S. Constitution.

Slavery damages societies, their economies, and their moral compasses. It's a dehumanizing and abhorrent system for the slaves, morally reprehensible for the slave owners, and causes severely restricted or nonexistent innovation and technological growth in society. Slaves have little motivation and ability to improve the techniques of labor, since their existence has been devalued to a miserable state of oppression and mere survival. Slave owners are not familiar enough or concerned with the intricacies the labor slaves endure, so finding more efficient and humane ways to perform that labor is not usually a priority, unless it is obvious and vastly improves output and profits.

The most horrific aspect of slavery is the suffering and impact it has on individuals and families. Loss of one's individual freedom and family through torture, death, or sale often becomes an overwhelming sorrow that breaks a person's will to live or to feel. Suicide and homicide become methods of escape for some people affected by slavery, which is a product of the numbing of their human senses and loss of hope. Death is often preferred to life when faced with a life of slavery.

General Douglas MacArthur once said that war is the "greatest sin of mankind," but I disagree. War is always horrific, but in the short- and long-term, slavery is far worse and more shameful than any other human failing.

These subjects and more are addressed specifically throughout our Freedom Charters beginning with the Declaration of Independence:

For cutting off our Trade with all parts of the world:

For imposing Taxes on us without our Consent: . . .
establish Commerce, and to do all other Acts and Things
which Independent States may of right do.

Our U.S. Constitution not only addresses some of these issues but also codifies them into law:

Representatives and direct Taxes shall be apportioned
among the several States which may be included within
this Union...

*All Bills for raising Revenue shall originate in the House
of Representatives; but the Senate may propose or concur with
Amendments as on other Bills...*

The Congress shall have Power To lay and collect Taxes, Duties, Imposts and Excises, to pay the Debts and provide for the common Defense and general Welfare of the United States; but all Duties, Imposts and Excises shall be uniform throughout the United States;

To borrow Money on the credit of the United States;

To regulate Commerce with foreign Nations, and among the several States, and with the Indian Tribes;

To establish a uniform Rule of Naturalization, and uniform Laws on the subject of Bankruptcies throughout the United States;

To coin Money, regulate the Value thereof, and of foreign Coin, and fix the Standard of Weights and Measures;

To provide for the Punishment of counterfeiting the Securities and current Coin of the United States;

No Capitation, or other direct, Tax shall be laid, unless in Proportion to the Census or enumeration herein before directed to be taken.

No Tax or Duty shall be laid on Articles exported from any State.

No Preference shall be given by any Regulation of Commerce or Revenue to the Ports of one State over those of another: nor shall Vessels bound to, or from, one State, be obliged to enter, clear, or pay Duties in another.

No Money shall be drawn from the Treasury, but in Consequence of Appropriations made by Law; and a regular Statement and Account of the Receipts and Expenditures of all public Money shall be published from time to time.

No State shall enter into any Treaty, Alliance, or Confederation; grant Letters of Marque and Reprisal; coin Money; emit Bills of Credit; make any Thing but gold and silver Coin a Tender in Payment of Debts; pass any Bill of Attainder, ex post facto Law, or Law impairing the Obligation of Contracts, or grant any Title of Nobility.

No State shall, without the Consent of the Congress, lay any Imposts or Duties on Imports or Exports, except what may be absolutely necessary for executing it's inspection Laws: and the net Produce of all Duties and Imposts, laid by any State on Imports or Exports, shall be for the Use of the Treasury of the United States; and all such Laws shall be subject to the Revision and Control of the Congress.

No State shall, without the Consent of Congress, lay any Duty of Tonnage, keep Troops, or Ships of War in time of Peace, enter into any Agreement or Compact with another State, or with a foreign Power, or engage in War, unless invaded, or in such imminent Danger as will not admit of delay.

No Person held to Service or Labor in one State, under the Laws thereof, escaping into another, shall, in Consequence of any Law or Regulation therein, be discharged from such Service or Labor, but shall be delivered up on Claim of the Party to whom such Service or Labor may be due . . . *[corrected by AMENDMENT XIII].*

Passed by Congress January 31, 1865. Ratified December 6, 1865.

Amendment XIII
Section 1.

Neither slavery nor involuntary servitude, except as a punishment for crime whereof the party shall have been duly convicted, shall exist within the United States, or any place subject to their jurisdiction.

Section 2.

Congress shall have power to enforce this article by appropriate legislation.

CHAPTER 2

Ancient Egypt

One of the oldest and better-known civilizations in human history is ancient Egypt. Egypt was important for its great accomplishments in agriculture, art, literature, construction, and religion. Egypt was also an extremely important producer and exporter of sorghum (wheat, corn to the Romans) and gold throughout the connected ancient world.

Aspects of free will in ancient Egypt are evident due to the enormous number of written texts we now call wisdom literature. People of ancient Egypt were taught to take personal responsibility for their actions from an early age, through adulthood and into old age. There are several cultural reasons for this special attention to good behavior from this first nation-state in history.

First is public order, but unlike civilizations along the Indus River and in Mesopotamia, Egypt became a unified nation much sooner. It was not simply a confederation of small villages sporadically occupying the banks of the Nile River. There was a broader central authority, and this presented a new dynamic between the people and their leaders.

Early societies settled as bands of people who had been tribes of hunters and gatherers for many thousands of years. They were tightly knit groups who relied upon each other for everything they had in life. These tribes settled into permanent homes, domesticated animals, and planted crops, but their worldview remained very tribal oriented. To a person who was born and grew up in a small locale, having never ventured far from home, it was almost impossible to conceptualize belonging to something as large as a nation-state.

Ancient Egyptians in their small villages knew each other intimately at almost every level, but people living tens or hundreds of miles away would not have been seen as belonging to the same society at all, in fact, they could have been seen as adversaries. So how could they all be seen as one people if they did not belong to the same tribe or even know each other personally? The concept of citizenship or even countrymen had very high barriers to overcome.

One way the ancient Egyptian leaders attempted to overcome this estrangement between people was to unify them through religion. This religion was based upon the mysteriousness and sacredness of the Egyptian gods. The strategy was to adopt certain god images that all people already knew or would accept. As this order was established, it took hold of the people's mindsets.

The Pharaohs (divine sovereigns of ancient Egypt), and their administrators (royal sovereigns), became the ultimate representatives of the gods and ruled by their desires and proclamations. Furthermore, established clergy would be recruited from local areas and would serve as the bridge between different villages, as well as the relationship to central authorities.

So how was this specific religion presented to the people? By studying the continuity of these ancient god images through the centuries, it is possible to see a common, very calm, yet powerful demeanor. Visually, the statues of the Egyptian gods demonstrate a divine order. This order was powerful, in control, reliable and stable. Ancient Egyptian artwork and god images presented strong, calm faces; and the benefits of Egyptian life and lifestyles were promoted to the people as being natural and good, with peace and plenty.

Without the ancient Egyptian administrative state and the Egyptian gods, people feared to suffer from natural disasters, raiders, starvation, disorder, and chaos. Ancient Egyptians saw themselves as blessed with security, surplus, serenity, and a sense of certainty. These were seen as gifts from the governmental and religious structures if the people continued to worship the Egyptian gods and follow the edicts of the Pharaohs and their administrators.

Most ancient Egyptian gods were believed to live in the cycles of agriculture. Ancient agrarian cultures were always on the edge of subsistence. One bad season and people died from starvation. These pre-mechanized societies did not have the benefits of modern scientific knowledge or technology. They did not have weather radar, refrigeration, pest control, antibiotics, machines, and other things that we in the modern world take for granted. Therefore, belief, worship, and obedience to the will of the gods and the Pharaohs were paramount to maintaining success and psychological sustainability of the society.

This vision of certainty, rooted in confidence, was essential for the ancient Egyptian civilization, and continued from that time forward in every other successful human civilization. Without it, people lose confidence and hope in their futures.

It's essential for every successful civilization to possess confidence and conviction in what they do; otherwise, the effort required to preserve and expand it appears futile and wasted. This is probably the most important lesson to the United States from ancient Egypt and all other great civilizations in human history, as a civilization cannot survive if the people who are charged with its preservation no longer believe in it.

Familiarity and family lines are extremely important in the minds of people throughout the world, and it was no different for American citizens who had only until recently been colonists in their now united states. Until the Industrial Revolution in the nineteenth century, technology was very limited and slow in bringing mass communication and a common national culture to the people of the new United States of America.

The difficulty of a local mindset among the citizenry was also present for the founders and framers of the American republic, as loyalty to one's state was often a priority over loyalty to the nation. Many Americans at that time saw themselves more as citizens of their state first and citizens of their nation second.

The founders and framers of the American republic also knew better than to have an established religion. Experiences with the Roman Catholic Church, the Protestant Reformation, and the continued branching of the Christian religion into various denominations and sects made a uniform religion unworkable and detrimental to freedom.

Instead, it was decided to simply adhere to the broader concept and faith in a single creator God that most American colonists recognized and understood. Utilizing the human value and dignity derived from our creator God, who formed human beings in His own image, the founders continued the processes begun many years earlier to state that natural rights exist as a gift from God and not from people or governments.

The founders and framers of the American system also understood the power of confidence and conviction. This confidence did not simply come from people believing in themselves. This is because people are fallible, weak, and suffer from vices. This new nation required the conviction of the people to put their faith in the God of Creation. This was essential to the nation's early success and future prosperity. Without God, a nation falls into a state of sin and debauchery, and like earlier civilizations, would disintegrate or be swallowed up by stronger forces.

―⁕―

The Declaration of Independence

When in the Course of human events, it becomes necessary for one people to dissolve the political bands which have connected them with another, and to assume among the powers of the earth, the separate and equal station to which the Laws of Nature and of Nature's God entitle them . . .

We hold these truths to be self-evident, that all men are created equal, that they are endowed by their Creator with certain unalienable Rights . . .

We, therefore, the Representatives of the united States of America, in General Congress, Assembled, appealing to the Supreme Judge of the world for the rectitude of our intentions…

The U.S. Constitution

. . . done in Convention by the Unanimous Consent of the States present the Seventeenth Day of September in the Year of our Lord one thousand seven hundred and Eighty seven …

Amendment I (ratified December 15, 1791)

Congress shall make no law respecting an establishment of religion, or prohibiting the free exercise thereof…

CHAPTER 3

Ancient Israel and Judaism

Just northeast of ancient Egypt was a collection of city-states in a land called Canaan (modern Israel). Canaanites were confederacies of tribes who had settled among the great lands of Egypt, Phoenicia, and Mesopotamia.

With all these influences, they developed a unique religious culture and worldview we call Judaism. Judaism teaches through scripture that the first man, Adam, was made by God the Creator from the dust of the ground. Later, God created a woman, Eve, by taking one of Adam's ribs. Both were occupants of a paradise called the Garden of Eden. This is unique in the ancient world because man and woman are made in the image of God, and like God, humans are self-aware creators with individual free will.

In Judaism, human free will is considered a gift from God, the creator of all things. It is what separates humans from animals, and it gives humans a responsibility that goes beyond our Earthly obligations. Free will in Judaism is not permission to do whatever is desired; rather, it is the power of individual choice. It is the power to freely choose to follow the will of God or not to follow the will of God—or how closely to follow.

God told Adam and Eve they may eat from any tree in the garden except from the Tree of Knowledge of Good and Evil. Adam and Eve chose not to follow the will of God and were forced to accept responsibility and consequences. Because Adam and Eve ate of the Tree of the Knowledge of Good and Evil, they stopped thinking like animals and started thinking like God. God then banished the couple from the garden, sentencing them to the toils of life on Earth.

—◁◁◁||()||▷▷▷—

The story of the Jews, followers of Judaism, begins in ancient Mesopotamia with a man named Abram. Abram was a poor shepherd. Scripture tells us that the Lord God spoke to him directly and commanded him to leave his home in Mesopotamia and venture through the land of Canaan and down into Egypt.

Abram could have refused to obeyed God's instructions, but instead he freely chose to follow. Each time God gave Abram new instructions, he obeyed and was more and more blessed by God. His faith and dedication to the will of God brought favor on him, and God changed his name to Abraham.

This God of Abraham became the God of the Jews, and His very specific and unique conceptualization remains with us today in the religions of modern Judaism, Christianity, and Islam, as well as "Nature's God," in our Freedom Charters.

—◁◁◁||()||▷▷▷—

When Canaan was attacked by northern tribes of invaders, some Canaanites must had fled into Egypt. When Egypt was attacked by the northern tribes, they had to repulse the invaders. Those tribes also settled in Canaan and became a civilization called the Philistines.

The Philistines settled along the coasts while the old Canaanite societies likely stayed in parts of Egypt and in the mountains of Canaan.

Many of these people were eventually called Israelites. Israelites were early Jews, who considered themselves a chosen people by God. People who were not Jewish were called Gentiles.

Jewish scripture states that the Prophet Joseph was taken to Egypt as a slave after members of his extended family attempted to murder him. Joseph was an interpreter of dreams, and when he impressed the reigning Pharaoh with his skill he was given important status in Egyptian society. Many Israelites fled to Egypt seeking Joseph to avoid famine in Canaan. While there, the Israelites prospered and multiplied, and their population grew to millions. To curb their numbers and secure their obedience, later Egyptian pharaohs had them enslaved.

Generations later, the Israelites were led out of Egypt, in an event called the Exodus, by the Prophet Moses. While in the desert, Moses went to the top of a mountain in Sinai where God gave him the Ten Commandments. These commandments are as follows:

1) "I am the Lord thy God, thou shalt not have any strange gods before Me,"
2) "Thou shalt not take the name of the Lord thy God in vain,"
3) "Remember to keep holy the Sabbath day,"
4) "Honor thy father and mother,"
5) "Thou shalt not kill,"
6) "Thou shalt not commit adultery,"
7) "Thou shalt not steal,"
8) "Thou shalt not bear false witness against thy neighbor,"
9) "Thou shalt not covet thy neighbor's wife,"
10) "Thou shalt not covet thy neighbor's goods."

The significance of these commandments would affect many future human societies. In Judaism, free will was not a simple choice for people to make in society. It became the choice to obey or disobey the will of God, the Creator. This line of thinking continued to affect the descendants of Abraham, who became known as the Children of Abraham, while impacting ancient, medieval, and modern civilizations more than any other statements of belief from ancient times.

Scripture also states that a prophet named Joshua led the Israelites into the land of Canaan, which had been promised to them by the God of Abraham. The Israelites then conquered many Canaanite cities. They established themselves in what scripture describes as the "land of milk and honey" with the city of Jerusalem as their capital. They also built their temple in Jerusalem through the leadership of a framer and royal sovereign named King Solomon, who was the son of King David.

It is important to note here that the sovereigns of ancient Israel were not seen as divine. Divinity was solely reserved for the one God of Abraham. The Lord God of ancient Israel was very different from the gods of the other ancient religions.

For centuries, Canaan, Jerusalem, and the Temple of Solomon would be the home of the Jewish people and the center of Judaism, ensuring their survival and prosperity if they freely chose to follow the will of God. This agreement to follow the will of God and, in turn, prosper is referred to as the Holy Covenant. The Holy Covenant is described in ancient scrolls called the Torah. The Torah is a guidebook revealing the mind of the God of Abraham, and it is considered holy and sacred to this day.

What is important for these writings is Abraham's God. Despite all the variations of the concept of God/gods throughout civilization, no religion has had such a lasting and profound impact on human perceptions of divinity as Judaism. This Jewish concept of God has shaped the minds and sensibilities of people throughout the ancient, medieval, and modern worlds.

There are many factors that made Judaism unique in the ancient world. First, was the radically new concept of a God who is one loving father. Most ancient religions were polytheistic (many gods), and their gods were very different in almost every aspect. The pagan gods, as we call them today, did not love humanity as many creation myths taught that humans were created as slaves. These gods engaged in intrigue and deception, opportunism, rape, and murder. They were extremely political and could destroy people and societies on a whim.

Judaism is monotheistic because the God of Abraham is one God, and He is not seen as our master, but our father, and He created us in His own image. This elevates humanity to universal importance. The God of Abraham does not operate on whims, but on laws that reflect His character. The Holy Covenant is a legal agreement between God and humans. Under the Holy Covenant, God rewards those who honor and follow his divine laws with prosperity and protection.

The God of Abraham also exists outside of linear time. For He not only travels with us throughout existence, as Creator of the Universe, He also exists outside of physical existence. He is not hostage to linear time and sees all things from a position of absolute truth. He knows the past, present and future because He is everywhere within and outside this Universe — the Universe He lovingly created. Ultimate truth is known to Him alone because He is the ultimate truth.

The concepts and worshiping of pagan gods were much different. The gods and people lived under the constraints of linear time and operated under arbitrary rules. The pagan god images were numerous and in every form. Statues of people, animals, hybrids, rocks, fire, and other things made up the pagan god images.

The God of Abraham was completely abstract with no images at all. The Jews considered it a great crime to create an image of a god figure or "the God" figure. Even Jewish art was very careful to avoid images of real objects, animals, or people.

Found in the Torah are the Holy Laws. Most people have heard of the Ten Commandments, but there were over six hundred commandments that regulated all kinds of behavior. Everything from worship in the temple to eating habits to circumcision were regulated by the Holy Laws of Moses. It was, and still is, believed that by keeping to the Holy Laws of Moses, God would keep to His promises of security, peace, and prosperity for the Children of Abraham.

The Holy Covenant in Judaism is paramount. It is the lifeline of blessings from God the Creator. Although life continues to be hard, due to the mistakes of Adam and Eve, the Holy Covenant proclaims that by keeping to God's instructions, Jews and the holy state of Israel will stand against all forces that attempt to destroy it.

Some influences ancient Judaism had on our Freedom Charters and the American republic are:

- There is one creator God (monotheism),
- He is a loving God,
- God is our Father,
- God is a lawgiver,
- Free will is choosing to follow, or not to follow, the will of God,
- God the Creator is an infinite, omniscient, omnipresent, and immaterial and not confined to a finite, physical existence,

- God ordains certain lands to people, and
- Through obedience to the Lord God any person can be blessed no matter his or her status in this world.

Believers trust they can benefit from the Holy Covenant as individuals, families, tribes, towns, cities, and nations, and this perception is very much with us today. Judaism also granted civilization a fervent dedication to religious study as a part of scholarship and was significantly influenced by intellectual concepts in the Egyptian and Mesopotamian cultures, from their concept of laws and lawgivers to the belief in a strong, stable, spiritual force that protects individuals, societies, and civilizations from chaos and destruction.

The founders and framers of the American republic also were very much influenced by the writings of these ancient peoples. A primary tenet of Judaism and the American system is the power of law. All just laws are derived from the first sovereign, God. Then through the establishment and enforcement of a civil administration consented by the popular sovereign, "We the People," justice becomes possible. People are corrupt, however, and behave in ways that are self-serving. Proper laws established by a legitimate governing body, under God, serves everyone.

———

While ancient Israel believed that God dictated His Holy Laws to Moses, the framers of the American constitutional system also believed that God created natural law and that human laws should be modeled after those examples. Human laws should not be dictated but derived through an equitable system of due process from leaders who are representatives of the people and empowered by their consent. These leaders might be elected or appointed by elected officials, but all are held to uniform standards established by our Freedom Charters and by law.

Many Americans have seen America as an emulator of ancient Israel, following in a similar cadence and rhythm. While the God of Abraham protected and rewarded the children of Israel if they followed His will, this same God would bless America as long as "We the People," remain faithful to Him and the American constitutional system. This is directly related to the idea that "We the People" have a covenant with our creator God just as ancient Israel did and, therefore, we are protected by divine providence.

There is nothing more important from ancient Israel than the belief in the creator God, the God of Abraham. Western civilization had been saturated by beliefs in the God of Abraham through their experiences with western Christianity, and whether the individual founders and framers were practicing Christians or not, their culture and worldviews had been dominated by the God of Abraham in western societies for over 1,500 years.

━━⊷⊶━━

Religion, faith, and God are very different things. Religions are organizations administered by fallible people. A person's faith is the individual relationship one has with their Creator. God is the Creator, a universal consciousness that is beyond any human ability to fully understand. Humans can only conceptualize God, but any conceptualization is flawed because human beings are not capable of knowing God in His infinite form. What we know comes from the prophets and scripture.

This is also why God is mentioned so often through American writings and referenced in its symbolism. God, as the creator of humanity and our natural rights, does have a place at every level of American society, from the individual to organizations to the population to government entities. Religions are free to exist, and people are free to worship, but religion in American society is separate from the government, and the establishment of a state religion is strictly forbidden by our Freedom Charters.

⤛⟁⟁⤜

Benjamin Franklin, The Constitutional Convention, 28 June 1787

Mr. President:

The small progress we have made after 4 or 5 weeks close attendance & continual reasonings with each other—our different sentiments on almost every question, several of the last producing as many noes as ays, is methinks a melancholy proof of the imperfection of the Human Understanding. We indeed seem to feel our own want of political wisdom, since we have been running about in search of it. We have gone back to ancient history for models of government, and examined the different forms of those Republics which having been formed with the seeds of their own dissolution now no longer exist. And we have viewed Modern States all round Europe, but find none of their Constitutions suitable to our circumstances.

In this situation of this Assembly groping as it were in the dark to find political truth, and scarce able to distinguish it when presented to us, how has it happened, Sir, that we have not hitherto once thought of humbly applying to the Father of lights to illuminate our understandings? In the beginning of the contest with G. Britain, when we were sensible of danger we had daily prayer in this room for the Divine Protection. —Our prayers, Sir, were heard, and they were graciously answered. All of us who were engaged in the struggle must have observed frequent instances of a Superintending providence in our favor. To that kind providence we owe this happy opportunity of consulting in peace on the means of establishing our future national felicity. And have we now forgotten that powerful friend? Or do we imagine that we no longer need His assistance.

I have lived, Sir, a long time and the longer I live, the more convincing proofs I see of this truth—that _God governs in the affairs of men._ And if a sparrow cannot fall to the ground without [H]is notice, is it probable that an empire can rise without [H]is aid? We have been assured, Sir, in the sacred writings that "except the Lord build they labor in vain that build it." I firmly believe this; and I also believe that without [H]is concurring aid we shall succeed in this political building no better than the Builders of Babel: We shall be divided by our little partial local interests; our projects will be confounded, and we ourselves shall be become a reproach and a bye word down to future age. And what is worse, mankind may hereafter from this unfortunate instance, despair of establishing Governments by Human Wisdom, and leave it to chance, war, and conquest.

I therefore beg leave to move—that henceforth prayers imploring the assistance of Heaven, and its blessings on our deliberations, be held in this Assembly every morning before we proceed to business, and that one or more of the Clergy of this City be requested to officiate in that service.

George Washington, Thanksgiving Proclamation, 3 October 1789

By the President of the United States of America. a Proclamation.

Whereas it is the duty of all Nations to acknowledge the providence of Almighty God, to obey his will, to be grateful for his benefits, and humbly to implore his protection and favor—and whereas both Houses of Congress have by their joint Committee requested me "to recommend to the People of the United States a day of public thanksgiving and prayer to be observed by acknowledging with grateful hearts the many signal favors of Almighty God especially by affording them an opportunity peaceably to establish a form of government for their safety and happiness."

Now therefore I do recommend and assign Thursday the 26th day of November next to be devoted by the People of these States to the service of that great and glorious Being, who is the beneficent Author of all the good that was, that is, or that will be—That we may then all unite in rendering unto him our sincere and humble thanks—for his kind care and protection of the People of this Country previous to their becoming a Nation—for the signal and manifold mercies, and the favorable interpositions of his Providence which we experienced in the course and conclusion of the late war—for the great degree of tranquility, union, and plenty, which we have since enjoyed—for the peaceable and rational manner, in which we have been enabled to establish constitutions of government for our safety and happiness, and particularly the national One now lately instituted—for the civil and religious liberty with which we are blessed; and the means we have of acquiring and diffusing useful knowledge; and in general for all the great and various favors which he hath been pleased to confer upon us.

And also that we may then unite in most humbly offering our prayers and supplications to the great Lord and Ruler of Nations and beseech him to pardon our national and other transgressions, to enable us all, whether in public or private stations, to perform our several and relative duties properly and punctually—to render our national government a blessing to all the people, by constantly being a Government of wise, just, and constitutional laws, discreetly and faithfully executed and obeyed—to protect and guide all Sovereigns and Nations (especially such as have shewn kindness unto us) and to bless them with good government, peace, and concord—To promote the knowledge and practice of true religion and virtue, and the increase of science among them and us—and generally to grant unto all Mankind such a degree of temporal prosperity as he alone knows to be best.

Given under my hand at the City of New-York the third day of October in the year of our Lord 1789.

Go: Washington

CHAPTER 4

Ancient Greece

Like the civilizations mentioned earlier, Greek history begins in pre-history, but this chapter begins around 1200 BC, which is when iron replaced bronze as the primary metal of weapons and tools, and when tribes of people called Dorians invaded the Balkans, Peloponnese peninsulas, and Anatolia.

It is likely that these tribes were part of a larger, and much older, contingent of Caucus Mountain people called Aryans. Aryans also invaded the peoples in the peripheries of the Indus River settlements, affecting their genetic makeup and written languages.

Ancient Greece occupied rough terrains of rocky and mountainous lands with many sudden drops into a sparkling aqua marine sea called the Aegean. Settlements in this beautiful but difficult area were sporadic, but eventually formed into lifestyles and cultures we call the city-state.

While Egypt formed much earlier as the first nation-state in history, city-states were far more common and were founded all around the Mediterranean Sea. The Greek city-states formed independent Hellenic and Ionic cultures. Ancient Greek culture was centered in the polis, which means city, and the individual person was often defined by that membership.

Each Greek city had its own set of cultural standards but did share ideas and trade with each other. Through this, sharing a common religious view was formed. The ancient Greek religion was polytheistic and based around the gods of Mt. Olympus. These gods lived high in the clouds and controlled the fate of humanity.

According to ancient Greek religion, people did not have free will to control their destiny. A person's destiny, or fate, was determined by the gods, who were very political entities and served their own egos before the welfare of people.

Ancient Greek religion also did not focus upon moral behavior toward others; rather, its focus was on dedication and sacrifice to the gods for favors. In ancient Greek societies, people could make individual choices, and they did have a will, but that will was only important in the task of imposing it onto other humans. Will in ancient Greece was being able to get other people to understand and follow ideas, and this was achieved through verbal and written discourse or physical battle.

Discourse was studied as the art of persuasion. The art of persuasion is the act of communicating with others for the purpose of convincing people to agree with you, while motivating them to follow or at least support/not oppose the idea. Depending how important the topic was, getting people to agree did not always remain civil. Even so, the art of convincing people through rhetoric was studied and expanded to serve in the areas of politics and philosophy, creating the concept of "freedom of speech."

Greek politics was intensely focused on the city-state, and while the freedom of speech was limited to a minority of people, it was the first time that self-governing was attempted in all human history. Politics in ancient Greece was extremely important, and "politicking" was a developed art form, which was promoted and rewarded.

Greek philosophies were numerous and took on many forms, but these ideas became the moral compass of the ancient Greeks rather than religion. Reason and logic were two virtues in Greek philosophy, and the art of convincing others through discussions was highly valued. While Greek philosophies were highly advanced for the time, they did not affect the majority of the populace. Schools of Greek philosophers were exclusive and limited to a very small fraction of the total population. Most people just lived the best they could while worshiping the Greek gods in Greek ways.

Being able to convince others to agree was considered much more civilized and productive than enforcing one's will through physical intimidation or battle. Even so, brute force was also a method used when discussions failed to reach an agreement. With Greek thought came a flourishing of intellectual curiosity about the world. Art, science, medicine, mathematics, technology, and governing (dictatorship and democracy), were just some examples of the vast imaginative powers that Greek philosophy released in the human mind.

Everything from Greek columns and methods of conciliation, to focused sunbeams and flamethrowers were invented during this time. The fullness and richness of the human imagination was opened with the ancient Greeks. Their culture and worldviews spread east and west across the Mediterranean. They spread to Spain, North Africa, Italy, Sicily, Anatolia, and the Black Sea through the establishment of Greek colonies. Greek became the international standard for intellectualism, and the alphabet they borrowed from the Phoenicians was expanded into a form that would forever influence civilization.

Athens is most famous for its assembly of citizens using a direct democracy. This form of government was designed to prevent an aspiring monarch or oligarchy from ascending to power and creating a dictatorship over the people. To counter this possibility further, magistrates were chosen by lot, not election, and served for only one year. This, in theory, would keep the popular sovereign from being dominated by a single personality who could impose his will over the masses in violation of the Athenian constitution.

The Athenians and other Greeks considered Greek philosophy, culture, and politics much more civilized than other forms of government. This separation of Greek culture from others did not go unnoticed by Greek-speaking people, especially when dealing with non-Greeks. In time, ancient Greek culture developed a sense of exclusivity and superiority to others. The Greeks invented the word "barbarian" to describe the cultures outside of ancient Greece. A barbarian is simply a person who does not speak Greek, but the word itself came to encompass much more than language. It became a way to distinguish "civilized" from "uncivilized" people.

Barbarians were considered less civilized or not at all. Barbarians did not know the Greek ways of civility and discourse. Barbarians were not sophisticated and refined like a Greek citizen. Being Greek was essentially part of an exclusive club, and barbarians could not be part of that club unless they adopted Greek ways of life. Thus, dressing, eating, entertaining, and learning the Greek ways was an essential part of the formula for being seen as civilized in Greek societies.

When competing thoughts failed, warfare was always an option, and Greek thoughts had produced some of the best military technologies and tactics in the ancient world. The ultimate power of Greek ideas and willpower enabled this very small group to stop the great Persian Empire from conquering Greece. After that occurred, however, infighting between the city-states started and continued for decades.

This warfare seriously weakened the Greeks and made them vulnerable to a powerful barbarian force that had developed to their north. A king named Philip of Macedon invaded and conquered all the Greek peninsula, forcing the separate city-states into a single empire under his own will.

Limited to an elite few, the prestige of Greek thought and education was highly treasured by people from all over the Mediterranean. Philip of Macedon, the founder of the Macedonian Empire, sought this gift for his son Alexander and had the most famous Athenian Greek philosopher of his time tutor his son. That philosopher was named Aristotle. In a typical Greek way, Aristotle taught Alexander all the dreams and ideas of Greek science and philosophy, including the Greek concept of willpower and the projection of it onto others.

Alexander was highly motivated and willing to learn all that his mentor would teach him. Through Aristotle's framing and influence, Alexander became a framer and fanatic of Greek culture. This fanaticism not only taught him that Greek culture was superior to all others, but also that he should impose this culture onto the rest of the world.

When Alexander became King of the Macedonian Empire, he decided to go on a crusade. This crusade was designed to bring all the greatness of Greek thinking to the rest of the world. This Hellenic culture was then projected onto the old world in a new way we call Hellenism.

Hellenism was a very specific worldview that covered every aspect of living, from art and architecture to food and entertainment and from religion and reasoning to government and warfare. Armed with superior Greek tools and tactics, Alexander's crusade conquered Asia Minor, Judea, Israel, Jordan, Egypt, Mesopotamia, Persia, and even parts of India. He only stopped from invading all of India because his armies threatened mutiny if he continued.

While in Babylon, Alexander was planning his next conquest, the Arabian Peninsula, when at age 33, he suddenly died. Although Alexander passed away at an early age, his effects on the ancient world were profound. Hellenism had spread internationally and was incorporated into every culture it conquered.

Egypt is one example. Egypt was transformed, as one of Alexander's generals took over as the administrative head of that land. Ptolemy was the man's name, and his decedents would frame the Egyptian nation-state as a Hellenized land for the next 300 years.

The Egyptian city of Alexandria (one of many cities named after Alexander) was an innovative city with all the advantages of Greek thought and culture. From our perspective, the most important part of Alexandria, Egypt, was its library. The Library at Alexandria copied and transcribed almost every human work of literature up to that point into the Greek language. This included the Hebrew Torah. That Greek transliteration is called the Septuagint.

Hellenism also changed Judaism in profound ways because, in many respects, it was the exact opposite. Hellenized Judaism was very different from Orthodox Judaism, and Jews living in a Hellenized world could not help but break the Holy Covenant daily. The rift between Orthodox and Hellenized Jews grew for centuries until the entire area was conquered and eventually subjugated by another pagan force, the Romans.

From the ancient Greeks, Western civilization and the American republic inherited:

- Greek thought and philosophies,
- a fervent curiosity about the world and the universe,
- science,
- medicine,
- mathematics,

- democracy,
- freedom of speech,
- trial by jury,
- poetry,
- theater,
- athletics,
- grand building projects, and
- the concept of individual power.

Confederacies of city-states replaced tribalism as a dominant worldview within the Greek domain, and imposing one's will through politics and warfare became an accepted model for change.

———⟨⟩———

Literature was abundant in ancient Greece; and writings such as *The Republic* by Plato, *The History of the Peloponnesian War* by Thucydides, and *Nicomachean Ethics* by Aristotle are just a few of the many influences ancient Greek thought had on the American founders and framers. Greek thought had a significant philosophical impact on the intellectuals of Britain and the American British colonies before, during, and after our founding.

The influences ancient Greece had on our Freedom Charters was not just in their written texts but also in their cultural worldview. The American colonies were part of Great Britain until they rebelled, and Great Britain, like many of the Western European powers of that time, was engaged in a process known as imperialism. Imperialism is the attitude and process of building an empire from lands that were never part of their place and culture.

Like Alexander the Great of Macedon, the British Empire had been colonizing foreign lands with a "superior culture." Areas such as the Americas, Africa, Asia, and Australia were "discovered" and incorporated into the vast imperial structure. All Western European nations were empire building at the time. These powers did so with a sense of entitlement, showing truly little (if any) respect for the people who were already occupants of those lands.

Americans continued that process after the founding by continuing to allow slavery of African peoples and the conquest of indigenous peoples and their lands as a "Manifest Destiny" ordained by God. This is difficult for twenty-first century Americans to process. No one wants to think of atrocities committed by their ancestors, but history is what it is, and this author believes that ignoring or minimizing it does a disservice to all.

Americans developed a brilliant system, and this system has been instrumental in saving the world from evils such as Nazism, Japanese Imperialism, and Soviet Communism. Those philosophies began and ended with evil. The American system is quite different, and regardless of its flaws and errors, it began and will end with goodness in mind and action. This being stated, Americans and supporters of our Freedom Charters cannot be intellectually and morally honest with themselves and others if the errors and crimes of American slavery and conquest are not recognized, addressed, and understood in its totality.

These historical travesties should not be addressed to attack white-Americans or America. They should not be ignored by Americans either, but like ancient Mesopotamia, Egypt, Greece, and Rome, they must be discussed and recognized so they are understood in their historical context and their effect on today. If not, they will only fester in the emotions of good people and be used as fuel for attacks from our enemies. The issues of American slavery and genocide will turn into dishonest, energized arguments, turning people against America, the American system, and each other.

While many ideas and practices in ancient Greece are found in our Freedom Charters, ancient Greece also taught our founders and framers what *not* to put into the American system. One of the biggest misnomers about the American system is the idea of democracy. Ancient Athens was a direct democracy, in which every recognized citizen could vote on political issues facing Athens. The problem with this is that society can be just as despotic as any dictator. The "will of the people" can very quickly descend into "mob rule." Gross violations of property rights, slavery, and genocide were supported by the ancient Greek democracies. Tyranny does not require one-person rule.

Another major problem with democracy is that it can easily divide into factions and those factions can do great damage and commit terrible crimes toward individuals, organizations, societies, and governments. This was demonstrated in Greece by the confederacy called the Delian League, in which Athens used its influence to intimidate and bully other members of the league for its own profit. This growing empire caused the city-state of Sparta, an ally of Athens during the Persian Wars, to create its own league of city-states and go to war with Athens and the Delian League. This, after 26 years, left the Greek world exhausted and open for conquest from Macedonia.

<hr />

The Declaration of Independence:

    The history of the present King of Great Britain is a history of repeated injuries and usurpations, all having in direct object the establishment of an absolute Tyranny over these States. To prove this, let Facts be submitted to a candid world.

He has refused his Assent to Laws, the most wholesome and necessary for the public good.

He has forbidden his Governors to pass Laws of immediate and pressing importance, unless suspended in their operation till his Assent should be obtained; and when so suspended, he has utterly neglected to attend to them.

He has refused to pass other Laws for the accommodation of large districts of people, unless those people would relinquish the right of Representation in the Legislature, a right inestimable to them and formidable to tyrants only.

He has called together legislative bodies at places unusual, uncomfortable, and distant from the depository of their public Records, for the sole purpose of fatiguing them into compliance with his measures.

He has dissolved Representative Houses repeatedly, for opposing with manly firmness his invasions on the rights of the People.

He has refused for a long time, after such dissolutions, to cause others to be elected; whereby the Legislative powers, incapable of Annihilation, have returned to the People at large for their exercise; the State remaining in the mean time exposed to all the dangers of invasion from without, and convulsions within.

He has endeavored to prevent the population of these States; for that purpose obstructing the Laws for Naturalization of Foreigners; refusing to pass others to encourage their migrations hither, and raising the conditions of new Appropriations of Lands.

He has obstructed the Administration of Justice, by refusing his Assent to Laws for establishing Judiciary powers.

He has made Judges dependent on his Will alone, for the tenure of their offices, and the amount and payment of their salaries.

He has erected a multitude of New Offices, and sent hither swarms of Officers to harass our people, and eat out their substance.

He has kept among us, in times of peace, Standing Armies without the Consent of our legislatures.

He has affected to render the Military independent of and superior to the Civil power.

He has combined with others to subject us to a jurisdiction foreign to our constitution, and unacknowledged by our laws; giving his Assent to their Acts of pretended Legislation:

For Quartering large bodies of armed troops among us:

For protecting them, by a mock Trial, from punishment for any Murders which they should commit on the Inhabitants of these States...

For depriving us in many cases, of the benefits of Trial by Jury:

The U.S. Constitution:

To promote the Progress of Science and useful Arts, by securing for limited Times to Authors and Inventors the exclusive Right to their respective Writings and Discoveries;

To constitute Tribunals inferior to the supreme Court;

To define and punish Piracies and Felonies committed on the high Seas, and Offences against the Law of Nations;

To declare War, grant Letters of Marque and Reprisal, and make Rules concerning Captures on Land and Water;

To raise and support Armies, but no Appropriation of Money to that Use shall be for a longer Term than two Years;

To provide and maintain a Navy;

To make Rules for the Government and Regulation of the land and naval Forces;

To provide for calling forth the Militia to execute the Laws of the Union, suppress Insurrections and repel Invasions;

To provide for organizing, arming, and disciplining, the Militia, and for governing such Part of them as may be employed in the Service of the United States, reserving to the States respectively, the Appointment of the Officers, and the Authority of training the Militia according to the discipline prescribed by Congress;

To exercise exclusive Legislation in all Cases whatsoever, over such District (not exceeding ten Miles square) as may, by Cession of particular States, and the Acceptance of Congress, become the Seat of the Government of the United States, and to exercise like Authority over all Places purchased by the Consent of the Legislature of the State in which the Same shall be, for the Erection of Forts, Magazines, Arsenals, dock-Yards, and other needful Buildings;—And

To make all Laws which shall be necessary and proper for carrying into Execution the foregoing Powers, and all other

Powers vested by this Constitution in the Government of the United States, or in any Department or Officer thereof.

The Bill of Rights:

Amendment I:

Congress shall make no law respecting an establishment of religion, or prohibiting the free exercise thereof; or abridging the freedom of speech, or of the press; or the right of the people peaceably to assemble, and to petition the Government for a redress of grievances.

Amendment IV: The right of the people to be secure in their persons, houses, papers, and effects, against unreasonable searches and seizures, shall not be violated, and no Warrants shall issue, but upon probable cause, supported by Oath or affirmation, and particularly describing the place to be searched, and the persons or things to be seized.

Amendment V: No person shall be held to answer for a capital, or otherwise infamous crime, unless on a presentment or indictment of a Grand Jury, except in cases arising in the land or naval forces, or in the Militia, when in actual service in time of War or public danger; nor shall any person be subject for the same offence to be twice put in jeopardy of life or limb; nor shall be compelled in any criminal case to be a witness against himself, nor be deprived of life, liberty, or property, without due process of law; nor shall private property be taken for public use, without just compensation.

CHAPTER 5

The Roman Republic

Tradition states that the city of Rome was founded in the year 753 BC. It was nothing more than a collection of villages settled on and around seven hills overlooking the Tiber River in a land called Latium on a peninsula called Italia. During early Roman history, Rome was commonly threatened by Greeks and barbarian tribes and eventually conquered and ruled by their Etruscan neighbors. Ancient Romans were resentful of being subjects of foreign invaders and became fanatically obsessed with their permanent removal.

After they freed themselves from the grip of the Etruscan kings, Rome established a republic. This republic was a representative form of government in which laws were established for all to follow, and individuals were selected to stand in for constituents of the general population to make decisions at the governmental level. These decisions, however, followed an established due process.

Individual people were voted into certain offices, and power was divided between three branches and two classes of Roman citizens (patricians and plebeians). It was thought that these divisions of powers would protect the Senate and People of Rome from internal tyranny.

Free will in ancient Rome was often seen as the will of the people (popular sovereignty). Rome developed an unwritten constitution that created a representative government. The three branches of this sovereign entity were the Magistrates, who elected consuls; the Senate, who elected judges and made financial decisions; and the Assemblies, who represented the people by approving or rejecting laws and electing magistrates and tribunes.

Patricians could serve for one year as a magistrate and indefinitely in the Senate, as they held most of the land and wealth. Other patricians and plebeians served in the Assemblies. Assemblies held the numbers, elected the magistrates and tribunes, and could declare war.

Tribunes who were elected by the Assemblies could serve one year and veto anything the Senate wanted to do. So, the Senate was very attentive to the will of the Assemblies, who represented the popular sovereign body, the people of Rome.

These people were citizens of the city of Rome, not the subjects of an unelected king. This republic was founded upon the ideals of civic virtue, which are the individual's obligations to society. These obligations included:

- serving in the Senate or Assembly,
- voting in the Senate or Assembly,
- serving seasonally in the military, and
- following all Roman law.

Non-citizens also had obligations to the citizen classes, and fulfilling these obligations could help them to gain Roman citizenship. Citizenship was a prized possession in ancient Rome, granting that person and their family members many rights and responsibilities, one of which was the right to due process found in the *Twelve Tables of Roman Law* (451-450 BC).

The primary obsession in ancient Rome was the fear of tyranny from within and the fear of being conquered by outsiders. Civic virtue was thought to be the solution to both quandaries. Foreigners could earn citizenship and benefits through service in the Roman army. Even slaves could earn emancipation over time.

A republican system tends to excel in organization, as its structure is varied and nuanced. The Roman military became a very well organized reflection of the republic, and the will of the Senate and People of Rome (SPQR). This made it very successful in achieving the military and political goals of the Roman republic with fervent attention to discipline, technological innovation, superb organization, advanced military tools and tactics, tenacity of will, and a vicious willingness to use extreme violence against any enemy real or imagined.

Rome's fanatical attention to foreign powers that might potentially conquer the republic led to many aggressive wars. These military actions were not seen as aggression by the populace but as defensive in nature, designed to protect Rome from foreign invasion. These wars brought greater power, prestige, and wealth. Wars, of course, kept reoccurring because there was always some other power adjacent to the expanding territories.

Competition from the African city-state of Carthage, which was founded centuries earlier by the Phoenicians, posed a particularly important time in the history of the Roman republic. The three Punic Wars would test Rome's constitutional structures but also expand Rome's dominion out of Italy and into Iberia (modern Spain and Portugal) and Numidia (modern Libya and Algeria). Later, Rome conquered lands east such as Macedonia, Greece, Asia Minor, Egypt, Judea, Jordan, and even Mesopotamia.

The pagan Roman religion, which had initially been an incorporation of the Greek religion with little more than names being changed, simply adopted the gods and goddesses of any territory they conquered or encountered, if they did not supersede the gods of Rome. Greek philosophy and style also were taken from the Hellenized East, and Roman conquests were eventually seen as emulating Alexander's conquests.

Roman consuls like Julius Caesar were very ambitious and egocentric men who looked to outdo Alexander's conquests. Caesar documented his wars in Gaul (modern France) and Breton (modern United Kingdom) in a book entitled *The Gallic Wars*, which catalogs the ruthless nature of this leader who would eventually turn his armies, and his personal will, against the city of Rome itself.

Caesar eventually attacked another consul of Rome, Pompey. Caesar defeated Pompey's forces, but Pompey escaped to Egypt. Caesar then left a contingent force of war-hardened veterans in Rome to maintain order, while he took the rest of his army to Egypt.

The Ptolemaic king of Egypt had Pompey murdered to impress Caesar, but while in Egypt, Caesar was bewitched by the king's adversary, half-sister, and wife, the queen of Egypt, Cleopatra VII. Cleopatra and Caesar became lovers and had her brother executed, and later had a child together.

Caesar returned to Rome, and under the watchful eye of his army, the Senate voted him the constitutional title of Dictator, which in fact, granted very limited powers. Caesar planned to institute his own title Dictator for Life when on March 15, 44 BC, he was assassinated by republican members of the Roman Senate. Caesar's written will promoted his great nephew Octavian to leadership status and gave him control over his Roman fortunes.

In the last battle of the Roman civil wars, Octavian defeated the Roman general Marcus Antonius in a sea battle near Actium, Greece, in 31 BC, while he and Cleopatra VII later committed suicide, thus ending the Ptolemaic line in Egypt. Octavian then took on the title Caesar Augustus, establishing himself in a new position he called the Principate,

meaning "first among equals." We know this leader and all future principates as the Roman emperors.

—◈—

The ancient Roman republic gave the American founders and framers many ideas and concepts. Some of which were:
- the Roman calendar,
- constitutional republicanism,
- the idea of civic virtue,
- a distaste for tyranny,
- a concept of the populace as a sovereign entity,
- superb organizational skills,
- sophisticated law codes,
- city planning,
- public welfare (basic food, housing, and sanitation),
- military order and discipline,
- incorporated businesses,
- indoor running water, plumbing, and sewage disposal,
- the concept of innocent until proven guilty in court trials, and
- early concepts of property rights, liability claims, court-ordered
  compensation, and due process rights.

—◈—

The Roman historian Livy was recorded to have said, "…the Twelve Tables
form the fount of all public and private jurisprudence." They were originally
etched into 12 bronze tablets and displayed outside the doors of the Roman

Curia (Senate). While they do not constitute a written constitution by our standards, the twelve tables became and remained the basis of procedural law for civil governing throughout the republic and into the empire.

While we currently only have fragments of the original tables, historians have been able to piece together a representation of what those tablets might have been in their entirety. This was useful to the founders and framers of the American republic many centuries later.

Without going into the specific nuances of the twelve tables, each one dealt with procedures established for trials. This included preliminary procedures to trial, procedures in the actual trial, rules for debt payments, family law, inheritance law, guardianships, ownership and possession, property rights, tort law, wrongful conduct, criminal law, burial rites, marriage law, theft, consumer law, and commercial law.

⸺⸺

One important aspect of Roman law addressed by the American framers was the concept of civic virtue. Much of Roman law depended upon civic virtue, which is people putting their assigned public roles ahead of their own personal interests. This dependence on personal integrity was noble, but obviously flawed, as people cannot always be trusted to put the good of society before their own personal interests. The framers of the American constitutional system saw this as a fatal flaw of the Roman republic cited by many delinquent actions by Roman public officials, culminating with the illegal acts of Julius Caesar and Caesar Augustus that ended their republic.

The American republic could not depend on the civic virtues of its leaders, so it was decided that the U.S. Constitution itself would be the roadblock to dishonest governing and tyranny. Taking from much of Roman law, the American federal government was separated into three branches. Then each branch was given very specific importance and responsibilities. Each has its own roles and the power to check the powers of the other two.

The powers of the federal government were also limited to what is written into the Constitution, while granting powers not written to the states or the people of the United States. This aspect of our constitution is called federalism.

<hr/>

We the People of the United States, in Order to form a more perfect Union, establish Justice, insure domestic Tranquility, provide for the common defense, promote the general Welfare, and secure the Blessings of Liberty to ourselves and our Posterity, do ordain and establish this Constitution for the United States of America.

Article I.

Section 1.

All legislative Powers herein granted shall be vested in a Congress of the United States, which shall consist of a Senate and House of Representatives...

Article II.

Section 1.

The executive Power shall be vested in a President of the United States of America. He shall hold his Office during the

Term of four Years, and, together with the Vice President, chosen for the same Term, be elected, as follows

Each State shall appoint, in such Manner as the Legislature thereof may direct, a Number of Electors, equal to the whole Number of Senators and Representatives to which the State may be entitled in the Congress: but no Senator or Representative, or Person holding an Office of Trust or Profit under the United States, shall be appointed an Elector.

Section 2.

The President shall be Commander in Chief of the Army and Navy of the United States, and of the Militia of the several States, when called into the actual Service of the United States; he may require the Opinion, in writing, of the principal Officer in each of the executive Departments, upon any Subject relating to the Duties of their respective Offices, and he shall have Power to grant Reprieves and Pardons for Offences against the United States, except in Cases of Impeachment.

He shall have Power, by and with the Advice and Consent of the Senate, to make Treaties, provided two thirds of the Senators present concur; and he shall nominate, and by and with the Advice and Consent of the Senate, shall appoint Ambassadors, other public Ministers and Consuls, Judges of the supreme Court, and all other Officers of the United States, whose Appointments are not herein otherwise provided for, and which shall be established by Law: but the Congress may by Law vest the Appointment of such inferior Officers, as they think proper, in the President alone, in the Courts of Law, or in the Heads of Departments.

These laws are counterbalanced with protection of the people from misuse of these armed forces through the adoption of Amendment II in the Bill of Rights.

Amendment II (ratified December 15, 1791)

A well-regulated Militia, being necessary to the security of a free State, the right of the people to keep and bear Arms, shall not be infringed.

Article. III.

Section. 1.

The judicial Power of the United States, shall be vested in one supreme Court, and in such inferior Courts as the Congress may from time to time ordain and establish. The Judges, both of the supreme and inferior Courts, shall hold their Offices during good Behavior, and shall, at stated Times, receive for their Services, a Compensation, which shall not be diminished during their Continuance in Office.

Article. IV.

Section. 1.

Full Faith and Credit shall be given in each State to the public Acts, Records, and judicial Proceedings of every other State. And the Congress may by general Laws prescribe the Manner in which such Acts, Records and Proceedings shall be proved, and the Effect thereof.

Article. V.

The Congress, whenever two thirds of both Houses shall deem it necessary, shall propose Amendments to this Constitution, or, on the Application of the Legislatures of two thirds of the several States, shall call a Convention for proposing Amendments, which, in either Case, shall be valid to all Intents and Purposes, as Part of this Constitution, when ratified by the Legislatures of three fourths of the several States, or by Conventions in three fourths thereof, as the one or the other Mode of Ratification may be proposed by the Congress; Provided that no Amendment which may be made prior to the Year One thousand eight hundred and eight shall in any Manner affect the first and fourth Clauses in the Ninth Section of the first Article; and that no State, without its Consent, shall be deprived of its equal Suffrage in the Senate.

Article. VI.

All Debts contracted and Engagements entered into, before the Adoption of this Constitution, shall be as valid against the United States under this Constitution, as under the Confederation.

This Constitution, and the Laws of the United States which shall be made in Pursuance thereof; and all Treaties made, or which shall be made, under the Authority of the United States, shall be the supreme Law of the Land; and the Judges in every State shall be bound thereby, any Thing in the Constitution or Laws of any State to the Contrary notwithstanding.

The Senators and Representatives before mentioned, and the Members of the several State Legislatures, and all executive and judicial Officers, both of the United States and of the several States, shall be bound by Oath or Affirmation, to support this Constitution; but no religious Test shall ever be required as a Qualification to any Office or public Trust under the United States.

CHAPTER 6

Early Christianity

There was one other gift that came to humanity during Roman rule. His eventual influence over the Roman Empire would change the future of the entire world more than any principate could ever hope to have accomplished.

During the reigns of Caesar Augustus and Caesar Tiberius, something very important but extremely obscure happened in the Roman province of Judea. Occurring almost anonymously and certainly unnoticed by the great powers of the empire was born a male child to a poor Judean couple. The story of this child will not be told here, but it is often referred to as the greatest story ever told, and certainly had a greater impact on humanity than could have ever been imagined by anyone living at that time.

The boy was named Jesus. He was later known as Jesus of Nazareth and would eventually be known by the people of earth as Jesus Christ. Jesus Christ was a poor Jewish carpenter who later became a preacher and rabbi around the orthodox Jewish faith. While He never held an official position in ancient Judaism, He was, and still is, regarded by Christians to be the Son of God and the promised Messiah (Savior) of the God of Abraham promised through prophecy to come to earth for the forgiveness of human sins. His conception, birth, life, death, resurrection, and ascension into Heaven has been compiled in the most-read ancient texts of all time, collectively called the Holy Bible.

Christ claimed that His purpose for existing on earth was what we call the New Covenant. The New Covenant is rooted in the idea that Jesus was, and is, the Son of the God of Abraham, a sinless man who took upon Himself the punishment that all people deserve for their sinfulness.

As the Son of God, He was Himself divine. His example of following the will of God the Father (rather than His own human will) is a core example of His obedience to the ancient Holy Covenant. The New Covenant began for humanity with Jesus' resurrection from the dead on a day now called Easter Sunday. As the Son of God, Jesus was divine, but as a fellow human being, He also was afforded the gift of free will. Jesus demonstrated His loyalty and dedication to the Father by obeying the will of God and not the will of His human self.

This continued throughout His suffering. Throughout Jesus's torture and execution He never cursed God or His persecutors, but remained loyal to God while forgiving His oppressors and His disciples who denied and abandoned Him.

The New Covenant achieves several objectives. First, it pardons all offenses toward the God of Abraham from the inherited original sins of Adam and Eve, and later to when people inevitably fail to follow the Ten Commandments and the Holy Covenant.

The Laws of Moses have very strict and deliberate rules of physical and moral conduct. The directives of the Holy Covenant are still in effect, and the New Covenant is not meant to negate the Holy Covenant, but the New Covenant removes the "burden of sin," which comes from our inevitable failures to follow the Holy Covenant and its consequence, death of the soul.

Second, the New Covenant condenses the hundreds of original Commandments into two primary commandments. "This is the most important: 'Hear O Israel, the Lord our God is One Lord, and you shall love the Lord your God with all your heart and with all your soul and with all your mind and with all your strength.' The second is this: 'Love your neighbor as yourself.' No other commandment is greater than these" (Mark 12:29-31).

Another accomplishment of the New Covenant is God's pardon from the punishments of Hell. Christianity teaches that Hell is a real level of existence where God's love is willfully rejected by those who inhabit it. Souls in Hell are completely disconnected from God by willful rejection of Him and His Son Jesus Christ, suffering terrible torments for all eternity. Through the acceptance of Jesus Christ by baptism and belief, the New Covenant spares humanity this divine justice and provides individual human-beings with an escape from eternal damnation with, in, and through the sacrificed body and blood of Jesus Christ.

Finally, the New Covenant gives humans a specific directive. This directive is found in the Lord's Prayer. It is asking God to "forgive us our trespasses, as we forgive those who trespass against us." This means that to be truly forgiven for missing the mark with God, we must forgive all others who miss the mark with us.

This places individual human salvation directly in the hands of each conscious individual and is specifically dependent upon each person's God given free will to accept Christ into their heart and choose love, forgiveness, and belief over hatred, discord, and rejection of Christ.

This tends to be a difficult task for humans because the pain we feel when wronged by another person can strike us to our core, and the pain of loss is a negative primal reaction. So, forgiveness typically goes against every natural sensibility and survival instinct in our biological makeup.

We also live in a scientific age where belief is supposedly supported by scientific proof. The error in this line of thinking is that relationships are not based on scientific proof, but faith. All human relationships are inevitably supported by the faith we have in others and the faith they have in us. Faith is the foundation of human relationships and our personal relationship with Christ through faith is paramount in Christian teachings.

Jesus Christ has, without doubt, been a greater impact on humanity than any known person in human history. He not only gave humanity new concepts of love and forgiveness, but He redefined what a human being and a leader should be.

Jesus claimed to be a king, but not of this world. His example of a king is one who is loving, kind, understanding, humble, and forgiving. Jesus Christ saved the world from eternal damnation and grants us a hope that cannot be found from anything we know or possess in this life on earth.

—◆—

From Christianity, the founders and framers of the American republic received instructions in the virtues of self-sacrifice, compassion, charity, piety, faith, forgiveness, empathy for human suffering, deliverance from the world's problems, salvation of the soul, and the concept of unconditional love for one another (even those who are our enemies).

Even so, other than referencing the year 1787 as "the Year of our Lord," our Freedom Charters make no reference to Jesus Christ. This is not surprising, however, because our Freedom Charters are not religious documents but an expression of an idea. This idea is on the natural rights of people and how a country should be framed and implemented based upon those rights of self-governing.

Even so, every one of the founders and framers of the American republic were products of a Judeo-Christian culture going back over five thousand years. This culture was framed, shaped, and performed according to the images and rhythms of the Western Christian Bible and faith in Jesus Christ.

The Judeo-Christian heritage of the United States and our Freedom Charters cannot be erased. It can be attacked, denied, distorted, ignored, minimized, and scorned, but it cannot be undone because all of it is cemented in human history. While faith in Jesus Christ is a personal decision made through God-given free will, the effects of Jesus Christ and Christian thinking is an influence that can never be erased from the American mindset or worldview.

Belief in the God of Creation and His gifts to humanity through nature is the very root of the American republic. Without this, every natural right can be arbitrarily thrown away and the whims of a faction, mob, or dictator can be implemented instead. This is the greatest danger "We the People" face in the twenty-first century, and it is the primary motivation of why so much time, resources, and effort has been applied to the writing, editing, and publishing of this book.

CHAPTER 7

Ancient Christianity and the Roman Empire

To perpetuate His teachings, Jesus Christ established the universal Church. The Church began in Jerusalem, but Jesus' followers ventured out into the Roman Empire and beyond, establishing Christian communities and apostolic churches that would one day transform the Roman world.

For the first two centuries AD, Jews and Christians were persecuted sporadically because they openly refused to obey the will of the principate and consider him divine. But Rome and the Roman Empire were relatively sturdy and constant for that time, called the Pax Romana. This worked in Christianity's favor, as peace and stability allowed for the rapid spread of the Christian message with relatively little resistance.

Two people who took full advantage of this reality were the followers of Jesus and framers of early Christianity whom we now call St. Peter and St. Paul. St. Peter and St. Paul are considered two of the most important founders and framers of the early Christian church but had very different backgrounds and viewpoints.

St. Peter believed in orthodox Judaism and was a simple countryman and fisherman from the town of Capernaum in Galilee, Judea. St. Paul was a Hellenized Jewish person and a highly educated scholar from the city of Tarsus in Asia Minor (modern Turkey).

The two men came from completely different backgrounds and had completely different ideas on where the Church should be going. Their battle of wills would reverberate throughout early Christianity until St. Peter capitulated to St. Paul on several issues. Then the blending of both men's beliefs came to be the accepted doctrine of the universal Church, which is the whole entity of all apostolic churches that were in communion with each other.

St. Peter was a traditionalist, and he was one of the first disciples of Christ. Jesus had probably lived with Peter and his family in Capernaum for some time. Shimon bar Yona, his original name, was from a very rural community next to the Sea of Galilee where fishing was a common profession. Peter's sensibilities were rugged, conservative, and very earthy.

St. Peter was primarily concerned with integrating the teachings of Christ into Judaism. He believed that all Jewish laws and sensibilities should be followed by converts to Jesus. He did not even see Christianity as a separate religion from Judaism, and at that time it really wasn't. St. Peter was following a path of integrating the teachings of Jesus into the Jewish faith and not expanding the Church outside of the faith. According to St. Peter, a follower of Jesus must first be Jewish, this meant that Gentiles first had to convert to Judaism and be circumcised (not always an easy sell).

St. Paul saw things differently. He was a convert to Jesus and one of the newest followers. Saulos Tarsus (or in Greek Paulos) was urbanized. He was not only a Hellenized Jewish person but also a Roman citizen. He came from a very stylish, Hellenized city named Tarsus, and had grown up with all the benefits of Greek philosophy and learning. While a pious Jew, he was part of the upper class. The Holy Bible says he was "a

Pharisee, the son of a Pharisee." Essentially, his worldview was the culmination of every ancient topic covered in these writings so far.

St. Paul turns out to be a pivotal person (perhaps the most pivotal person) in ancient times, whose work and views had a profound effect on human history. If the Gospels of Matthew, Mark, Luke, and John can be considered the keel and hull of the Christian New Testament, then the speeches and writings of St. Paul were the propellers, the rudder, deck, and helm of this great ship.

While St. Paul is arguably the most effective person in early Christianity, he begins as a most unlikely candidate for the role. As a Hellenized Jewish Roman citizen, St. Paul was at first no fan of these new followers of Jesus. He already had to be very careful growing up in a Hellenized Roman society, where breaking the Holy Covenant was almost a daily occurrence.

These new disciples of Jesus were greatly offensive to him. He most certainly looked down upon them as silly and even stupid people, while engaging in lethal persecutions of Christ's Church. Paul's conversion on the road from Jerusalem in Judea to Damascus in Roman Syria was perhaps the most world-changing event to occur to a mortal man. This was a trip he took to arrest Christians. It is described in the Book of Acts of the Holy Bible. Paul states that he heard Jesus in Heaven who asked why he was persecuting Him. Paul was then knocked off his horse and temporarily blinded. He did not have his sight restored until he met with a specific Christian leader in Damascus.

St. Paul's objective was to convert gentiles as well as Jews without going through Judaism. This was a fundamental change in the direction of the early Church. St. Paul was completely at home with gentiles and their ways. While a pious Hellenized Jew, Paul's sensibilities were inclusive of Jewish and gentile people. Peter would not even sit down and eat with gentiles, and there was a big conflict in Antioch in Asia Minor between Paul and Peter. The two men had an open adversarial relationship, but both are important for our purposes, being instrumental in the founding and framing of the cultural perspectives of the Greek Churches and the Church of Rome.

—⁓⁓—

Today we speak of Christianity as one religion. While there continues to be thousands of different denominations in modern times, the Christianity of the first three centuries was very different in many ways. The books of the New Testament were still being written and chosen for inclusion and exclusion. There were many more books we now call apocryphal testaments. What we now call Christianity (Nicene-Christianity) was the winner of 300 years of disputes that could had ended very differently.

The Christianity of the first century was an amalgamation of various apostolic churches and gnostic cults, each with very different and radical ideas about the nature of Jesus. There were many in existence that were very bizarre to modern sensibilities, but the preaching and writings of St. Paul the Apostle were instrumental in the foundations and development of most perspectives within the early Christian church that remain with us today.

—⁓⁓—

As stated earlier, divine sovereignty has been used by the leaders of all the great empires since ancient Mesopotamia and Egypt, and the pagan Roman Empire was no different. From Julius Caesar and Caesar Augustus on, the Roman Emperors presented themselves as divine sovereigns. They claimed to have descended from the Roman gods or were even gods themselves. The Divine Caesar was a cult of worship that fluctuated and changed through the centuries but always remained the justification for the ultimate authority and will of the Roman principates.

In AD 64, the Roman Emperor Nero was the first head of state to institute an official policy of persecution against all the different forms of Christianity in Rome. A fire had burned a sizable portion of the city, and rumors began that Nero had ordered the fire himself.

To counter this accusation, Nero blamed the fire on Christians and responded with mass arrests and executions. It was during this time that St. Peter and St. Paul were martyred (St. Peter was crucified upside down and St. Paul was beheaded).

Six years later, Judaism was also targeted for its exclusivity and oddness compared to other religions in the empire. They eventually revolted with armed force, and the emperor Vespasian destroyed the ancient Jewish state, Jerusalem, and the Second Temple.

The Romans also renamed the entire area Palestine/Syria to permanently remove Jews as the accepted owners and occupants of that land. A moving historical commentary entitled *The War of the Jews* was written by the Jewish Historian and Roman collaborator Flavius Josephus. While difficult to stomach, the fate of the Jews in the last days of ancient Israel is vividly recorded.

After the destruction of Jerusalem and the Second Temple in AD 70, Judaism and Christianity were forced to become intercultural. While exclusivity was maintained at certain levels, Judaism and Christianity had to adapt to the realities of existing within pagan, polytheistic world cultures.

This would forever shape and change both religions in cultural sensibilities, language, and practice.

Sporadic persecutions continued against both religions and even between each other at certain times, but the Roman crisis of the third-century AD was a real game changer for the Christians. The Pax Romana was ending, and the empire faced tumult from many enemies internally and externally. The crisis of the third century changed all this because the Roman Empire was beginning to feel the pressures of decline.

The need to obey the will of the principate and worship him became more important psychologically as the stresses and strains of third-century realities pushed the Roman world into chaos and self-doubt. This divine sovereignty of the Roman Emperors became a very necessary thing for all people to recognize, and it came to a head with an emperor named Diocletian.

The Roman Emperor Diocletian came to power over a very degraded Roman Empire. His solution as leader was to reorder the administrative state so it would function more competently and more efficiently. This required a sharing of power with others, so the empire was reordered based upon new administrative areas called dioceses.

These dioceses established new administrative heads of the empire while remaining loyal to the divine sovereign, Diocletian. He appointed others and anointed them with sovereignty to administer different sectors of the Roman Empire in Diocletian's name. This was called the Tetrarchy.

These new administrators were called Vicari (Substitutes) and would serve the will of the emperor for the good of the empire. It also created a new class of sovereigns who received their power from the divine sovereign, Diocletian. One such administrator was a man now called Constantius Chlorus, a military general by profession and co-emperor appointed to rule over the areas of Roman Britain and Gaul.

Diocletian then ordered all people living in the Roman Empire to offer a universal sacrifice to the divinity of the emperor. This, he believed, would bring the favor of the gods, cement the people together with commonality, and bring about greater respect and dedication to the Roman Empire's sustainability and preservation.

This new administrative structure Diocletian created was designed to preserve and perpetuate the Roman state through a system that shared power but remained loyal to him through recognition of his "divine will." It also was seen as the Roman Empire's attempt at self-preservation, and for many reasons it was.

Pagans did not have such a hard time with this universal sacrifice. They simply integrated it into their already bloated pantheon of gods and went about their normal business. Jews and Christians were very different, of course, and could not simply integrate worship of the emperor into their theologies. On 24 February of AD 303, Christians became the focus of Diocletian's wrath. Constantius Chlorus was Vicar in the West when the order of persecution came.

Constantius Chlorus was a faithful general to Diocletian but did not enforce all the persecution orders against Christian sects probably because his first wife Helena was a pious woman who was a Christian sympathizer. Even so, wherever these persecutions did take place, it was so intense and so atrocious that the results had a profound impact on the entire Roman world.

The impact on Constantius Chlorus' son was somewhat different than the original intent Diocletian had, however, which was to demonstrate pagan Roman superiority over the Christians, to alter or eradicate Christianity from the empire by force of will, and to install a permanent universal sacrifice to the emperor. The son of Constantius Chlorus, whom we now call Constantine the Great, had a very different take on the persecuted Christian faith and the dedication they had to their God.

Constantine must have seen something in those persecutions, something that was enviable to any aspiring leader. The boy saw and heard of steadfast faith and dedication in the face of horrific circumstances. All these Christian men, women, and children had to do to avoid being butchered, fed alive to wild animals, or burned alive in an open amphitheater, was to openly perform and give a statement of universal sacrifice to the emperor.

Even though they could have simply performed the sacrifice and made the statement of loyalty to Diocletian in public, while worshiping Christ in secret, which some did, many others would not budge from their convictions. Thousands were brutalized, tortured, and killed in some of the most grotesque ways possible. These sickening displays were also showcased and documented across the Roman Empire.

The Roman persecutions of the third century came down to a battle of wills between the Christians and the pagans—the will of pagans to see Christians submit to the emperor, and the will of individual Christians who refused to give up their faith, even to enduring torture, dismemberment, and death. This was carried out in gruesome public spectacles.

Strangely enough, while thousands of Christians were slaughtered, their unique dedication to Jesus Christ and their own power of will was too innovative for the sensibilities of the pagan Roman authorities to process and understand. While the Christians never fought back, they endured, the will of the Christians survived, and they eventually outlasted the pagan Roman state, the emperors, and other Roman leaders, who capitulated.

In a strange and ironic testament to Christian will, a pagan Roman leader, the Imperial Vicar Galerius, who strategized and encouraged

Diocletian's persecutions, became extremely ill with horrible suffering and infectious oozing from several orifices of his body. This was likely bowel cancer, but Galerius considered it a punishment from the Christian God. Galerius rescinded his orders of persecution toward the Christians and then asked for Christians to pray for him before he expired.

—⟨⟩—

Roman Christianity will be discussed in future chapters, but from the pagan Roman Empire, the American founders and framers learned about:
- the concept of interlocking territories connected by a vast road system,
- early concepts of a decentralized administrative state that shares governmental power and authority,
- public health projects,
- an extension of Greek cultural achievements,
- the organization of large standing armies,
- retirement benefits,
- international trade practices,
- a standardized intercultural language (Latin),
- and a more advanced code of laws with the continuation of due process rights for all citizens.

CHAPTER 8

Christendom and the End of Ancient Times

Upon the death of Vicar Constantius Chlorus, Constantine became co-emperor and was crowned vicar of the areas once given to his father. Constantine was an extremely bright and insightful leader. He saw how the reordering of the administrative state by Diocletian was genius but still had a fatal flaw. The weakness was that the cult of Emperor worship did not really have the faith and backing of the Roman people, or even the royal sovereigns of the empire.

Most people followed Diocletian's orders for imperial worship but only in a mechanical or lackluster way. Even Diocletian himself got tired of it all and retired to a fortress alone, rejecting any attempts by others to return to duty. Upon retirement, Diocletian did not want anything more to do with Roman matters, and he was more interested and obsessed with growing cabbages in a huge garden fed by an enormous aqueduct.

Constantine then made war on his fellow sovereigns and was very successful. As his army surrounded Rome itself and was about to do battle with another royal sovereign named Maxentius, he claimed to have had a vision. Constantine claimed to have seen a symbol of Christ Jesus coming down from the clouds, instructing him to paint the Greek letters Chi

"X" and Rho "P" (for Christ the King) on their shields to be victorious in battle. In AD 312, at the Battle of the Milvian Bridge, Constantine utterly defeated Maxentius, who drowned in the Tiber River.

The next year, Constantine issued the Edict of Milan, which instituted Christian tolerance within his realm of the empire. For the next 10 years, Constantine made war on the other royal sovereigns until his victory was complete throughout the Roman Empire. At this time, Constantine became the sole emperor of Rome and was recognized as the rightful, supreme, and sovereign leader. He was expected to claim the divine mantle of Roman power, become a god, and rule his subjects through direct divine authority, but this is not what he did.

Constantine could have simply assumed the mantle of divine sovereign. That would have followed exactly what so many others before him had done, and it would have cemented his place as ruler of the Roman world until his death. Upon the death of Constantine, most everything would have been up for grabs with competing egos and interests. This would have continued to damage the Roman Empire as aspiring leaders pursued their own personal power and greed. But Constantine was looking further into the future than his own life. He was, in fact, looking to the coming centuries and not just the limited time of his own lifespan.

Constantine did not take the mantle of divine sovereign. Instead, he "willed" it to Jesus Christ and the God of Abraham. So here was the beginning of widespread acceptance of Christendom and the next step in the evolution of people's perceptions of the Christian and Jewish God of Abraham.

Christendom used the concept of divine sovereignty to justify its very existence, but it was a line of supremacy beginning with God in Heaven and relying on a very specific and deliberate process. This symbiosis of church and state was believed to have been instituted when the universe was first created.

It was built into every aspect of God's creation, and it was essential for humanity's survival, progress, and salvation. From God to government and from the church to businesses and organizations and from societies and cultures to each individual human person, everything had its place in God's divine order.

Constantine called a meeting that would settle disputes and shape the evolution and progress of the Christian Church and the future of human civilization. It was a council of Christian bishops from all over the Roman Empire known as the First Ecumenical Council of Nicaea, convened in AD 325.

Constantine attended this council, too, and although he did not direct its religious decisions about the nature of the Holy Trinity: God the Father, God the Son, and God the Holy Spirit—he made sure his position as earthly sovereign was next in line from the divine authority of the Holy Trinity to the governing of "God's Will on Earth."

Constantine had the bishops agree that the principate was the first royal sovereign of the new Christian Roman order, and that this power sat in complete dominance on earth, ordained by the Creator of the universe from the beginning of time. This is the fusion of religion and government called Christendom that continued to directly shape the course of Eastern and Western civilizations for the next 1,200 years.

This also began a change in the view of free will. While free will under ancient Judaism and early Christianity was seen as a gift from God, free will under Christendom was a problem for humanity. It was argued that free will caused humanity's fall from grace and that it continued to threaten human salvation from Hell. A new order of Christianity was established with the Church as the focal point and the only path to salvation.

Free will was then seen in a negative light as the occasion to sin, and these sins attacked God's divine order. Obedience to the Church and its interpretation of God's will was paramount and seen as the only path to salvation. Furthermore, anyone outside of the Nicene Christian faith — Christian heretics, excommunicated Christians, pagans, Jews, and later Muslims—were believed to be automatically damned to Hell.

⸺⁂⸺

Constantine the Great had the Greek city of Byzantium (modern Istanbul, Turkey) established as the new Christian capital of the Roman Empire, and he declared its new name to be Constantinople. There are several probable reasons Constantine chose that location to set up this new Rome. First, Byzantium was strategically set as a land and water border between Europe and Asia. This gave it tremendous advantages in economic trade and physical defense.

Second, it was in the eastern (Greek) portion of the Roman Empire and, at that time, the New Testament was written only in Greek. Since Constantine was ruling via the faith of Christianity and the "Will of the Holy Trinity," he needed to rule from an area where people could know and understand the teachings of the Holy Bible firsthand.

Third, being far away from Rome, Constantinople had a chance to establish its own Christian culture, which was still a minority and a very tough sell in the western (Latin) portion of the Roman Empire.

⸺⁂⸺

Most Latin Romans still had not accepted Christianity, and Rome had been the seat of pagan power for centuries. The pagan Senate and People of Rome were not yet on board with this new religion, which, just one generation earlier, had been persecuted and despised. Pope Damasus I was Bishop of Rome during the time when the Church of Rome had accepted Nicene Christianity as its official doctrine, but the Senate and People of Rome had not accepted Christianity at all. Thus, another battle of wills began between the leaders of the Western empire and of the universal Church.

One major obstacle to Christianity in the West was that the Holy Bible was only available in Hebrew and Greek; therefore, only the intellectual class was able to read it. The Council of Nicaea had established the Church of Rome, founded by St. Peter, as the head church of Nicene Christianity, and the Bishop of Rome (inheritor of the seat of St. Peter) as Pope of the universal (catholic) church.

The Pope's secretary, Jerome, was commissioned and ordered to translate the entire Holy Bible into Latin. While this took many years to accomplish, Jerome (now St. Jerome) translated the entire Hebrew and Greek texts, while using references in Aramaic, to write a standard Latin version called the Vulgate.

On 27 February 380 AD, the Roman Emperor Theodosius I issued the Edict of Thessalonica, officially making Nicene Christianity the religion of the entire Roman Empire. This permanent acceptance of Christianity by the Roman authorities was part of a transformation that essentially ended ancient times and began medieval times. While no single event can be cited as the moment this transition started, the capitulation of the pagan Roman Empire to the universal Church was certainly an instrumental moment in that long process.

Over time, the political divide between the Greek and Latin halves of the Roman Empire became more pronounced. The permanent split of the Roman administrative state became official in the year AD 395, with Rome as the capital of the western empire and Constantinople as the capital of the eastern empire.

Christian emperors continued to rule over both halves, but the cultural differences grew as different leaders were educated and coronated, different languages were spoken, and different cultures infiltrated and changed the composition of each side.

The Western Roman Empire officially fell as an entity on September 4, 476 AD, with the removal of the last Western emperor named Romulus Augustulus, whose crown was sent to Constantinople. Barbarian tribes had so infiltrated and conquered the Western empire that it effectively ceased to exist. Even so, the Eastern Roman Empire continued to function independently for another millennium.

Societies and sensibilities were intensely altered due to the wide acceptance and empowerment of Christendom, but this acceptance at a governmental level also changed Christianity and the role of the Church. The transition from the ancient to the medieval world was profound for civilization and for the concept of free will in imperial Roman Christianity. The concept of free will that began as a gift from the Creator became something to reject and to shun, giving way to the power of the Church and the state as representatives of God's will over the wills of individual people and the people as a sovereign entity.

Popular sovereignty, the will of the people, was replaced entirely by a hierarchy of bureaucrats who shared the same worldviews. Deviation from this line was considered a threat, not just to the state, but also to the established "Order of God." Anyone who seriously questioned or refuted those in charge were not just seen as deviants, but enemies of God. This, of course, took centuries to build and culminate in events such as the Christian Crusades and the Inquisitions, but the seeds for such events had been planted, and it would inevitably lead to the dominance of the Roman Catholic Church in the West.

————

The creation of Christendom played a very important part in the inspiration and writing of our Freedom Charters, for it showed what a government fused to religion could do to the government, the religion, and the people, both as individuals and as a society. Following the edicts of the religious government became essential to the administration and survival of the state, and there was very little room for innovation or change, as a religious state is extremely top heavy in its power structure.

The founders and framers of the American republic knew these lessons well and put into place a federal system built upon no particular religion, just faith in the Creator, to avoid the pitfalls of a tyrannical, religious government. The framers of the constitution understood the dangers of a religious state and the idea that royal and holy sovereigns speak for God. To counter this possibility, they also adopted ten of the twelve proposed constitutional amendments. Each amendment defines constitutional rights of individuals, organizations, and populations within American jurisdiction, while limiting the powers of state and federal governments.

The Bill of Rights
Amendment I

Congress shall make no law respecting an establishment of religion, or prohibiting the free exercise thereof; or abridging the freedom of speech, or of the press; or the right of the people peaceably to assemble, and to petition the Government for a redress of grievances.

Amendment II

A well-regulated Militia, being necessary to the security of a free State, the right of the people to keep and bear Arms, shall not be infringed.

Amendment III

No Soldier shall, in time of peace be quartered in any house, without the consent of the Owner, nor in time of war, but in a manner to be prescribed by law.

Amendment IV

The right of the people to be secure in their persons, houses, papers, and effects, against unreasonable searches and seizures, shall not be violated, and no Warrants shall issue, but upon probable cause, supported by Oath or affirmation, and particularly describing the place to be searched, and the persons or things to be seized.

Amendment V

No person shall be held to answer for a capital, or otherwise infamous crime, unless on a presentment or indictment of a Grand Jury, except in cases arising in the land or naval forces, or in the Militia, when in actual service in time of War or public danger; nor shall any person be subject for the same offence to be twice put in jeopardy of life or limb; nor shall be compelled in any criminal case to be a witness against himself, nor be deprived of life, liberty, or property, without due process of law; nor shall private property be taken for public use, without just compensation.

Amendment VI

In all criminal prosecutions, the accused shall enjoy the right to a speedy and public trial, by an impartial jury of the State and district wherein the crime shall have been committed, which district shall have been previously ascertained by law, and to be informed of the nature and cause of the accusation; to be confronted with the witnesses against him; to have compulsory process for obtaining witnesses in his favor, and to have the Assistance of Counsel for his defense.

Amendment VII

In suits at common law, where the value in controversy shall exceed twenty dollars, the right of trial by jury shall be preserved, and no fact tried by a jury, shall be otherwise reexamined in any Court of the United States, than according to the rules of the common law.

Amendment VIII

Excessive bail shall not be required, nor excessive fines imposed, nor cruel and unusual punishments inflicted.

Amendment IX

The enumeration in the Constitution of certain rights, shall not be construed to deny or disparage others retained by the people.

Amendment X

The powers not delegated to the United States by the Constitution, nor prohibited by it to the States, are reserved to the States respectively, or to the people.

CHAPTER 9

Medieval Times

The culture of the Eastern Roman Empire did not remain solely in the realm of Byzantine society but influenced societies in every direction of the connected world. Advances in Byzantine art, architecture, and literature had an impact on the Near East, Arabia, Africa, Western Europe, and Russia.

The Byzantine Empire produced strong and weak leaders throughout its long history, and like any society, a certain combination of people, environments, and events needed to occur for certain individuals to shine. One example of this had a deep impact on Western civilization and the creation of our Freedom Charters.

The emperor Justinian took power in AD 527. While a cultural outsider to Roman heritage and politics, Justinian quickly became a fanatic of Roman law. The *Code of Justinian* would remain the basis of law in Byzantium and become the root of civil laws in Europe for centuries after Byzantium.

While Justinian achieved much in his lifetime, it would never have happened if it were not for the strength and fortitude of his loving wife, Theodora. Justinian and Theodora's primary importance was the new framing of Roman civil laws under the categories of Persons, Things, and Actions. Simply stated, the Code of Justinian was a new arraignment of old Roman laws and legal opinions that had passed down through the centuries.

After Justinian's death in AD 565, Roman emperors continued to rule over their provinces, but they gradually formed their own Eastern identity and followed their own path. From that time on, the Eastern Roman Empire was really the Byzantine Empire, and the many ancient forms of civilization it influenced gave way to new and different models of religion and government.

Byzantium's influence on the world was multifold. Its contribution to civilization is similar to, yet different from Islam's, which will be covered next. First, the city of Constantinople continued the royal sovereignty of the Christian Roman Emperors in the Greek east. The Byzantine Emperor was seen as Christ's will on Earth and ruled as a royal sovereign backed by the divine sovereignty of God (the Holy Trinity) and the Blessed Virgin Mary (the Mother of God).

Second, Byzantium preserved all the learning of the ancient Greeks and Romans, which essentially preserved the thoughts, beliefs, and advances of the ancient classical world. Greek learning was still at the center of this Christian Roman Empire, and the thoughts of every connected ancient culture that had been translated into Greek during the Ptolemies was available for any literate person to read and contemplate. This included the ancient Greek concept of individual free will.

Third, Byzantium was the only force powerful enough to stop the spread of barbarians in its territories; thus, it did not experience the Dark Ages that occurred in Western Europe. Byzantium and the walls of Constantinople kept back non-Romanized and non-Christianized barbarian tribes who would have destroyed the Christian culture and civilization founded by

Constantine the Great, and framed by the influences of Theodosius the Great, the emperor Justinian, and the empress Theodora.

Fourth, the Byzantine Empire was the only military counterbalance against the armies of Islam throughout the early Middle Ages (until the recovery of Western Christendom centuries later). Islamic armies flooded out of Arabia one generation after the death of Justinian, taking many Eastern Roman provinces, including parts of Asia Minor, Lebanon, Palestine/Syria, Jordan, Egypt, and north Africa. Islamic armies even continued into the Western Christian Visigoth Kingdom in North Africa and Iberia, only being stopped in Gaul by a Western barbarian Christian tribe, the Franks.

Finally, although they could not sustain any expansion of their empire through military conquests, they did spread their prestige and influence through Christian missions. The Christian Roman emperors of Byzantium could not enforce their direct will outside of their realm or stop much of it from being overrun by foreign armies over the next thousand years. Even so, the Eastern Orthodox churches of the Byzantines sent missionaries to every area of the connected world.

<hr />

The Eastern Orthodox churches operated in cooperation and in communion with the Byzantine Church. Eastern churches were, and still are, Nicene Christian, with each bishop being the head of that Orthodox church. While Orthodox theology is maintained, separate nuances continue to make each Eastern church unique unto itself.

The Church of Rome was beaten and battered by the tumultuous end of antiquity in the West, and the desires of the Popes in Rome had very little material weight to back their political will outside of Latium and the peninsula of Italia.

The Eastern churches within the Byzantine realm then looked to Constantinople as the only head of their eastern faith, but disputes over the nature of Christ caused the first schism in Nicene Christianity. The churches of the Greek East and the Latin West also had continued to distance themselves from their early unity. The official split in communion took place in AD 1054. The Pope and the Church of Rome had excommunicated, and been excommunicated by, the Patriarch of Constantinople. At this point, the Nicene Christian Church was officially split into the Greek and Oriental Orthodox Churches of the East and the Roman Catholic Church of the West.

The contributions of Byzantium and its churches to Western culture were many. Most important for this book are the collection and coding of Roman law by Justinian and the preservation of classical documents. These laws and documents would serve as the initial catalyst for shaping of our modern concepts of law and justice in Western civilization and, inevitably, the American republic.

———

The Byzantine withdrawal from Western Europe in AD 565 left a very open and weak Western empire void of central authority. The barbarian tribes that had officially ended the rule of the Western Roman Empire a century earlier, were at least Christianized (although not Nicene Christian) and were familiar with, and interested in, continuing the successful nature of Roman administration.

The barbarian invaders of the sixth century, however, were not Christianized and not interested in anything related to Roman culture or even classical antiquity. Their conquests brought about a dramatic change in the administration and culture of Western Europe.

It can be argued that Western civilization stopped for more than two centuries. People could not safely travel on the Roman roads, all international trade ended, and entire Roman cities were abandoned because they could not feed large populations. Western Europe depopulated, and Christianity and classical learning disappeared in many areas. In its place were very localized "towns" made of mostly mud, dung, and straw buildings that operated as independent fiefdoms.

The loss of classical civilization and Christianity in the West had a deep impact that severed it from the ancient worlds of Greece and Rome. Rome itself depopulated and the Roman Catholic Church was the only entity strong enough to have any influence.

Christendom, the ancient Roman Empire, and classical antiquity seemed to have disappeared in the West, and for all practical purposes it did, but something outside the borders of the Western empire had been planted centuries earlier and began to grow. This was the Christianity of Scotland and Ireland. What is today known as the Celtic Church remained a bastion of Western civilization that kept the dream of a literate, Christian West alive for two centuries.

⁓⁓⁓

Roman armies never conquered and held Scotland north of Hadrian's Wall or the western island of Ireland; however, Christian missionaries during the late Western Empire had done just that through mass conversions of those populations to the Christian faith. Without anyone's notice, the Celtic Church kept civilized living alive in the West. They transcribed Jerome's Latin Bible in the old Latin language and spread the Christian message to areas outside their lands. It was very dangerous, and the pagan barbarian tribes had no hesitation murdering Celtic missionaries. Slowly, however, Christianity was again spread to areas that had been the Western Empire.

The English legends of King Arthur began during this time and continued to evolve for a millennium. While the story, in all its many versions, is mostly fantasy, it was apparently inspired by real people and real events that occurred in those dark centuries. The story is significant because it kept alive the idea of the divine sovereignty of a single royal sovereign ruler of a Christian world in the West.

Many symbols in the legends of King Arthur reflect the obsession with this shrouded ideal. The old ways of sorcery and paganism were on their way out, while the quest for the Holy Grail of Christ demonstrated the desire to reunite the lands of the West under a single Christian ruler.

The Sword of Power, Excalibur, was another symbol of this king who was, or would be, an enlightened and just ruler, ordained by Christ and the God of Abraham. Through the centuries, several people appeared momentarily that suggested this dream was transpiring. Some of them were the Western Roman Emperor Constantine III; some obscure defenders of Sub-Roman Britain against the pagan Saxon invaders; the Emperor Charlemagne, King of the Franks; Alfred the Great, King of the Saxons; several kings of Normandy, and others.

Monasticism began in Christendom long before Benedict of Nursia was born around AD 480. Although he did not invent this lifestyle, he did codify the standards and worldview, which would take shape throughout the West during the Middle Ages.

The Holy Rule of St. Benedict documented the precise order, expectations, attitudes, and behaviors of people in the monastic clergy. St. Benedict's writings became the established standard of ecclesiastical living for more than a thousand years.

Benedict's rejection of individual free will and complete surrender to God's will was the essence of his Christian standards. These standards were based on asceticism. Asceticism is rooted in the abandonment of the material world for the purpose of dedicating all of one's time, space, and body to spiritual pursuits. Ascetics swear off all material possessions and earthly pleasures of the body in pursuit of spiritual pleasures of the soul.

While many people living outside the monastic lifestyle find the ascetic philosophy of self-denial inconceivable, monks who are truly dedicated to its beliefs often find an inner, spiritual peace not generally experienced through the physical, material world.

Christian ascetics have an age-old dilemma between the individual pursuit of living an isolated life and the Christian calling for serving others. St. Benedict found the compromise through the establishment of monasteries. Monasteries are isolated communities of monks who live and work among each other but still provide services to nearby communities. The leader of a monastery is called an abbot. Abbots are essentially the chief executives of the monastery.

Benedict's primary importance for Western Christendom is his establishment of very specific standards for clergy who would eventually fill the administrative void created by the dissolution of the Western Roman

Empire. This new role of the clergy as public administrators was promoted by a benefactor of St. Benedict who we call Pope Gregory I.

Pope Gregory was born around AD 540, ten years after Benedict established his monastery on Montecassino. He was the first pope to come from the monastic lifestyle, and his experiences both as monk and emissary to Constantinople gave him a broad perspective from personal self-discipline to the administration of civil laws.

Pope Gregory's primary importance stems from his conversions of barbarian kings to the Nicene Christian faith. Most barbarian kingdoms were either Arian Christian—who were considered heretics—or pagans.

Pope Gregory the Great initiated contact and sent out emissaries like what Byzantium had done in the East. His successful conversion of many tribes to Nicene Christianity, with sworn loyalty to the Roman Church, immensely aided the re-Christianizing of the west. They also expanded the power and influence of the Roman Catholic Church through use of Catholic clergy for reviving, directing, and managing the emerging administrative state(s).

This, of course, was a slow process that took much longer than one lifetime. But in a few centuries, the policies of Pope Gregory I paid off immeasurably as the barbarian kingdoms of Western Europe all swore loyalty and spiritual submission to Christ and the See of St. Peter.

While Gregory brought northern and western tribes back into Western Christendom, future popes and their emissaries followed his guidelines, which eventually established Roman Catholicism in the emerging nations of Italy, Spain, Germany, France, and Britain.

On December 25, AD 800, a small coronation took place in Rome's old St. Peter's Basilica. It was the crowning of Charlemagne, King of the Franks, with the title "Augustus, Emperor of the Romans." Charlemagne was the grandson of Charles Martel, who stopped the Islamic invaders from conquering past Iberia. Charlemagne is considered the first Holy Roman Emperor of the Holy Roman Empire.

This ceremony was significant not only because it reinstituted a Western empire with Roman law, but also because it was instituted and executed by Pope Leo III, demonstrating the accepted power and prestige of the papacy in northern and central Europe. Charlemagne was the first royal sovereign crowned by the Bishop of Rome, and he ruled the first unified empire of the Christian West since the fall of the Western Roman Empire over three centuries earlier.

Charlemagne presided over a time of continuous war between kingdoms in the West, but he commissioned literate monks to transcribe not only the Latin Holy Bible (Vulgate), but also all the works of classical antiquity that had survived in monasteries since before the Dark Ages, as well as ancient Greek and Roman learning preserved by Byzantium and Islam.

Charlemagne also reinstituted civil laws in the West, using law codes from the Byzantine Empire as a model. Charlemagne's law codes became the foundation of civil law in the West for centuries. Charlemagne's royal sovereignty not only reestablished Roman administration in the West, but also affirmed the power and prestige of the Roman Catholic Church, which was responsible for his coronation.

The power of the papacy and the Bishop of Rome also went from a religious model to include a model for governing. The clergy had, in fact, become holy sovereigns whose power was claimed to be derived from the God of Abraham, Jesus Christ, and the Holy Spirit of God—the Holy

Trinity. While still weak compared to Byzantium, Latin Christianity and the Holy Roman Empire was growing in power and influence in central and western Europe.

These events caused western civilization to become dominated by one Nicene-Christian church, The Roman Catholic Church. The powers of the Church of Rome, founded by St. Peter and St. Paul, took on the spiritual mantle of Christendom in the West. While the Emperor of Byzantium was seen as "Christ's will on earth" in the East, the Roman Catholic Church proclaimed itself "God's instrument on earth" in the West. This was the beginning of an era of history and Christendom now known as the Gothic Age.

⚜

The Gothic Age saw the pope and his bishops claim moral authority over all Western Christendom. The power and will of the Latin Church became absolute, and any royal sovereign who wanted to be a king or emperor needed to be affirmed and ordained by the papacy in Rome.

Popes even raised their own armies and made war with those who dared threaten their claim as the Holy See of Christ's Church, founded by the first pope, St. Peter, who they believed had been specifically named by Jesus Christ as "the Rock" on which He had built His Church.

Any ideas of individual free will were automatically negated. The "Will of God in Heaven" became paramount, and the Church was God's instrument on earth, with the Bishop of Rome as its head. Thus, the will of the Roman Church was determined by the will of the papacy in Rome, led by the infallible Bishop of Rome—the Pope. This was proven through the might of the Christian emperors and kings who ruled through the sovereign powers of the papacy and its administration, as well as the armies that enforced the will of these leaders.

The Roman Catholic Church became the moral authority and civil administrators for much of the Western world. While royal sovereigns often fought among themselves, all gave allegiance to the Church of Rome and its bishop, the pope.

The reason for this ability to grab and hold power over so many people came from the fact that the Church leaders were literate and had the most advanced administrative system in the West since the fall of the Western Roman Empire. Centuries earlier, the Church of Rome had adopted almost every administrative advantage from the genius of Diocletian's system. The pagan Roman Emperor Diocletian, a persecutor of the Christian faith, invented the administrative system, which the Church had adopted for itself and later imposed on the kingdoms of the West.

The Latin Church was also seen as a reflection of ancient Roman imperial power. Its priests were the only literate people in Western Europe. They traveled the old Roman roads in safety. They were learned people who had the advantages of a classical education. They studied and learned the thoughts of the ancients and had the powers of influence and persuasion that others in the illiterate royal class could not hope to wield.

They also were protected by the aura of the Holy See of Rome, and since the Church of Rome was God's instrument on earth, attacking it, or any member of that organization, was considered an attack on God Himself.

The Gothic world survived for six centuries, and while improving life for many inhabitants of its lands, its people were still a very closed and superstitious society. The barbarian culture of personal glory through the brute force of physical battles stayed with the people in the West, and the winners of contests, battles, and wars were often seen as being right according to God's will. Sporadic and violent persecutions of Jews and Muslims living in, or near, their lands also were commonplace.

Political and military planning of the Crusades was hatched and implemented by powerful clergy and royalty who obviously had more than religion on their minds but used religion in a way to justify these endeavors and the slaughters. Medieval torture was quite inventive, cruel, and more in line with pagan Rome than the messages of Jesus.

Even so, Gothic Europe was a step forward out of the Dark Ages, and renewed interactions with the old faiths of Judaism, Byzantine Orthodoxy, and Islam gave Gothic Europe the tools and knowledge required for their next great step—exploration of the world.

⋙⋘

The law codes of Justinian and Charlemagne became the template of Western civil law. This, plus the contributions of English common law, became the standards that the American founders and framers used for their blueprint of a new constitutional republic. While the substance of those laws was of interest, it was the order and organization of the laws that had the greatest impact. As stated earlier, ancient law codes were more like abstract principles of justice that the rulers wanted for their realms. Coded law books saw the beginning of structured formats for laws. This gave rise to our modern definitions of civil, common, and constitutional laws.

CHAPTER 10

Islam

The Byzantine Emperor Justinian died in AD 565, which can be identified as the official end to the ancient classical world. About five years later, a prophet was born further east on the Arabian Peninsula. This prophet proclaimed to be the last of the prophets of the God of Abraham. His name was Muhammad, a middle-class merchant, born in the city of Mecca (now in the Kingdom of Saudi Arabia) which, at that time, was still controlled by the old pagan orders of Parthia (The Sasanian Empire). In the span of one lifetime, Muhammad's teachings impacted the Near East, Far East, Byzantine Empire, Africa, and Iberia with a new belief, which became the religion of Islam.

Islam translates most closely to the English word "submission" and is meant as "submission to the will of God." Islam is an intensely systematic dedication to faith, prayer, charity, fasting, and pilgrimage. Unlike Jesus Christ, who Muhammad considered another prophet of God but not divine, Muhammad penned the Holy Book of Islam called the Koran, "The Recitation."

According to the followers of Islam, the Koran in the language of Arabic is considered a direct revelation from the God of Abraham, dictated by the Angel Gabriel for Mohammad to transcribe. These new ideas caused a deemphasis of tribes and clans worshiping many gods and promoted the idea of humanity as a whole, worshiping one God, or The God, "Allah."

Muhammad's teachings of Allah threatened the pagan power structures in the city of Mecca, which at that time, was led by his own family tribe, Quraish. Persecutions by the Quraish in Mecca eventually caused Muhammad to leave his tribal home for a city now called Medina. Medina is approximately 210 miles from Mecca.

While travelling one night, Muhammad was intercepted by an envoy of multitribal leaders (pagan and Jewish) who were desperate for his assistance. Tribal and clan violence had made life intolerable in Medina, and this envoy was very interested in hearing the message of Muhammed that the tribes of Mecca had rejected. Upon hearing Muhammad's testament, the members of the envoy converted to Islam on the spot and agreed to meet with Muhammad again.

After leaving his ancestral home and tribe, Muhammad was welcomed by the tribes of Medina as a great political leader and mediator. Muhammad later authored and produced a document called the Constitution of Medina. The original Constitution of Medina is lost to history, but this composition was successfully developed by Muhammad to bring peace to the warring tribes and clans of Medina.

Muhammad's success as a mediator between tribal minds brought great respect from the people. The Constitution of Medina brought all the tribes and clans together through ideas, not bloodlines. This is its primary significance. Never before had a broad group of diverse people adopted a union enshrined by an ideology.

This ideology was written into the constitution by Muhammad, not to be an Islamic document, but a universal declaration for all residents of Medina. This document was based on Muhammad's desire to unite the tribes and clans of Medina under the common benefits of peace and protection.

It did not establish Islam as a ruling religion, but rather a part of the community of tribes, clans and families who were Islamic, Jewish, Christian, and pagan. What Muhammad had established was a state that respected the universal rights of its citizens and was governed by the rule of law. These laws were based on the civil rights of the residents of Medina. Some of these rights and responsibilities included:

- the right to life,
- the right to property,
- the right to free religious practice,
- the responsibility to protect Medina from invaders,
- the responsibility to respect the rights of other residents regardless of tribal or clan affiliation,
- the responsibility to follow the rule of law set down in the constitution,
- and the responsibility to allow the law, not tribal tradition, to dictate responses to grievances.

The Constitution of Medina was a tremendous political achievement. Convincing tribal peoples to put the rule of law ahead of tribal tradition was an amazing feat. Tribes were still free to follow their own traditions, but these traditions were all expected to yield to the constitution and the rule of law when in conflict with it.

Unfortunately, this innovative idea was short-lived. Lasting less than a decade, the Constitution of Medina was eventually altered and later discarded. The tribes of Medina, as well as the rest of the world, were not yet ready for Muhammad's vision. Although abandoned, the Constitution of Medina proved it is possible for people to be united through shared abstract notions and concepts and not just family lineage and ethnicity.

—⊶⊷—

Muhammad was not just the accepted leader of Medina, but also a political genius who was able to use his position to make alliances with other tribes of Arabia. The Quraish tribe of Mecca were still very bitter and engaged in numerous plots to overthrow and assassinate Muhammad.

When the Meccans attacked a tribe allied with Muhammad, the city state of Medina rallied ten thousand men and marched on Mecca. Arab tribal tradition dictated that the conquered men of Mecca were to be executed and the women and children enslaved. This is not what Muhammad did.

Convinced that his new view of humanity was a genuine revelation from the God of Abraham, Muhammad believed in his spiritual revelations before tribal tradition. In these revelations people were not identified by tribal affiliation, but by their common humanity.

Muhammad's revelations also taught that free will was a gift from God the Creator and that no person should be forced to convert to Islam. Conquered Meccans were not killed or enslaved but had a choice to convert to Islam or to leave Mecca forever; thus, Mecca became the first truly Islamic city in the world.

Today Islam is its own religion, but Muhammad saw it as a continuation of Judaism and Christianity. Muhammad taught that Jews and Christians were "People of the Book," and much later they were granted special treatment called dhimmi. Muhammad taught that faithful followers of Islam, Christianity, and Judaism were all Muslims, i.e. submitters.

Dhimmi constituted permission for Jews and Christians to worship in their own ways, but they had to pay a special tax, and they were not allowed to convert Islamic Muslims, or challenge Islamic dominance with the building of new churches, or to worship outside the church and private homes, nor to ring church bells where the sound could be heard outside.

⊷▯▯▯⊷

While Muhammad had been very successful in uniting the multitude of Arabian tribes under one religion, there was a split that occurred upon his death. That split continues to this day, and it is a very destructive aspect within and between the followers of the Islamic faith.

Muhammad died teaching that no Muslim should ever take up arms against another Muslim, but this split between what we call Sunni Islam and Shiite Islam has been responsible for much suffering and death within the Islamic world since the physical death of Muhammad.

After the death of Muhammad in AD 632, the united Arab tribes conquered civilizations in every direction. Islam was spread to India, Persia, Mesopotamia, Lebanon, Palestine Syria, Egypt, Africa, and Iberia. Muslims not only brought their religion, but also their new ideas and ways of looking at the world.

Along their conquests, Muslims had found and translated all the ancient Greek works into Arabic. Many Islamic leaders became fascinated with Greek thoughts in everything from technology, physics, mental health and medicine, to art, architecture, literature, and music. Islam also advanced knowledge in the areas of science, through new studies and discoveries, as well as a new numeral system borrowed from India: 0, 1, 2, 3, 4, 5, 6, 7, 8, 9; thus, these Arabic numerals—Indian numerals to the Arabs—became the new language of clocks, calendars, and mathematics.

The Islamic armies became the most powerful fighting forces in the early Middle Ages. Islam is most important here for briefly demonstrating that a constitutional republic can be founded through an ideology of law and due process and for helping to preserve the knowledge and wisdom of the ancient classical world through the translation and scholarship of ancient Greek works.

Many Arab-influenced cultures in Persia, Mesopotamia, Lebanon, Syria, Palestine, Egypt, north Africa, and Iberia (called Al-Andalus) copied and extended ancient Greek thoughts through science, mathematics, and poetry, but all remained submissive to their faith through Islamic law. Free will in medieval Islam was very similar to free will in ancient Judaism, in that people were allowed to freely choose the interpretation and extent they would submit to the will of God.

While following their own individual will, people in early Islam were allowed to make choices that benefited themselves, which brought "prosperity and pleasure to the soul." All thoughts, words, and actions, however, must be for the glory of God and not the glory of man. Giving thanks to God several times daily was, and still is, a critical part of the Islamic faith.

Medieval Islam was very similar to ancient Judaism in many ways. Muslims did not believe in making graven images, so they rejected statues or depictions of God and Muhammad in art. Islamic art remains abstract with vibrant colors and patterns, which are very dynamic and pleasing to the eye. Dietary restrictions in Islam also are like that of ancient Judaism, as well as the active practice of men wearing beards and prayer and fasting for repentance and cleansing of the soul.

110

The most important idea in Islam to Muslims is found in their declaration of belief, "There is no God but God, and Muhammad is his prophet." While Jews and Christians under medieval Islamic rule were often allowed to continue their worship of the God of Abraham in their own ways, pagans were not permitted to continue to worship in the old ways. Despite the universal teachings of the prophet, many millions of pagans as well as some Jews and Christians were forcibly converted to Islam, enslaved, or executed.

The geopolitics of Islam starts in Mecca and Medina, where the first Islamic caliphs resided. In later years, different cities became the power centers of the Islamic world. Damascus was a far-reaching capital of a dynasty known as the Umayyad Caliphate, but these Sunni Muslims were conquered by Shiite Muslims from Persia. The new Shiite Muslim dynasty called the Abbasid Caliphate built a new capital called Baghdad, which became a cultural center to every art and science.

Other Islamic caliphs ruled areas further west in Syria, Lebanon, Palestine, Egypt, north Africa, and Iberia. A sole survivor of the Umayyad, Abd al-Rahman I, made his way to Iberia and established a new dynasty that was eventually centered in the city of Cordoba, Al-Andalus (modern Spain and Portugal). This very advanced and tolerant society would last several centuries and become a vital link to Western Europe's rebirth.

Islam was the largest international influence in the Middle Ages. The science and technologies produced were vital to Western Christendom from the tenth century forward. Sea trade was especially fruitful for Islamic and Christian empires alike, and while the Christian Crusades did irreparable harm to the relationship between Islam and the West, the knowledge that was exchanged during those times benefitted both cultures.

For our purposes, Islam's most impactful technological contributions to the West were found in their number system, sailing, navigation, and warfare. Algebra was an essential mathematical invention, and the triangular lateen sail allowed ships to sail against wind currents, which meant that sailing was no longer solely dependent upon wind direction. The Chinese compass was adapted and improved, and navigation by the stars was a perfected skill and technique with devices called the alidade and astrolabe. Islam also brought the West another Chinese invention called gunpowder.

Use of gunpowder in China was limited to fireworks and a few experimental weapons, but some in the West saw a greater potential. The technology of firearms and cannons started with small, unreliable weapons, but eventually improved with deadly efficiency, changing warfare and the world forever.

Islam was essentially the medieval equivalent to ancient Judaism, Greece, and Rome in that it advanced art, architecture, science, mathematics, philosophy, medicine, and more. Medieval Islam kept the spirit of innovation alive in the world. While Byzantium was grand and very rich, it was also static. Islam was a much more dynamic and diverse religion of invention and trade, which would help preserve and transmit to Western civilization the richness and majesty of their lost ancient heritage, as well as the heritages of the Far East, Near East, and new Middle East.

—◦◦◦—

Islam's contribution to the founding and framing of the American republic was indirect. It's doubtful that white American colonists in the eighteenth century had much knowledge of Islam and its history. The fact remains, however, that there were many Muslims in the Americas during the founding of the United States.

It's surprising to most Americans as this is rarely mentioned in our history books, but many African slaves came to this country as members of the Islamic religion. Dehumanization and conversion to Christianity obscures this history, but the contributions of African slaves and African American citizens of the United States have been grossly underappreciated for much of American existence.

This is because native Africans did not arrive in the Americas like most other people from the Eastern hemisphere. Coming to this country as slaves was a degradation that robbed so many of them from their historical roots. The process of dehumanization of the slaves caused most free Americans to not even realize that their human property had a culture, let alone religion.

This on-going crime for almost 300 years completely separated Africans and African Americans from their Islamic roots, and it has only been in the last five or six decades that African Americans have been reintroduced to their lost culture.

Most African Americans today are Christians, but their Islamic cultural past has remained with us in obscure forms, and all the contributions to the American republic from African Americans is certainly reflective of their heritage that goes back much further than the days of Western slavery.

CHAPTER 11

The First Source of Causality

While human concepts of a divine order go back to the beginnings of human self-awareness, certain philosophical thinkers and historical writings have been specifically instrumental in the development and application of our Freedom Charters. While their philosophies are built from the works of yet earlier people, examples described here are fundamental in understanding the viewpoints and motivations of the founders and framers of the American republic.

This chapter will begin with a man named Abu ʿAli al-Husayn ibn Sina (aka Avicenna). Avicenna was born around AD 980 in central Asia. He was a Muslim philosopher, scientist, mathematician, and physician. He is important for his thoughtful and profound exploration into the nature of human beings and their Creator. This work is called *The Physics of The Healing* (aka *The Cure*).

Avicenna believed that a creator God is a "necessary existence" in understanding human beings and the existence of a rational human soul. The rational soul is not considered a part of the human body, but rather it is a quality of divine essence. Evidence of this rational soul is found in the fact that it is self-aware, and that it is constantly questioning itself. The most fundamental principle of Avicenna's work is called the first source of causality. Understanding this is vital to understanding everything in existence from the moment of Creation, and Avicenna identifies the God of Abraham as this source.

The rational soul allows humans to conceive and perceive ideas that are not directly related to information gained from the physical senses; rather, it is the human ability to create abstract conceptualizations of life and the universe from insight beyond the physical senses. This allows and causes people to generate ideas gathered from divine inspiration. This makes the existence of a divine creator, as the ultimate source of the rational soul and its abilities, indispensable.

Avicenna's contention was that a rational soul cannot create itself; therefore, a creator God becomes a necessary existence for human creativity, reasoning, and self-awareness. This is evident in that many of our abstract conceptualizations about life and the universe are not based on direct observations, but rather imagined, rationalized, and explored through inspiration, faith, and reasoning.

Sometime later came an enlightened thinker of medieval Judaism named Rabbi Moses Ben Maimon (aka Maimonides) who lived in Cordova, Al-Andalus (Spain) from AD 1138 to 1204 under Muslim authorities. Maimonides built upon Avicenna's nature of origin (the nature of God and the nature of the soul), but he also questioned the nature of nature and the nature of man. His book, *Guide for the Perplexed,* is a work that causes the re-evaluation of ancient religious perceptions using faith and reason.

On page one of his book, he lays out the idea that the image of God is not physical but abstract. Humanity is not made in the physiological image of God the Creator, but the spiritual and intellectual image. The human frame does not apply to this abstract God, but rather the human soul does. Since the God of Abraham is completely abstract in Judaism and Islam, our similarities to the Creator are derived from our self-aware consciousness, abstract conceptualizations, and creative abilities, not our corporeal bodies.

Rabbi Maimonides theorized that the God of Abraham, as the first source of causality, created the universe in one of three ways:

1) a free act of Creation where all was created from God directly. This is the most common interpretation of the Book of Genesis,

2) creation from already existing ingredients, where God took these raw materials and made His Creation. An example of this can be found in scriptures where God is said to have made the first man, "Adamah" (Adam), from the dust of the ground, as is in Judaism and Christianity, or from a clot of blood as is in Islam,

3) or eternal emanation, where God used other substances and structures to create the universe. This is perhaps best explained by modern scientific theories about quantum fields, quantum mechanics, and the "Big Bang" Theory.

A third thinker from the Middle Ages is a Christian saint named St. Thomas Aquinas (AD 1225-1274.) In his writings called Summa Theologica, St. Thomas Aquinas believed that as rational beings, humans can understand the God of Abraham and His Creation through the special human qualities of faith and human reasoning.

St. Thomas Aquinas studied under another profound thinker named St. Albert the Great, who was his senior. Both men were diligent in their investigations of the sciences and the natural world. Both also knew the medieval thoughts and writings of Avicenna and Maimonides, as well as the classical Greek writings of Plato and Aristotle. St. Thomas Aquinas built upon the ideas of Plato, Aristotle, Avicenna, Maimonides, and his contemporaries Averroes and Albert through the concept of natural law.

The concept of natural law began in the ancient Greek philosophy of Aristotle. Aristotle stated in his books on metaphysics that the laws of nature were present before the laws of man and that these laws do not change; therefore, the laws of man should be reasoned and based upon the laws of nature.

Medieval Muslim and Jewish philosophers took Aristotle to the next level, where they believed that natural law could be understood through reasoning being applied to holy scriptures. If the universe had been designed by a conscious and rational Creator, then the reasoning of that Creator's creation should be available for human study and understanding.

St. Thomas Aquinas took these beliefs even further by formulating a model that defined the results of human reason being applied to natural law to create human Law. Here, St. Thomas Aquinas laid out his belief that the rational human mind with God given free will can give human beings the ability and the knowledge to choose a reasoned path toward perfection. Note that while total perfection is solely reserved for the God of Abraham, humans have the capacity to aspire toward perfection as they attempt to emulate the Creator, being in his image.

This pursuit of perfection is essential as we study the path from eternal law to human law:

1) Eternal law is the entire being of God the Creator and is beyond any human ability to comprehend.

2) Divine law is the part of eternal law that has been given to humanity as divine revelation through the Old Testament prophets, Jesus

Christ, and His disciples with insights from the Holy Spirit of God and recorded in the Holy Bible.

3) Natural law exists in the natural order of things and is understood by humanity through faith and the reasoning of God's divine law.

4) Human law is thus created from human knowledge and reasoning of natural law.

St. Thomas Aquinas reasoned eternal law to human law:

1) God revealed aspects of His eternal law through divine revelations, which humans know as divine law.

2) Human faith and participation in divine law allows people to reason and understand natural laws, which are already in existence.

3) Natural law does not vary according to time but is unchanging.

4) Natural law applies to all humans in their imperfect state.

5) Human self-preservation is a product of natural law.

6) Natural law causes us to pursue good and avoid evil for the purpose of self-preservation.

7) Natural law is self-evident due to the promotion of one's well-being for the purpose of self-preservation.

8) Individual human acts of reason and free will are innate occurrences within natural law.

9) Natural law is judged by humans based upon human intellect and the human senses.

10) Active human reasoning allows for human knowledge of natural law.

11) Natural law is based on self-evident principles.

12) Human virtue is not naturally recognized but becomes apparent through reasoning of one's well-being.

13) Virtuous human behaviors are subject to natural law.

14) Human vice is a perversion of natural law.

15) Natural law can be blotted out of the human heart by evil or by instinctual mistakes.

16) Human law is derived from our understanding of natural law.

17) Human law is dictated from human reasoning.

18) The essence of human law is ordained in the common good.

19) The force of human law depends on its capacity for justice.

20) Human law is framed for humans, the majority of whom are not perfect in virtue.

21) Human law should repress grievous vices, but not all vices.

22) The purpose of human law is to lead people to virtue, not instantaneously, but gradually.

23) Human law does not prescribe all acts of human virtue and does not prohibit all acts of human vice.

24) Human law can be changed as it progresses toward perfection.

Human laws are derived from the instinct of self-preservation being subjected to human reasoning of the natural order of creation. The purpose of these laws is to curb the vices of individual free will while allowing the virtues of individual free will to flourish in the common good for the honorable pursuit of justice.

Human law is made by humans but is not simply a human invention. It is derived from the self-evident laws of nature, begun at the moment of creation by the first source of causality, God the Creator; emanated through the evolution of the universe, which brought about the powers of reasoning, virtue, faith, free will and God-given natural rights to the entire human race.

The writings of these three and other medieval philosophers from the Abrahamian religions form the blueprint of the Western worldview of the Creator God. This concept of God frames Him as the first source of causality, establishing laws that are to be emulated by human law for the pursuit of justice.

Proclaiming God to be the first sovereign and for all human beings made in His image, our Freedom Charters began the process of recognizing sovereignty of the individual. While our Freedom Charters were applied much more narrowly at their beginning, within our Freedom Charters was placed the mechanisms to expand and evolve, and to enhance the virtues and correct the faults of American society from its inception forward to greater perfection.

A very important aspect to remember is that the framers knew American society had a long way to go to fully actualize the benefits of our Freedom Charters. This is why adhering to them is so important for our current preservation and progress. The constitutional system of the United States is an enduring process, not something that changes on the whims of each generation.

Next, I will focus upon Western culture and the English system, which is the direct predecessor to the American system. While the American colonies departed from the British, the English philosophies and model for governing are the blueprint for the American system. Ironically, it was their loyalty to the British system that led the colonists to rebel against the ruling monarch, King George III, who was denying them their sovereign rights granted by the English system as British subjects.

Part II

CHAPTER 12

The English Charters

If there is a point in history to suggest the beginning of an elevated state of freedom as a practical application within a society, it would begin in AD 1100 with the coronation of the literate and classically educated King Henry I of England. King Henry was the embodiment of a classical philosopher king (such as described by Plato in *The Republic*). As the son of William the Conqueror, the Norman king who invaded and conquered England in AD 1066, he succeeded his brother William II as king of England.

Although of Norman line, King Henry continued the Anglo-Saxon Exchequer, which had been the system for collecting taxes in England for centuries. The Exchequer was also responsible for the act of auditing tax records, which established greater accountability between the collections of the King and others in the royal classes. This, plus the establishment of the Charter of Liberties, recognized the rights and responsibilities of English sovereigns from that time forward.

The Charter of Liberties was King Henry's attempt to bind the Roman Church and the royal sovereigns with a uniform law. Henry saw that accountability and fairness was necessary for the stability and strength of the new English nation on the Isle of Britain.

His Charter established:

- restitution for previous abuses by his brother,
- the rights of the Church and clergy,

- the rights of the royal classes,
- the rights of wives and widows,
- the rights of knights,
- holding the royal sovereigns accountable to the law,
- holding the holy sovereigns accountable to the law,
- maintenance of the land,
- restitution of his own properties.

The Charter of Liberties served two important purposes. First, it established the principle of the rule of law over the arbitrary will of royal and holy sovereigns, and second, it kept the peace for the rest of Henry's reign. Upon the death of King Henry, lawlessness and domestic wars ensued, and it was only the ascension of his grandson, King Henry II in AD 1154 that re-established law and order to the English realm.

Henry II had very bad relations with the Church of Rome. He had ordered the assassination of an archbishop and replaced him with an ally. He also was determined to hold the Church and its clergy accountable to the law just as the English royal classes. Henry II's reforms also established property rights among the nobles and the clergy. This, plus greater emphasis on legal impartiality through impartial judges, helped to stabilize and secure order and justice for those in the royal and ecclesiastical classes.

King Richard I (the Lionhearted) was a son and successor to Henry II. Richard was a successful soldier and dedicated his talents to serve the Roman Catholic Church in the First Crusade. Although successful in that endeavor, Richard died in France while returning from Jerusalem. His brother King John I was then coronated King of England. John was not a very good sovereign, as he continually raised taxes arbitrarily to pay for all his losing wars in France.

On 15 June AD 1215, King John I of England was left no option but to sign and seal a profound document at a meeting field we know today as Runnymede. While its effects were minimal at the time, its conception was essential for our Freedom Charters. This was a document called Magna Carta, or Great Charter.

The symbolic significance of the Magna Carta is found in several very important aspects. First, it again established the concept of rule of law over the will of kings and of the Roman Church. This meant that leaders from any organized entity were held responsible for following established law and not just their own personal whims. Second, it cataloged the rights of every class of person who found themselves within sovereign English territory.

This included:

- the royal classes,
- the clergy,
- the merchant classes,
- the peasant classes,
- convicts,
- soldiers,
- widows, and
- foreign travelers.

Other important aspects of the Magna Carta were the concepts of jurisprudence and common law, due process rights, taxation through law (not by royal decree) and trial by jury. In England, the will of kings and the clergy were no longer considered absolute. Issues were decided through representation, regulated by established law and not the arbitrary impulses of the ruling classes.

Sovereigns also had the right to own property, which was secured by laws and not subject to random seizures by the king or any others in the ecclesiastical or royal classes. Although the first Magna Carta was barely implemented at the time, the philosophy and vision behind it was planted in the English psyche. Under the Great Charter, royal and holy sovereigns were ideally held just as accountable to the law as all other classes in the realm.

King John died one year later, and his nine-year-old son Henry III took the throne. This event allowed the Magna Carta to be more fully implemented with the approval of the papacy and the eventual creation of the English Parliament (representatives who were elected to embody the will of the lords of England).

The coronation of Edward I occurred upon the death of Henry III. During that time Magna Carta was expanded again to include the amendment of taxation through representation. Slowly, and bit-by-bit Magna Carta became a template for many rights found in our Freedom Charters.

Magna Carta was revolutionary in the twelfth century but would require many centuries to be fully realized. It is important to note that all these charters with amendments were not originally founded to grant rights to every person, but primarily to establish limits on the power of kings and the Church toward other sovereigns.

Even so, these charters can be cited as a tangible starting point in the evolution of ideas where royal and clerical sovereignty began to see legal limits on their powers, and that the implied rights of common people were at least mentioned and given written recognition, although not fully implemented at the time.

Magna Carta was an essential component to the development of our Freedom Charters. Many of its premises were instituted by England and later transferred to the English colonies in the Americas. While originally written in Latin, excerpts of the AD 1297 Magna Carta in modern English translation are available for perusal at: http://www.archives. gov 5 and https://www.archives.gov/files/press/press-kits/magna-carta/ magna-carta-translation.pdf

CHAPTER 13

The End of Sanctioned Arbitrary Rule in England

Magna Carta was the first document established to reign in arbitrary powers of royal and clerical sovereigns. While its original intent was to grant greater rights to wealthy landowners called barons and to the Roman Church, it set into motion a philosophy that no sovereign had limitless powers and that anyone could be held accountable through enforcement of just laws.

Before King John I died, he had already written to the pope asking to be released from the limits on his powers through Magna Carta. The Pope agreed, since he also saw the threat of losing his authority to powerful barons, but eventually the papacy supported expanding Magna Carta to balance the Church's rights against future abuses of the kings and queens of England.

During the reign of Henry III (AD 1207–1272), a parliamentary system was instituted, where meetings could be called, and representatives of the barons had the right to discuss and debate issues which could affect them. Magna Carta was reissued under the new king's name with the blessings of the papacy. The next meeting of Parliament instituted an instrumental change through an amendment that one day would reverberate throughout the American colonies. It established the principle "No taxation without representation."

Other principles followed through the centuries, but there was always uneasiness between Parliament (the barons) and the royal sovereigns (kings and queens). This uneasiness broke down into strife with the crowning of King James I, aka King James III of Scotland (AD 1451-1488) and with civil war during the reign of his son King Charles I (AD 1600-1649.)

James and his son Charles did not recognize Magna Carta, since it was only instituted in England, and both were kings of England, Scotland, and Ireland. James believed Magna Carta had no jurisdiction in Scottish lands, and his son Charles eventually rejected the entire document.

James and Charles believed that all kings and queens throughout Christendom were ordained by God Himself. The "divine right of kings" was thought to have gone back to the time of creation and given to the first man/prince, Adam, and passed down through the kings of Israel to the kings and queens of Christendom. James and Charles both believed their powers were derived directly from the God of Abraham and could not be managed or changed by any human document.

In medieval Europe, absolute authority of the royal sovereigns had often depended upon the authority of the Roman Church. While the concept of royal divinity reached back to the beginnings of civilization, events over the centuries had eroded and changed popular perceptions of its meaning. Magna Carta was a vital step in this very long process.

The papacy initially resisted Magna Carta, as they knew perceived limits on the divine right of royal sovereigns could also limit popular perceptions of the divine rights of holy sovereigns. Even so, abuses from the royal sovereigns against the Church would eventually lead to papal support of the document. This is an example of the balances and counterbalances provided by Magna Carta in Britain and much later by our Freedom Charters in the United States. The acceptance of these balances and counterbalances did not depend on the personal virtues of the sovereigns, but on the fact that adhering to the laws was essential for their own self-preservation.

With Magna Carta came the expansion of the powers of civil law, common law, and criminal law. Power was defusing from a top-heavy system of church law and royal edicts to a more pyramid-shaped system. Wealth and power continued to be centered in the royal and holy classes, but that power was much more divided among many and no longer absolute.

While establishing legal limits on royal and holy sovereigns was a major factor in the development of Magna Carta, this forward movement sometimes came at a certain cost that threatened to reverse this process in the interests of social order and societal stability.

One drawback in the weakening of the legal authority of the royal sovereigns was the disjointed legal system of localized and competing court systems found throughout the realm. Each court, which was based upon feudal models, attempted to assert their authority and supremacy over other areas and courts. One court went as far as issuing arrests for "trespass" on anyone they wanted to bring in for trial. Once the person was arrested and brought within the court's jurisdiction, the trespass charge would be dropped, and the intended charge would be applied.

By this time, England had also become a very litigious society, where the law and lawsuits were being used by unscrupulous people to attack their rivals. Lawsuits were often made not to administer justice, but rather to intimidate or punish people with the threat of having their reputations destroyed through vicious accusations. This not only removed the prospect for justice, but also caused the courts to jam up with ten times the cases or more than the intended capacity.

While our Freedom Charters were designed to avoid such things, it seems to be increasingly acceptable for government entities in the twenty-first century American government to use the force of law to attack and persecute private citizens with whom they have disagreements or dislikes. This is a dangerous precedent that, if left unchecked, could threaten the entire American system of justice.

No matter the person being attacked or persecuted, no American patriot should accept the use of government powers against an individual or an organization simply because that person or organization is unpopular with the powerful in government or a segment of society. This dangerous trend should be recognized, pointed out, and stopped wherever and to whomever it occurs.

CHAPTER 14

The Renaissance

An important change in Western culture that removed primary focus on the Roman Catholic Church and onto the human individual is a time known by many historians as the Renaissance. The Renaissance reshaped societies and used them in different and innovative ways. This includes increased knowledge of the mechanics of the universe, evolved ideas and concepts about our Creator God, the natural rights and responsibilities of the individual human person, new theories for economic prosperity, the role of government in the lives of the people, new social orders, and more intricate social hierarchies.

Climate change helped shape medieval times, just as it has in all other times of earth's history. From AD 900 through much of the 1300s, the earth had warmed approximately two degrees Fahrenheit (compared to today) in the northern hemisphere. This caused a rapid expansion of usable farmland in northern areas of Europe, Asia, and the Americas. In Europe, milder climates and a population explosion doubled the number of people in a very short period.

Cities of the northern Italian peninsula were positioned well to benefit from this change in climate and technology. All had innovative advances (many still in use today). This is everything from perspective art, architecture, and fashion, to trained professional armies, navies, and mercenaries, and from international commerce, trade, and banking, to grand basilicas, libraries, and universities. Much of what we identify today as modern began in Renaissance Italy.

The Renaissance is best known in popular culture for its advances in artistic and architectural style, but these two important aspects were the brilliant physical manifestations of a much deeper philosophical and intellectual movement sweeping various parts of the Italian peninsula. This chapter will focus upon the abstract philosophical and intellectual aspects of the Renaissance rather than the tangible artistic and architectural ones.

The greatest innovation in Renaissance Italy was a newfound emphasis on the human individual. Individualism became an idea and focus of the modern Renaissance person. This individualism allowed certain people to excel in ways once forbidden in medieval society. For most of the Middle Ages, the clergy were the influential and literate people, while the royal class held much wealth and power. The rest were pigeonholed into a place and status that was solely determined by their birth family.

In Renaissance society, individual people were encouraged to focus and hone their inborn natural talents into usable skills regardless of birth or status. This new emphasis upon individual merit led these societies in a very different direction than what had been experienced in times past or anywhere else up to that point.

The initial change of focus from Church and God to man and his God-given talents thrusted Italy into the forefront of the emerging modern age, and as their prestige and power became more obvious, others in Northern and Western Europe eventually imitated and followed. Man was becoming the measure of things, and his mind, emotion, soul, and even bodily proportions became the model for all that the Renaissance achieved in every subject and study.

Individualism allowed for more people from all types of backgrounds the freedom to explore and perfect their innate aptitudes and skills. These abilities could then be used for improving their own wealth and status in society, as well as the status of friends, acquaintances, and family members. So, the innate, God-given gift of free will ceased to be a shunned burden of humanity (as described by the medieval Roman Church) and returned to European culture as a positive source of human-centered innovation and change (as in some parts of classical antiquity).

Many people outside the clerical class learned to read and write, not just in Latin, but in their own language. The Roman Church had vacated Rome and Italy as the seat of the papacy for a city named Avignon. Avignon was in a southern part of the Holy Roman Empire, which today is southern France. When the papacy transferred residence to Avignon in AD 1309, Roman Church administration lost much of its presence in Italy, and secular leaders rose through the ranks of cities and towns to fill those roles.

With this de-emphasis of the traditional order, individuals were less restricted to seeking out their desired place in society, and often rewarded for their contributions through personal accomplishment regardless of birth family. This, in turn, improved the quality and diversity of goods and services, reduced market prices through competition, and encouraged new, independent businesses through increased prosperity.

Depopulation of Rome and southern Italy occurred as people who wanted to make money moved north to areas like Avignon, Marcelles, Valencia, Milan, Verona, Venice, Genoa, Bologna, Pisa, Florence, Urbino, and Siena. These cities expanded as they were organized and administered with great energy and efficiency, unbound by a stagnant, traditional order.

Strong merchant and craftsmen classes sprung up from the peasant classes. Prosperity ceased to be a monopoly of the clerical and royal classes and became more widely dispersed among the common people. With lots of new wealth and influence, ordinary people outperformed those static classes with much greater diversity of thought, innovation, and energy.

Many in the merchant class lived better than some royalty. Successful merchants and craftsmen also saw great upward mobility, prosperity, and influence as they organized into unions called guilds. These trade guilds had enormous influence over the newer secular governments that had taken root in northern Italy. In many cases, these guilds took over the functions of the government as the administrative state, replacing the Roman Church and their clergy.

These new guilds and the spirit of individualism also changed many social hierarchies. This time saw massive expansion of trade as the city-states along the coasts of the Mediterranean generated vast amounts of wealth in goods and services. This, in turn, granted the intellectual class something new. People such as poets and artists could now make a living through their trade alone, rather than just doing it on the side as a hobby.

⚜

In philosophy, the Renaissance is best defined as a mainstream return to Aristotle on logic, ethics, and politics. Technically, this began with St. Thomas Aquinas and his literary work *Summa Theologica*, but like many things in human history, the transition between eras of time do not come from a single person or event, but by a process which is multifaceted and continuous.

The Italian Renaissance was a product of the thoughts of ancient times being reintroduced to the thoughts of medieval people, then melding those viewpoints to form a bridge from medieval times to the modern age. The emerging philosophy of Renaissance humanism began to take hold due to the writings of several late medieval/early modern poets who today would be called writers or journalists, some of whom I will describe next.

First is a man named Durante degli Alighieri (aka Dante.) Dante was born around AD 1265 in the Republic of Florence. Dante wrote several books that influenced the development of our Freedom Charters. One entitled *humana civilitas* helped to define this new concept of the individual person. Earlier societies gave the individual substance only as a member of the larger group, Dante professed that all individuals have substance in their own right. This included Christian and non-Christian individuals alike.

Another written work entitled *de monarchia* illustrated how this new individualism changed the dynamic of sovereign leaders toward the people and the state. Individualism essentially reversed the roles of the leaders to exist for the sake of the people and the state, and not that the people and state exist for their leaders.

Dante is best known for his literary work entitled *comedia*, which comes down to us as *The Divine Comedy*. The Divine Comedy is written as a narrative poem that follows people from ancient pagan and medieval Christian times through the Roman Catholic Church's concept of Hell, Purgatory, and Paradise. It is meant to illustrate humanity's established pathway toward God and eternal salvation (or damnation).

Each of these works were instrumental in the transition from medieval to modern thought. Taking much of St. Thomas Aquinas' perspectives in *Summa Theologica* and placing it in his Italian writings continued the bridge begun by St. Thomas Aquinas with stories and allegories relatable to people of various callings and backgrounds outside of small intellectual circles.

Put simply, the "high" reading of the Latin *Summa Theologica* to the common people of medieval Europe would have been ineffective, but the "low" reading of Dante's Italian poetry allowed for the transference of those same ideas to the population at large.

His works were not only written to explain political and religious subject matters, but also presented scientific theories of the time. For example, while traveling through Hell, Purgatory, and Paradise, the characters in *comedia* are exposed to scientific concepts such as gravity, time, and spatial dimension. The idea of a circular Earth is implied, as well as the idea that time is different based upon one's location and is not universally the same everywhere.

Although subtle and rudimentary compared to today's knowledge of science, Dante's writings about scientific concepts moved the exposure of these ideas from tiny intellectual groups to a more broad-based assembly of common people.

Dante's literary works put the culmination of all medieval thought into relatable stories written in the vernacular of the local population. He also synthesized biblical and ancient pagan ideas into a context that defined them logically and even somewhat compatible with each other. From our perspective, the primary importance of Dante was his mainstreaming of *Summa Theologica* by spreading the complex thoughts and ideas of St. Thomas Aquinas to the less educated minds of the general population of that time.

Another great mind of the early Renaissance was a man named Francesco Petrarca (aka Petrarch), born in AD 1304 in the town of Arezzo (approximately 45 miles from the city of Florence). Petrarch is often credited with beginning the Renaissance movement with a return to scholarly assessments of people and society.

Like Dante, Petrarch was a professional Italian writer and poet who produced famous works that were embraced by the greater population. But unlike Dante, Petrarch's focus was upon human experiences of life on earth. Petrarch was the first medieval person of popular influence to look at this life in its many facets and nuances, not simply as a short transition to the next life, but as something important to be studied, discussed, evaluated, and enhanced.

Petrarch's writings were very human oriented and filled with real-life experiences, questions and theories about humanity, relationships, society, and civilization. He did not only read classical texts; he also subjected them to critical analysis. This change in emphasis started an avalanche of questioning and scholarship, which over the next two centuries, helped bring about the modern world.

Petrarch was the first person to examine the ancient classical world as a humanist Christian. While the thoughts of humanistic ancient philosophers like Aristotle had been studied throughout medieval Europe, there had always been a divide between pagan and Christian philosophies.

Aristotle's earth-centered views and explanations of the universe were an accepted doctrine of the Roman Church because they were compatible with their interpretations of the Book of Genesis. Even so, Aristotle's philosophies on the nature of man were de-emphasized and only viewed as an intellectual curiosity.

During the Middle Ages, the Church's point of view had prevailed, but as Renaissance humanism brought in greater attention and study of humanity through science and philosophy, medieval Church-centered beliefs were challenged and overturned. The Modern Age eventually embraced the viewpoints of Renaissance humanism, which was to reject Aristotle's view of the earth-centered universe in favor of scientific observations of a broader universe, and to accept this view of humanity, society, and human life on earth over that of the Roman Catholic Church of the Gothic Age.

Renaissance humanism also blurred the line between pagan and Christian thinking and simply looked at the human qualities of those two perspectives, not their religious doctrines. Suddenly pagan philosophies and Roman Christianity were not solely exclusive and separate from each other, but part of a much larger phenomenon of life experiences in the human condition. While not Petrarch's intention, this would start the ending of the medieval Roman Catholic Church as a political force and eventually destroy the form of Christendom it had established and enforced for many centuries.

Petrarch's mainstreaming of the classical humanistic worldview also caused him to take a greater interest in ancient Roman histories. While Aristotle symbolized the greatness of ancient Greek thought, Petrarch was looking for a humanistic philosopher closer to his Western, Italian culture. He found this person in a man named Marcus Tullius Cicero.

Cicero had been a great Roman orator, lawyer, legal scholar, and Senator who lived at the very end of the ancient Roman republic. Cicero's speeches and legal writings had been preserved in Christian monasteries since the Dark Ages, but few medieval people had shown interest in them because, like Aristotle, Cicero had been a pagan.

In AD 1345, Petrarch had rediscovered many written works by Cicero in Verona, Italy. Collections entitled: *Epistulae ad Atticum, Epistulae ad Quintum Fratrem, and Epistulae ad Brutum* were copied and restored by Petrarch and other scholars. Through these studies it was discovered that Cicero was as important to ancient Roman philosophy as Aristotle had been to the ancient Greek. Cicero was essentially a

Roman continuation of Aristotle's philosophy, demonstrating the continuity of ancient humanist thought.

Petrarch's Renaissance humanism allowed Cicero to be read and studied, not as a pagan outsider, but as a humanist philosopher of reason. In many of Cicero's writings were found ancient republican Rome's emphasis on law and the virtues of prudence, justice, and temperance. The collected works of Cicero became an obsession for Renaissance scholars, and later, the British American colonists, who mainstreamed the long-forgotten ancient humanist philosophies, bringing them back from obscurity to the forefront of the modern Western mind and worldview.

Authors Note: More excerpts of our Freedom Charters would be redundant at this point, so I will begin using my end-of-chapter commentary to better illustrate the key concepts written about in each chapter, how they compare with competing concepts, and how they translate in modern thinking.

— ⁙ —

Humanism:

Renaissance humanism is very different from secular humanism. Renaissance humanism does not reject the belief in our Creator God, while the term "secular" has made its way from a definition of non-religious to atheism. Secular humanists reject the idea of a creator God in favor of "pure science." While pure science is a noble and important process, it cannot answer every question of the human condition, and the idea of science being a permanent fact-based process is misleading.

Human biases are pervasive throughout humanity and human scientists are people with prejudices and biases that affect judgment. Scientific evidence, if discovered properly, is objective, but interpretations are not, and the meanings assigned to the evidence and facts can be very subjective. This is because interpretations of evidence and facts are very much influenced by the people performing the interpretations. Other scientists with the same prejudices and bias will, of course, support these interpretations and reinforce these conclusions based upon the same viewpoint.

One of the many examples of this kind of bias can be found in Albert Einstein's views on quantum mechanics when he described it as "spooky actions from a distance." Einstein rejected many theories of quantum mechanics because he believed adamantly that "God does not play dice with the universe." Einstein took his biases further when he altered one of his own equations with cosmological constant. Since Einstein believed we live in a static, rather than expanding, universe, he purposefully skewed one of his own formulas because it did not fit his preconceived notions.

—◦◦◦◦◦◦—

Individualism:

Individualism can be defined in different ways. Collectivism, the antithesis of individualism, defines it as self-consumed, selfish, or self-centered beliefs and behaviors with no concern or regard for others. This is not true; rather, the philosophy of individualism is one of personal dignity and free will granted to the individual by nature and nature's God. Individualism does not reject or minimize the importance of others; in fact, it provides greater respect for others, as individual sovereignty is recognized to exist by our Creator in every person. Collectivism devalues the individual, which inevitably leads to discrimination and persecution.

One essential distinction between individualism and collectivism is that the philosophy of individualism promotes the helping of others from a person's own free will, usually out of love, compassion, or empathy. Collectivism is compulsory, and not necessarily of a genuine desire", but through intimidation, peer pressure and shaming at best to seizures and confiscations of persons and properties at worst.

Individualism does not remove a person's responsibility to organizations, societies, and the state. Individualism simply recognizes the inherent sovereignty of the individual who can also be a member of organizations, societies, and the state. All are sovereign entities with designated rights and responsibilities.

Individualism establishes the natural rights of all, not of one or some. Collectivism establishes no natural rights for any individual, which places the strongest and most violent in charge of all others in the name of society and the state. This is often referred to as a "democratic republic," a "socialist republic," or a "people's republic." The United States is a constitutional republic as described by our second President, John Adams.

The Collectivist ideal is impossible to achieve because it goes against the nature of humanity. There will always be various classes of people because people are born with various gifts and inclinations. Collectivism attempts to control aspects of humanity and society that cannot be dictated, and the more it does so, the more damage it does to the individual, society, and humanity.

The American constitutional system works best because it takes the most basic truths of life and humanity into account. Instead of relying on people it relies on laws, and while people make the laws, human law under the

American system is rooted in natural law. People of various gifts and inclinations can hone their skills and aptitudes. This, in turn, promotes the best of what humans have to offer themselves and each other. Freedom is the fuel that allows the American system to evolve and prosper. Changes occur over time. These changes are not forced upon the people as dictates but unveil themselves as sensible forms of what is right and best for self-preservation.

⚯

Journalism:

Journalism and freedom of the press is an individual and organizational right that should be cherished and protected. A free and independent press allows the open exchange of ideas and debate. This helps to keep the American population an informed citizenry.

Few things are more important in a free society than a free and independent media. The problem is that many in today's media have voluntarily given up their role to report events and keep those in power accountable. They have decided to take sides in every squabble based on political sympathies. They then protect those individuals and groups they support while savaging those they do not. The people who follow the media then choose the media outlets that support their own biases and prejudices, which reinforces their thoughts and feelings without any serious challenge.

Media cannot be objective because people cannot be objective. Every person who cares about issues in our world is shaped by cultural and personal sensibilities that cause prejudice and bias. This cannot be avoided. Instead of attempting to find or create an objective media, the goal should be to honestly identify the subjectivity of each media outlet and take that into account while subjecting all of it to critical analysis.

CHAPTER 15

The Great Mortality (Black Death)

It is now necessary to depart from the advances of the early Renaissance for an important event that took place in the mid-fourteenth century. This event dramatically reshaped and restructured European thoughts and sensibilities as perhaps nothing else would or could. During this time, Europe experienced a biological catastrophe, a plague of sicknesses for reasons unknown at the time, on a scale difficult to fathom for people living in any age since.

The first wave of this plague, known to later generations as the Black Death, came to Europe in AD 1347. Genoise and Venetian merchants brought the sickness west from the port city of Kaffa, a Crimean city on the Black Sea, through Constantinople, and onto the Italian peninsula. Genoise sailors brought devastation to the southern Island of Sicily in late 1347 and later to the city of Genoa itself. Venice, another mercantile city-state on the northeastern side of the Italian peninsula also brought plague and devastation to the continent of Europe, as well as everywhere they had stopped on the way.

Giovanni Boccaccio (AD 1313-1375) a Florentine poet/journalist at the time wrote, " . . . many dropped dead in the open streets . . . many others though dying in their homes, obtained their neighbors attention by the smell of their rotting corpses more than by any other method . . ."

The plague seemed to attack quickly and in various forms. One type would begin with an uncomfortable prickling sensation over the body and a severe chill. Next would come agony in the armpits and/or groin with severe swelling. This would sometimes be accompanied by blistering or blotching of the skin, but all would follow with high fever and throbbing headaches. This form of the plague would take several days on average to run its course. Many would become delirious and die, while some would be permanently traumatized, but physically recover.

Another form of plague worked more rapidly, with similar chills and fever, then difficulty breathing, brutal chest pains, coughing up of blood, and death within hours of the initial symptoms. Both forms would affect most people in towns and cities throughout most of Europe, with and without direct contact with other infected individuals.

This pandemic was so sudden and so harsh that people believed it signified the end of the world and was God's final judgment upon them for their sins. In the eyes of many, this was the Armageddon that had been preached to them from the Book of Revelation in the Holy Bible and the sentence of sudden death to all the unrepentant.

As this sudden and shocking event worked from Genoa to Pisa to Florence, intellectuals of the Renaissance were able to document a description of the illnesses, how they manifested, when they devastated certain areas, and their effects on the thoughts and sensibilities of those who endured it.

These Italian city-states had once brought wealth and prosperity to a Europe still recovering from the fall of the Western Roman Empire and the following Dark Ages. By bringing death and devastation in the form of illness and disease, many people interpreted this event as God's retribution for the prosperity and changes in lifestyle that these new ideas and markets had created, as well as the Renaissance humanism focus on the individual, and a society not solely centered on God and the Roman Church. Of course, this plague did not discriminate between the peasants, craftsmen, merchants, knights, clergy, or royalty. People from all walks of life were equally susceptible as the plague ravaged cities, towns, and the countryside.

This made the initial return of focus to the Roman Church short-lived, as people witnessed monks, priests, and bishops contracting plague and sudden death in significant numbers. The clergy of the Roman Catholic Church was just as susceptible to plague and appeared just as powerless to stop the spread, suffering, and dying as anyone else, regardless of status. In the end, this seriously weakened people's faith in the powers of the papacy as well as their faith in the old hierarchy of Western Christendom.

As the initial plague left Italy for Northern and Western Europe, the fatality rate typically ranged from 25 to 50 percent of those infected, but also went as high as 80 percent in some places. The plague continued to follow land and sea routes to other cities and islands on the northern Mediterranean coastline. Marseille was infected, as was Barcelona, Valencia, and the Islamic kingdom of Grenada.

The social dynamics of medieval society changed due to the Black Death. Several important aspects of this change dealt with individual opportunities, societal sensibilities, and the role of organizations such as the Roman Catholic Church, private and public businesses, and administrative governments.

Opportunities for healthy individuals to move up in society were present in every area. Mass death created all kinds of vacancies that needed to be filled by people who could perform such tasks. Due to necessity and lack of other options, common people were recruited directly.

Anyone with the skill already present could be fast-tracked into positions ranging from shoe repair to parish priest. This included males and females regardless of background. Those who did not possess the skills, but the interest and aptitudes, were accepted into institutions of higher learning.

Before the Black Death, education was reserved primarily for people in the noble classes who were most likely going to join the clergy. These people would then operate the administrative state. Early education usually came in the form of personal tutors, and higher education was mostly monastic. Education after the Black Death became somewhat more democratized as the practical need for live bodies outweighed older sensibilities about class structure.

Merchants and craftsmen had already established sophisticated guild systems. While the existence of guilds cannot be attributed to the Black Death, the ability to organize and handle this calamity boded well for the importance of guilds during and after the first wave of infection. Some guilds were the forerunners of universities of higher learning. Universities were much less focused on religious instruction and more in line with the training required for vocations. Many towns and cities lost all their experienced tradesmen, as well as the advanced knowledge of certain techniques.

More sophisticated professions were lost to the plague and had to be reinvented by people who only possessed the natural aptitude for that skill. Higher learning also transformed from focus on the narrow subject of theology to more general and practical studies of vocation.

A humanistic education was instituted due to the need to accommodate many people from diverse backgrounds. The subject matter studied needed to involve a secular nature (non-religious, not atheistic) because their practicality was rooted in certain skills and not in social status and family relations.

Guilds were also well organized due to the importance of the new and emerging middle classes, which had been growing before the Black Death had reached Italy. With the death or abandonment of duties by so many in the royal and clerical classes, urban areas had no choice but to find survivors from any background to competently take on the responsibilities of the government entities.

In many cases, these guilds also took on the role of the government when most or all government positions in certain areas were vacant. The royal and clerical classes traditionally held these positions, but with their absence, only merchants and trade guilds had the organizational structure and practical knowledge to effectively take the levers of power.

Guilds had not only provided the beginnings of the modern university system and a sound administrative state, but they also provided concern for the general welfare of the population through public and private charitable sources.

Assistance to people who had been displaced by the plague is one example of this modern sensibility. Widows and orphans had once been wives and children of prosperous working husbands and fathers. But with the death of so many men, many women and children were left without support.

Tradition dictated the giving of an advantageous dowry from maidens' families to bachelor men to convince them to settle down into marriage and to procreate. Widows and orphans could not afford enticing offers since their entire livelihood had been extinguished. Guilds collected much of the wealth that was left without heirs and distributed them as enticing dowries to bachelor men for marriage.

As the labor class became more valuable, they also became bolder with their wage expectations. So many dead meant new opportunities for the living. The old orders could not sustain themselves, as people once pigeonholed into serfdom could begin marketing their labor for higher wages and greater shares in the estates they worked. Sharecropping replaced serfdom because laborers could negotiate improved conditions due to greater labor competition between estates.

The Church had little choice but to recruit from the lower classes to fill the ranks of missing clergy. This, of course, brought new perspectives and a greater diversity of experience to a once protected class that had been static for centuries.

Procreation was profoundly affected, as women who might have assisted their father's and husband's work became the head of household and the primary breadwinners. After the plague devastated the population, women who stepped into the places vacated by the dead did not remarry and have children in numbers that could replace the missing population. Young women also waited longer to marry and had fewer children during their childbearing years. This became a permanent trend in the Modern Age.

This fact, along with generational recurrences of the plague and the creeping in of another major climate change (the "Little Ice Age") kept the population levels much lower for the next few centuries than in pre-plague times. With lower populations, everyone brought more value to their skills and labor, which in turn kept wages at higher and more competitive levels.

This new way of living would eventually have a major effect on the entire world. As international commerce was revitalized, the new cultural sensibilities of early modern age Europeans was also transmitted to much older cultures, who had difficulty keeping pace with the innovations in technology and the economic prosperity this focus on freedom for the individual provided. This edge made it only a matter of time before Europeans would break out onto the world stage, and this new culture with its tangible and abstract innovations would have a global effect over the next five centuries.

—◦◦◦—

American Freedom:

The founders and framers of the American republic were beneficiaries of these changes to society. The focus on the individual and individual sovereignty was a principal component to the American system and our Freedom Charters. Focus on individual merit is central to American capitalism, as banks and other lending institutions needed a universal standard for credit and loans that funded building projects and entrepreneurial ventures.

While pressures from family members pigeonholed some people into a life of professional redundancy, American society welcomed entrepreneurs who could provide goods and labor in affordable ways. Any free person with talent and willpower could break away from traditional roles and create a living based on their own skills and merit. In time, many more people would join the ranks of freedom through their own personal efforts and belief in the premises of our Freedom Charters, should eventually apply to all people living within the borders of the United States.

—◦◦◦—

Charitable Giving:

Helping the poor and downtrodden is an important aspect of the teachings of Jesus Christ. Every individual, organization, and society should dedicate a portion of their labor toward helping those who earn very little or cannot earn a living through gainful employment.

Government Welfare Programs:

Generally, government programs to help the poor are a positive aspect of our society. The government can provide funding and finances in greater amounts than individuals or private and public organizations, and it is an extension of the will of our popular sovereignty.

Trouble occurs when assistance becomes dependence. People dependent on government have just enough to survive but not enough to thrive. Dependency on government entities places people in a position of high vulnerability and open to greater exploitation by unscrupulous individuals and public officials.

Gainful Employment:

No government welfare program can substitute for the many benefits of gainful employment. Gainful employment of the individual generally brings greater personal pride in achievement, proper use of talents and abilities, better income or income potential, productivity rather than just consumption, and much less dependency on the government.

While government does have a role in the "general welfare" of people and society, our constitutional republic is not meant to be a "welfare state." Individuals and organizations are numerous, and demeaning or oppressive ones can be avoided. There are fewer government entities, and these entities have the powers of law making, law enforcement, and military control.

Large segments of the population who are dependent on government welfare can bring about unintended consequences (or sometimes intended) that threatens the sovereignty of the individual and society as well as the viability of organizations and government entities. Nothing is better for all than free people earning an honest living. Those who disagree usually have ulterior motives that are not honorable or based on freedom for the individual.

CHAPTER 16

The Age of Exploration and Discovery

The Age of Exploration (aka the Age of Discovery) was a Western European venture that began in the mid-fifteenth century. This was during the height of the Renaissance in southern Europe, the fall of the Byzantine Empire to the Ottoman Turks in Eastern Europe, as well as the early beginnings of Protestantism in northern Europe. The Western European nations of Portugal, Spain, France, Holland, and England were the primary beneficiaries of this period, as their locations gave them great maritime advantages. Just the same, the discoveries of these seafaring nations made them significant because of the role they played as the early engineers and cultural founders of a global modern world.

The massive expansion and conquest of the world by Western Europeans began in the tiny Kingdom of Portugal on the newly reconquered Iberian Peninsula. The Kingdom of Portugal had been established many centuries earlier but its location in the new power center gave it great advantages in westward and southern exploration. While few things in human history begin with a single person or event, the life of a man named Infante D. Henrique (AD 1394-1460) is important for our purposes. Henrique, who today is called Prince Henry the Navigator by the English-speaking world, was an early Western European mariner who explored lands west and south of Western Europe.

While tiny islands called the Azores had been discovered by an earlier Portuguese mariner named Diogo de Silves, Prince Henry the Navigator set his sights on western Africa to establish trade with the Muslim Berbers. When one of his captains passed Cape Bojador in the western Sahara Desert for the first time, it can be said that the Age of Exploration was well underway.

Conquest of the Berber city of Ceuta on August 21, 1415, was a significant event in the Age of Exploration as well as the beginnings of the Portuguese empire. It was ordered by Henry's father, and Henry was present (and even wounded) during the battle. While the city was a strategic success in flanking Spanish rivals, Ceuta did not deliver the trade benefits that had been planned. Another nearby city was unsuccessfully attacked, and eventually the Portuguese withdrew.

This failure did not deter the Portuguese travelers from their desire to establish lucrative trade routes on the continent of Africa. They continued to explore further south via a new type of ship called a caravel. Caravels were based on successful Arab sailing ships, enhanced for greater maneuverability and longer sustained voyages.

Up until that time, Europeans were dependent on Arab technologies to navigate the seas, but many of these ventures relied on known star charts of the northern hemisphere. The north star, Polaris, was the fixed point of reference for all mariners to calculate their coordinates. Eight degrees south of Sierra Leone, however, Polaris was not visible over the horizon. To make matters worse, the visible stars of the southern hemisphere were completely different, with no known fixed positions to rely on.

Thus, Sierra Leone became the southernmost sailing point for some time due to the limits of star navigation, but trade with the sub-Saharan

Africans quickly became extremely lucrative. Sub-Sahara Africa was very wealthy in gold, and the exchange was so pleasing that the Portuguese established a colony there and gave the area its current name.

One objective of the Portuguese monarchs was to successfully navigate around Africa and establish direct trade with India and China. The Crusader States had fallen to the Arabs centuries earlier, and the markup of goods from Arab and Turkish middlemen had become very costly. Even so, the combination of the lucrative trade in Sierra Leone and the limits of star navigation made it difficult to find people willing to keep sailing south of the equator.

The Genoese mariner named Christopher Columbus was pitching to the Portuguese that one could travel to China and India by sailing west across the Atlantic Ocean. Although tempting, the Portuguese remained obsessed with sailing around the southern end of Africa to reach Asia. Just as Columbus was about to convince them to finance a westward voyage in 1488, another mariner named Bartolomeu Dias de Novais sailed around the newly named Cape of Good Hope, and the Portuguese lost all interest in Columbus and his ideas.

Columbus then pitched his idea to the monarchs of Spain, who were in the process of completely removing the Muslim Berbers from the Iberian Peninsula. In 1492, the capitulation of Grenada tossed out the last vestiges of Muslim rule in Western Europe and brought about great confidence in the bold Spanish monarchs Queen Isabella and King Ferdinand. Just as Columbus was about to give up on Spain, the monarchs decided to finance his voyage with two ships. Columbus was then able to charter a third ship, and in August 1492, he and a handpicked crew sailed south and west into the Atlantic Ocean.

Spain was an emerging Catholic power, but like Portugal, the Spanish monarchs were in the process of secularizing their governments from the Roman Church. Publicly, they remained loyal and true to Roman Catholic Christianity, as did the general population but, behind the scenes, they began to operate much more independently. Spain and Portugal were becoming very wealthy military powers, while the power of the papacy was waning. This reality would have a profound impact on the future.

Human slavery has been a reality since the first cities of ancient Mesopotamia. By the end of ancient times, the Roman Empire had used slavery to build its vast and lasting civilization. The Roman Church shunned slavery as being extremely un-Christian due to its obvious flaws. While condemned by the Spanish monarchs and the Roman Church, Muslim Berbers were very active in the slave industry. They had raided areas of Europe and taken tens of thousands of people back to Africa as slaves. This was resented by the church for moral reasons and the sovereign monarchies of Europe for economic ones.

Slavery in sub-Sahara Africa was also accepted. Captured slaves were traded alongside gold and other treasures in Sierra Leone. The Portuguese began taking African slaves in trade when they realized the wealth that their labor generated. While still shunned by the Church, the new independent governments of Portugal and Spain only saw the economic gains to be had in slavery, so they condoned and encouraged its use despite its immorality.

It can be said that the greatest rediscovery of the Renaissance was the dignity and worth of the human individual. It also can be said that the greatest flaw in the Age of Discovery is the implementation of societal dehumanization. Dehumanization begins as a mental construct, discounting the humanity of certain people and reducing their perceived place in society to that of property or livestock. Dehumanization is arguably the starting point of any crime a person can commit against another, as it opens the door to a completely amoral view of that person, entirely disregarding a person's humanity and the moral value of their own dignity, free will, and freedom.

With a perspective of dehumanization, one does not feel compassion, empathy, or obligation toward certain others because their value has been reduced to that of an object to be possessed. By seeing people as property, all the moral and ethical standards usually reserved for others ceases to apply in the minds of slaveowners. Slaves are not considered human, so like any other objects or property, the owner can do with them as he or she sees fit.

While the flaws of slavery have existed for thousands of years, there was something different and distinct about it in the Age of Exploration. Until AD 1450, human interactions had been very regional. With brief exceptions, most cultures remained within their part of the world. The Romans, for instance, subjugated and enslaved peoples such as the Greeks and Celts, but Romans, Greeks, and Celts were of European ancestry. Sub Saharan African tribes subjugated and enslaved each other, too, but that remained among Africans, and the sub-Saharan African culture of communalism gave slaves quite a different place and status in their societies.

The Age of Exploration saw the enslavement of black native Africans by white native Europeans. The distinct physical differences in racial backgrounds became the easiest method to identify each other and the source of the attitudes concerning dehumanization that were cultivated then and continue even to today. This allowed what was to come next, while the amoral attitudes and behaviors of slavery were ignored, excused, and sometimes justified by the larger Christian population of Western Europe.

Columbus returned to Spain at the end of 1492 with news. He claimed to have found the westward sea route to Asia. He believed to have landed in the East Indies off the mainland and brought back gold, plants, and native "Indians" with him as proof. While this earned Columbus a knighthood and a permanent place in human history, there were some things about his discovery that did not make sense at the time.

Europeans had been trading with Asia via the Silk Road, which crossed the entire Asian continent to Europe. The gold and artifacts brought back to Spain by Columbus looked somewhat different than what they had expected to find in Asia. Next, Columbus had not found the Asian mainland where he thought it should be, and the native islanders of the Indies had never heard of the Great Khan, who ruled Asia at that time. Third, the translator who Columbus brought with him to interact with the natives could not easily decipher their languages, even though he had been trained in several known Asian languages.

While these peculiarities remained a mystery, Columbus appeared to have found exactly what he had promised, which was a westward trade route to Asia. The Spanish quickly financed more and greater voyages with Columbus and several other professional mariners. Columbus made three Atlantic voyages in all. Having not reached the mainland until very late in his last voyage, it took years to realize that he had not discovered a new route to Asia, but an entirely different hemisphere that was apparently unknown to ancient and medieval Europeans.

Another Italian mariner name Amerigo Vespucci had sailed west from the coast of Africa and had discovered the mainland and the current day Amazon River Delta. Vespucci was also under the impression that he was in Asia, but as he sailed north, he began to realize this was not Asia but an entirely new continent altogether. Thus, the name America was given to this new continent rather than the name Columbia. Later it was discovered that they were, in fact, two continents that were renamed South America and North America.

The discovery of the Americas opened a "new world" for European exploration, and all the intellectual and cultural traits of this new modern age gave them the technological skills and advantages to exploit the riches of this newfound land. Spain and Portugal immediately began empire building and established lucrative wealth through trade and conquest.

The Americas were, of course, inhabited by native "Americans," but by the time the Europeans had realized they were not in Asia, the term "Indian" had stuck. Until the twentieth century, native Americans were commonly referred to as Indians and, even now, the term "American Indian" is widely used. Since the native peoples of the Americas did not call their land America, it has been suggested that they be referred to as indigenous peoples or first peoples.

While the Americas of today are filled with modern, technologically advanced nations, the Americas during the Age of Exploration were much different. The security and comfort of Western Europe was not found in the Americas, and great efforts were required for the Spanish and Portuguese to establish sustainable colonies. At first, many Western Europeans were hired to help colonize the American continent, but it soon became evident that the manpower necessary was affordable only through the institution of slavery.

The native Americans were offered trade deals, but the reality was that the Europeans had no qualms about taking what they wanted by force if diplomatic negotiations were not to their liking. Native Americans were sometimes subjugated and enslaved, but it was much cheaper and easier and more productive to purchase native African slaves for the task of colonization. This was the beginning of the Transatlantic Slave Trade, which continued for several centuries. During the next 300 years, native Africans and native Europeans began pouring onto the American continents. With them, they brought all the technologies and human labor of the modern age, which were established to reap all kinds of wealth from jewelry to sugar to silver, but much less gold than anticipated.

While European firearms were far superior to the arrows and spears of the native Americans, the native Europeans simply did not have the manpower required to take lands exponentially larger than their home countries. Unfortunately for the Native Americans, the native Europeans brought two other things that devastated their societies. These were alcohol (for which the native Americans had no biological tolerance) and old-world diseases (which the native Americans had no biological immunity.) Very high percentages of native American societies were eradicated simply through fatal illnesses.

Many Christian Europeans questioned the morality of this, but they also viewed it as evidence that God was on their side and that the atrocities committed against native Americans and native Africans were morally justified due to their non-Christian "savagery." All this happened while the Spanish and Portuguese empires continued to expand in land and riches at the heavy expense of native American and native African lives and freedom.

The Roman Church remained present, but its views were only slightly more humane than the secular authorities, for they worked to convert the local populations from their native religions into Catholic Christianity. The cultural traditions of the native Africans and native Americans were discounted and ignored. Dehumanization made all

162

this possible and palatable to Christian sensibilities of the time and beyond. Native Americans were eventually conquered, absorbed, and/ or displaced into concentrated areas called Indian reservations.

The exploitation of African slaves continued and expanded at the expense of the native Africans and their descendants, African Americans. While recognized by some European Christians as an abhorrent system, the economic benefits were too great to make emancipation of slaves a serious issue for many centuries. Dehumanization made all this justifiable in the minds of many European Christians, although it was a direct violation of the teachings of Jesus Christ. Enslavement of Africans and conquest of native Americans continued with far-reaching effects on modern- and present-day America.

⏤⏤

Western Colonization:

Laissez-faire capitalism became a hallmark of the Age of Exploration and Discovery, and the primary motivator for people who wanted to improve their lives and lifestyles through increased wealth. This economic philosophy took hold of Western Europe and transferred to the Americas.

The British colonies in the Americas were chartered and offered to the population on the promise of a better life through greater religious freedom and economic prosperity. While not all individuals were able to achieve these lofty goals, enough did to inspire others, and the idea of heading west for greater freedom and fortune is an outlook that continues to motivate and engage people today.

Most cultural sensibilities in the new world colonies were shaped by the Age of Exploration and Discovery. These included the great achievements people produced with freedom and willpower as well as the worst crimes many of the same people committed with those same tools. So much wealth, prosperity, and freedom ran alongside deprivation, dehumanization, and slavery. There was such a stark contrast between the two that it is difficult for modern people to understand how it was even possible, let alone factual (but it is).

—◦◦◦—

The Transatlantic Slave Trade:

No words can express or detail the horrors of the Transatlantic slave trade. The abductions, beatings, starving, imprisoning in small coffin like spaces, transporting, raping, selling, and working of black Africans is beyond our abilities to fully understand. The segregation of families from one another and separating them immense distances for all time. Showing them no compassion, empathy or even a small consideration for their humanity or even as conscious beings.

Many colonists deprived them of every dignity or pleasure in life to a point where death was preferred and longed for; with occurrences happening daily to thousands and, in years to millions of human beings. This cannot be fully ascertained except by those who directly experienced it. Where it is preferred by us to avoid contemplating the fear, loss, loneliness and hopelessness that must have been experienced, we must, even though this injustice goes beyond all that language and human imagination can possibly muster.

—◦◦◦—

The Freedom Charters Ended Slavery:

The American republic inherited the best and the worst aspects of the ages of discovery and exploration. It would take time and the genius of our Freedom Charters to enhance the finer aspects while reversing the abhorrent ones. Both these blessings of our Freedom Charters began in the eighteenth century but continued forward to the nineteenth, twentieth, and twenty-first centuries.

Despite all the problems the American republic inherited from the times of colonization, it is our Freedom Charters and people's dedication to these principles and documents that provides our best chances to continue a forward movement. Forward can be measured in several ways, but one factor is the evolution of a society that provides opportunities for all who live within its borders regardless of their background or status. Another is the formation and enforcement of laws that provide everyone with the same protections and the same responsibilities for self-improvement, societal improvement, and government accountability.

The crimes of slavery and conquest cannot be erased from history, but the effects of these insidious events can be reduced over time. This is an extremely long and difficult process for several reasons.

First, many people do not believe crimes committed before they were born are their responsibility. While this is true at a personal and legal level, society has an obligation to correct the negative effects because society is a true continuation of that time. Government entities also have a responsibility because they are an extension of the will of the people through representation.

Second, poverty and destitution created by slavery and conquest is not limited to material lifestyle. In fact, much of material lifestyle is not the central issue with the poor since government programs began in the

1960s. Poverty and destitution also exist in the human mind. People who blame history and society for their ills, rightfully or not, are not taught the powers inherit in their individualism. Many look to society and the government for their material benefits and cannot conceptualize anything outside of those means. Self-improvement and self-sufficiency are seen as impossibilities mainly due to the harshness of life and the negative impacts of centuries of dehumanization.

Third, dehumanization continues to plague individuals and society as the thought processes that produce it have continued in one form or another since colonial times. There are many people who continue to see others as less human, and it is extremely difficult to challenge and overturn that line of thinking. Others see no chance of changing their circumstances due to the power of racial and societal discrimination, so they simply do not try, or worse, attempt to tear down the physical and abstract structures in place that can bring about greater positive change.

—◦◦◦◦—

Multicultural America:

Cultural differences and expressions of anger and frustration come out at inopportune times, creating a polarization of people's ideas and attitudes. These vulnerabilities in American society and culture are often exploited by America's enemies for their own agenda. Education is the inevitable solution to this quandary, but what kind of education? Who is qualified to provide it? This is by far the most enduring barrier to our progress, as many different people with various philosophies are in constant competition for the role.

The answer, of course, is a return to the principles of our Freedom Charters and all that came before to produce them. First and foremost is recognition of our Creator God, who granted us our natural rights. Without this there is no path to success. Next is belief in free will and the human ability to reason. The power to correct our problems is in our hands, not the hands of fate or others. Third is virtue. This includes personal virtue, integrity, and civic virtue, putting the needs of others on an equal par with our own needs. Finally, it is the personal disposal of pride, ego, prejudice, and intolerance. All of us possess these vices at one level or another, and it is the personal abandonment of them as a way of thinking and feeling that must take place before communication and understanding can begin.

This is an extremely difficult task, as it requires people of very diverse backgrounds to come together for the enhancement of an abstract principle, "We the People." This goal also requires the abandonment of personal, political, and religious agendas not rooted in the tenets of our Freedom Charters.

Of course, our Freedom Charters themselves prevent the eradication of alien influences, as freedom of conscience is paramount. Eradication of collectivist philosophies, such as Marxism, Fascism, National Socialism, and Communism, does not come from outlawing it. Rather, it comes from the proper understanding of our Freedom Charters and the belief that all people possess the divine essence of our Creator God, making them sovereign individuals with natural rights that must be respected regardless of anything else. It's my hope that these writings might play a part in that process.

CHAPTER 17

The Protestant Reformation

While southern and western Europe were experiencing the Ages of Renaissance and Discovery, central and northern Europe were beginning a time in history now called The Protestant Reformation. The Protestant Reformation is often viewed as a split in Western Christendom from international Roman Catholicism to national, independent, Protestant churches. The causes are often cited as centuries of abuse in the Roman Church for the ways they held political power and material wealth over the populations of northern, central, southern, and western Europe.

As the confidence and power of individualism had taken hold in the minds of people during the Renaissance, people began questioning papal doctrines and activities. As the Roman Church resisted what was essentially an indefensible position, humanism and individualism became powerful forces for protest and revolt. This manifested itself in the fourteenth century with two primary thinkers whose names were John Wycliffe and Johannes Huss (aka Jan Hus).

John Wycliffe (AD 1320s–1384) was an English religious professor and advocate for ecclesiastic reform at the University of Oxford. During his tenure, Wycliffe attacked many aspects of the medieval Roman Church. Two of his most impactful writings were *The Twelve Conclusions of the Lollardy*—which were highly critical attacks on the sovereignty and importance of the papacy—and his direct translation of the Latin

Vulgate Bible into the English vernacular of the time, now called Middle English. All this was illegal and punishable up to, and including, torture and death.

This may seem strange to modern sensibilities, but control of language is a powerful force for those in charge of keeping control and dominance. First, the church had been teaching for centuries that the Latin Vulgate, translated by St. Jerome, was the literal "Word of God." Therefore, any translation of that word could be flawed and/or distorted. Second, since only the Church-educated population was taught Latin, only people who had been vetted and approved by the Church could read, understand, and transmit the word to the population. Third, and most importantly, the Latin Bible continued to be a justification for the authority and positions of the royal and holy sovereigns. This had become an ingrained tradition since the time of Constantine the Great over 1,000 years earlier.

The Latin language was much older and much more formal than the vernacular languages of that day. Latin demonstrated an heir of sophistication and gave the Holy Bible an aura of sacredness that could be degraded or even lost through translations into modern languages. Translations also were a threat to the Church's power because people could better understand and challenge certain church doctrines, allowing it to be openly discussed and debated by all.

Geoffrey Chaucer (AD 1343-1400) is often referred to as the father of English literature. He was fluent in Middle English, Latin, and Italian. He travelled to Italy and was exposed to the writings of Dante and Petrarch. Their style of narrative poems appealed to him, as he focused on stories and subjects that involved everyday life in England.

Chaucer served the royal classes as a civil servant and experienced great danger during the Peasant Revolt in 1381. This pseudo-revolution was part of the great restructuring of society that began with the effects of the Black Death in the late 1340s. Chaucer's greatest work, *The Canterbury Tales*, was a collection of stories commenting on English medieval life, pointing out the many problems, discrepancies, and weaknesses of the Roman Church and the royal classes before and after the first wave of plague from AD 1347 to 1351.

Chaucer used satire in the Middle English vernacular to make examples of all kinds of people and their follies. Writing in Middle English and not Latin allowed anyone to hear and understand the stories he wrote. His primary targets were the powerful people of the royal classes, merchant classes, and clerics. It's not exactly known how he was able to survive casting such insults and mockeries toward the powers of the time, but he appears to have died as an older man from natural causes.

Chaucer essentially turned many perceptions and opinions of English subjects from viewing the Roman Catholic Church as sacred to being profane and corrupt. With the loss of many exclusive powers after the Great Pestilence, Chaucer's works put England in a new and unique direction politically, socially, and scholarly.

While the Isle of Britain had a unique experience with the Protestant Reformation, the main thrust of that movement initially took place on mainland Europe. Jan Hus (AD 1369-1415) was a Czech priest, professor, and advocate for church reform at Charles University in Prague. During his tenure, Hus translated the writings of Wycliffe into his native language and continued the critique with further challenges of the papacy and the Roman Church.

An extraneous event taking place at that time was a divide in the Church called the Western Schism. This occurred when more than one person claimed sovereign authority as pope, causing a divide in loyalties between royal sovereigns. It was resolved by a meeting called the Council of Constance, but during this council, John Wycliffe was posthumously excommunicated as a heretic, while Hus was arrested, tried, excommunicated, and executed by burning at the stake. Hus's friend and supporter named Jerome of Prague came to his defense; however, he also was declared a heretic and executed by burning. While the protest aspect of the Protestant Reformation had begun in the 1300s, it seems the reform aspect waited a few centuries.

It's not possible to describe all the influential people and ideas in the age of Protestantism, as it is an entire subject unto itself. It is possible to describe the lineage of thought and change of focus, which brought about a new, modern view of life and society during that time in history. Like so many changes in human history, these new eras of thought were possible and very rapid because of emerging technologies.

It is rare that a technological achievement can have such an intense impact that it changes the culture of almost every society on Earth. In prehistory, the harnessing of fire was one of these discoveries. Ancient times saw inventions such as the plow, the wheel, writing, and the alphabet. There are many more in modern times, including more recent inventions such as the personal computer, the internet, and the smart phone. But in Medieval times, one would be hard pressed to dispute the importance of printing (pun intended).

Johannes Gensfleischzur Laden zum Gutenberg (AD 1394-1404?-1468), known today as Johannes Gutenberg, was a German blacksmith born around AD 1400. He is best known for his movable-type printing press that allowed the mass production of papers, books, and theses. Gutenberg's printing press was an adaptation of several technologies from Europe, the Middle East, and Asia.

Gutenberg was motivated by the emerging economic philosophy of capitalism. He saw printing as a very important technology that, if successful, could benefit everyone involved and make him a very wealthy man. Unfortunately for Gutenberg, he did not fully understand the nature of this new business and his investors did not recover their full investments.

Capitalism can be a winning system for the investor, the inventor/manager, and the population at large, whose lives and lifestyles can be improved through the integration of the new products, services, and technologies that would otherwise not exist. Even so, capitalism also comes with certain risks that can damage and even cause calamities if something goes wrong with the lender/borrower relationship. There are, of course, different versions of capitalism. American capitalism is generally defined as free market capitalism, which is a blend of open competition between providers and government regulation or oversite. An earlier form of capitalism with fewer protections was called laissez faire capitalism.

—◦◦◦—

Due to the untried nature of printing at that time, Gutenberg miscalculated how much money could be made from printing books compared to the total cost of the venture. When he could not repay the loan as promised, Gutenberg was sued in a court of law and lost almost all his property.

While his backers did not recover their expected investment and he died obscure and impoverished, Gutenberg's invention eventually revolutionized and democratized knowledge for literate people everywhere. The printing press he invented took what was usually a long and costly endeavor of transcribing books by hand into a faster and cheaper process of copying them by machine.

Gutenberg was based primarily in the German town of Mainz, which, at that time, was part of the Holy Roman Empire of central Europe. Mainz had a very large Jewish population for the time, and banking had been a profession in which European Jews excelled. This was not only due to the intellectual literacy and scholarship ingrained in Jewish culture, but also because banking was considered a sin by medieval Christianity.

The sin of usury was the act of loaning money and charging interest. While today usury is the act of charging unfairly high interest rates on loans, usury in Medieval times was the act of charging any interest at all. In business, not charging interest removes the incentive for lending money in the first place, and since according to the teachings of the medieval Church, Jews were already going to Hell for rejecting and executing Christ, it was extremely convenient for the Christian leaders at that time to allow Jews the practice of banking.

Ironically, antisemitism, which is the hatred of Jewish people, was widespread in Europe and especially within the German culture of that time. This prejudice would fester in central Europe for centuries, becoming violent intermittently until its horrific climax in the 1930s and '40s.

—◦◦◦—

Martin Luther of Germany (AD 1483-1546) is another pivotal person of modern times. Like St. Paul in ancient times and St. Thomas Aquinas in medieval times, Martin Luther's religious writings altered the course of world history. His life and effect on civilization was only possible due to many factors covered in this book thus far.

He was born in the new middle class to a family whose business was mining and copper smelting. The old medieval system of the Middle Ages would have likely kept his family poor, obscure, and illiterate. Fortunately, however, the Renaissance, the Great Mortality, and new economic opportunities and prosperities had changed everything.

Martin Luther's parents wanted more for their son. Instead of being a craftsman and merchant, his parents sent him to university to become educated as a lawyer. While in school, Martin Luther was taught to read and write, and his keen mind made him a great litigator. Fortunately, Martin Luther did not want to be a lawyer and left his legal studies to become a monk. This took him on a collision course with the Roman Catholic Church that reverberated throughout Europe and eventually the entire world.

Martin Luther's life had two profound effects. First, his new way of looking at Christianity and the Bible freed individuals from the corrupt domination of the medieval Latin Church. The Roman Church had left its focus on Christian teachings in the Bible and had become very focused on ritual and ceremony. The Church was teaching that salvation could only be attained through obedience to the Church and its clergy, rather than belief in Jesus Christ. Elaborate ritual Masses in the Latin language were performed across Europe. This left the general population with little understanding of what was being preached from the pulpit.

What it meant to be a Christian was further obfuscated with near worship of relics. Relics are bones, clothing, or other artifacts claimed to have belonged to Christ or a saint. These relics were said to have special powers and that they were evidence of Christ's divinity.

Instead of faith in Christ and knowledge through the Holy Spirit to serve the will of God the Father, people depended on superstitions for their salvation. The selling of indulgences was a moneymaking scheme in which people would give large amounts of money and other valuables to the Church, believing this would free the souls of loved ones from Purgatory and/or Hell.

While Martin Luther's desire was to change the Catholic Church, not to break away from it, Pope Leo X excommunicated Martin Luther on January 3, 1521. This act severed Martin Luther from all ties to the Roman Church and left him with no alternative but to lead his fellow German countrymen full force into the Protestant Reformation.

This aspect of Protestantism began in AD 1515 when Martin Luther had a revelation. It came from a passage of St. Paul's letter to the Romans where it is stated that humans are saved by "grace." God's grace, he realized, did not come from the Church, but from faith and belief in Jesus Christ. Luther called this his moment of "rebirth."

On October 31, 1517, Martin Luther posted his 95 Theses. This was a docket for intellectual debate that was posted to the door of The Church of All Saints in the German town, Wittenberg. Several versions and multiple copies of the theses in German and Latin were printed and distributed. Because of the printing press, within two months, various versions had spread across what is now Germany and into Italy, France, and the Netherlands.

Luther did not consider his theses to be controversial. He simply intended them to be a discussion about indulgences, penance, and relics, and how church practices needed reform to return to their original mission. Even so, it was considered a grave threat to the established powers of the popes. By that time, papal control was built on the powers of the Christian Crusades. After the Crusades, the Church continued these processes, which brought the papacy greater wealth and power.

The papacy became a business that raised money from wealthy and poor people alike to support church projects. It was corrupt, and many people knew that, but since the eleventh century, these processes and procedures had become so ingrained that it was impossible to separate from them without a significant loss of power over people and politics.

Martin Luther was eventually condemned by the Roman Church, excommunicated, and ordered arrested. What saved Martin Luther, and the Protestant Reformation were the Dukes of Wittenberg. These royal sovereigns had become disgruntled with the powers of Rome reaching from central Italy all the way into Germany. Whether each royal sovereign was motivated by spiritual piety or raw politics (or both) is a matter of discussion. The effect, however, was that many in Germany and elsewhere left the Roman Catholic Church and established a new German Church, later called Lutheranism.

Once that initial break had been made, there was no stopping it. The Lutheran Church, which eventually inspired many different Protestant faiths, became an entity unto itself. This entity changed many of the thoughts, processes, and perspectives of Western Christianity.

Emphasis on rituals was de-emphasized, as was the complete elimination of relics, confessions, and absolutions to and from priests, indulgences, Latin Masses, and even the Latin Bible. Translations of the Bible from its original Hebrew and Greek into the German language was initiated, and printing allowed tens of thousands of these new portable German Bibles to be distributed very efficiently far and wide.

The most important impact of the Protestant Reformation was the dissolution of mass conformity and the loss of a single, central religious authority in Western society. This was replaced with a new order and an emphasis on individualism in the form of modified churches rooted in nationalism and a complete focus on salvation through baptisms, personal faith, and belief in Jesus Christ. Salvation of the soul and individual relationships between God and man became very personalized in Western Christianity.

This new system also destroyed the collective powers of the Church of Rome over foreign lands in northern Europe and Britain, creating a Protestantism grounded in national identity. This set individuals free to read, interpret, and understand the Holy Bible in their own manner and in their own language. Barring the inherit problems with the translation of languages, this was a very liberating and enlightened time for Western Christianity. But it was also a time of great strife as people and royal sovereigns chose sides. Propelled into high gear by printing, the Protestant Reformation caused wars that were much deadlier because of the greater use of newly improved firearms.

⫸◆⫷

Another powerful force in Protestantism was the works of John Calvin (AD 1509-1564). Calvin was a French philosopher who was part of the Reformed Church. The Reformed Church was started in Switzerland a generation earlier by a man named Huldrych Zwingli (AD 1484-1531). Zwingli never challenged the legitimacy of the Roman Church, and he was never targeted for persecution. John Calvin, on the other hand, had radical beliefs about Christianity that did make him a target.

It has been said that John Calvin and his preaching of the Reformed theology made him the founder of America. While this statement is meant symbolically, his philosophies on religion, politics, and economics were the basic template of the American founding and framing. Through the migration and settlement of the Pilgrims and Puritans who were steadfast believers in his doctrines, John Calvin's Protestantism became the most influential religious philosophy of the British Americas.

Calvin believed that human beings were so immersed in the state of sin that nothing good could come from the choices of free will. Calvin believed in divine providence, which is essentially that God created the universe and controlled it by His will. God's will is always good, but humanity's choice to disobey the will of God brought about a terminal condition that prevents any person from being good by God's standards. When humans believe they are doing good, it is a distortion caused by a very limited understanding of the nature of God.

Our inability to understand God in our minds distorts the desires for goodness in our hearts, immersing us in a "bondage of sin." This severity in outlook had moderated quite a bit by the time of the founding of the American republic, but the perspectives of John Calvin have always remained in the psyche of the American Christian culture in the United States.

The Pilgrims and Puritans of the Reformed Church were some of the first English settlers in the Americas. They immigrated to escape the persecutions of the Church of England. They were a mixture of English-speaking peoples seeking to establish their own religious state. More of their settlements and worldview will be discussed in the next chapter.

England was changing from the Medieval class system to a more modern system with a larger and more powerful middle class. The English middle class was becoming so successful that they were challenging and sometimes outperforming many of the royal sovereigns in dress and lifestyle. King Henry VIII of England (AD 1491-1547) passed a law restricting what materials a person could wear based upon their social class, and this could even be enforced through execution.

King Henry VIII is infamous for his divorces from various wives, but his most relevant consequence is the English Reformation. This began when the pope decided not to honor his request for an annulment to one of his marriages. King Henry simply quit the Catholic Church and started the Church of England, also known as the Anglican Church.

King Henry was fortunate that the Bible had already been translated into old English by a British follower of Martin Luther named William Tyndale. Tyndale had already been executed on the mainland of Europe for his translation of the Holy Bible from its Hebrew and Greek versions to English. King Henry simply adopted the main body of Tyndale's translation, with modifications from other literary scholars, and implemented it as the first English Bible for the English Church and the British nation.

Henry VIII took a grave risk by allowing English Bibles into his churches. This was because the Latin Bible was considered the literal Word of God and the divine justification for sovereignty of kings. People were told that not honoring "God's Order," would have them sent to Hell either when they died or certainly upon Christ's Last Judgment. This kept most people in line even under the most incompetent or despotic rulers. Both leaving the Catholic Church, and the English translation of the Bible could be seen as a dissolution of the "divine right" of the sovereign classes.

Leaving the Catholic Church also left behind its authority of interpretation of the English Bible texts. Interpretations of Bible passages became much more personal, as people felt that God was talking directly to them when they read it in their own language. This loss of control of information through translation and interpretation would serve as the inevitable downfall of the principle of divine sovereignty of most kings, queens, and emperors in the Modern Age.

⬦

Queen Mary the First of England (AD 1516–1558) did not directly follow her father as ruler of England. His son Edward VI "ruled" from age 9 to 15, then a pretender named Lady Jane Grey was installed by elite members of the Protestant movement. Lady Jane Grey lasted five days before Mary was able to claim her legal right as Queen of England. Once Mary became the leading English royal sovereign, she began ruthless executions of many of the Protestant conspirators and strongly swerved back toward the Roman Catholic Church.

While this was likely due to her Catholic piety toward the Virgin Mary, the Roman Catholic Church had also been doing much soul searching since the breakup of their northern power base and instituted certain changes that brought it into line with many traditional Christian teachings and proceedings. This essentially saved the Catholic Church from further schisms and preserved it as an influential power.

There was still great reverence for the Church of Rome because it had been founded by St. Peter, a direct apostle of Christ. Queen Mary believed in many of the traditional teachings of the Catholic Church, especially in the line of papal succession and veneration of the Virgin Mary as the blessed Mother of God. The Roman Catholic Church's long history and international prestige was enviable to Protestant monarchs who continued to experiment with various religious forms, reforms, and processes.

Queen Mary died young without having produced a royal heir. This brought her sister Queen Elisabeth I into power. Queen Elisabeth the First of England (AD 1533-1603) was Mary's younger half-sister and was held in the Tower of London awaiting possible execution for some months before essentially being under house arrest for several more years. Elizabeth survived due to her keen wit and masterful ability to play the game of politics correctly. Elizabeth was an amazing sovereign who not only survived in a world run by alpha males, but also thrived in practically every area of necessity.

When Queen Mary died young and childless, Elizabeth was proclaimed Queen of England almost immediately. This is a time where the very course of world history was influenced by one single event. Queen Elizabeth I not only ruled longer than any other English monarch up to that time, but she was a very shrewd and powerful ruler in her own right. Not relying solely upon divine right to justify her position, her strength and longevity as the ultimate royal sovereign of England cemented the fact that Britain would favor Protestantism from that time forward.

Elizabeth's successor, King James I of England (AD 1566-1625) unintentionally oversaw instrumental progress in the journey to our Freedom Charters. First was the establishment of a permanent British settlement in the Americas. Second was the translation of the Holy Bible into a consistent English format called the King James Bible.

The King James Bible became the universal Bible translation for the Church of England. This is relevant because the King James translation set into motion a certain structure in language and meaning that was interpreted in a very specific manner. This manner used words that promoted the concepts of individual dignity and freedom as God-given gifts. The syntax of the King James Bible offers much more individualized interpretations to each reader, rather than having a universal church defining and enforcing its perceptions through the Latin language.

King James I did see the threats that an English Bible could levy against his sovereignty. Therefore, he wrote two books: one entitled *The True Law of Free Monarchies*, which focused on what he called "the Divine Right of Kings," and the other entitled *Basilikon Doron*, which focused upon the rules of kingship. While his writings helped to justify his royal sovereignty for the rest of his rule, they were much less helpful to his son Charles I.

<hr />

With Roman Catholicism yielding power to the Anglican Church and Protestantism in Britain, recognition of the individual in our Freedom Charters came even closer to fruition. Protestantism is now at the heart of English and American society. While Roman Catholicism has changed significantly since Medieval times, it is still built on a hierarchy not rooted in individual freedoms. American Roman Catholics are a sizable portion of the American population and are just as acculturated to the American constitutional system (including the author). Still, Roman Catholics who are serious about their religion can feel the influence of the papacy and its bishops, who have a strict dogma entrenched in the conformity of papal rule.

Protestantism is a counteraction to Catholic international conformity and is much more rooted in the powers of the nation state and the individual. Martin Luther and John Calvin led the way in this new type of Christian thinking, which reverted to scripture for guidance rather than tradition. British Puritanism was an even more refined version of Protestantism. Equipped with Bibles in English, Puritanism opened all kinds of interpretations of scripture not available to Roman Catholics or Anglicans at the time.

Roman Catholicism:

I would like to also note that these writings are not an attack on Roman Catholicism. Quite the contrary, it should be recognized that without the established orders and administration of the Roman Catholic Church, the emerging Modern Age would not have been possible. If there is one thing the Dark Ages proved, it was that disorder and the power of random wills by those who can commit the most violence is not conducive to justice or a state of security and freedom for the populace.

Without the holy sovereigns of the Latin Church and their competent administration of power, society would have been a continuing hodgepodge of individual wills combating for supremacy, with no center except that of personal egos. Winners of violent battles do not necessarily establish competent leadership and sound governing. While this was true for many pagan and Christian leaders during the Western European

Dark Ages (AD 565-800) the Roman Catholic Church remained a bastion of stability and conviction that was required to reign in so many of the random evils that all human beings can commit.

—◦◦◦◦◦—

American Capitalism:

The founders and framers of the American republic and our Freedom Charters knew these lessons well and made economic regulation a part of the constitutional duties of the government to ensure economic and societal stability. These regulations can seem, and possibly be, excessively controlling at times, but the need for regulatory powers in government is essential for many reasons. They include quality and safety of products, environmental impacts of production, laws governing the treatment of labor, antitrust laws preventing monopolies, and much more. These governmental powers are designed to offset possible abuses from individuals and organizations damaging other individuals, organizations, and society in general.

Even so, attention must also be paid to the government entities executing regulation and oversight, as they are also operated by people who are fallible and corruptible. Oversight of the government is the responsibility of individuals, organizations, and the public at large. A free media is again required for proper accountability, but this appears to be a continuing problem in the modern, mass-media age, where information has ironically become much more subjective and limited.

—◦◦◦◦◦—

American Pamphleteers:

The American revolutionaries also excelled in use of the printing press. Many, called pamphleteers at the time, printed and distributed scores of papers condemning the British government for their illegal behavior toward the colonists. These documents fueled the fire of revolution in the American colonies and brought cohesion to the cause. Pamphleteers also existed on the loyalist side, but their influence was limited at the time due to geographic factors.

Freedom of the press became a vital part of our Freedom Charters, as printing allowed a wide, fast distribution of news and ideas. This was instrumental in coordinating the American Revolutionary War across hundreds of miles of diverse terrain within and between the various colonies.

Printing continued to have an impact on our Freedom Charters after the Revolutionary War. This is especially true through the writings of James Madison, Alexander Hamilton, and John Jay, as they wrote many published articles describing, defining, and explaining the need for a new constitutional system. These writings are collectively called the Federalist Papers and are a must read for anyone interested in understanding the premises and reasoning of the American constitutional system.

Historical Processes:

It is important to remember that each event in history is part of a much larger process. Defining and describing this process in all its details is impossible. This process began at the moment of creation and will continue until the end of existence. We are only a minute portion of this process, but we are vital to it because all of us are members of a link in a long chain that is still being made but is connecting us all.

Our link in this chain is connected to the previous ones and will be attached to the next ones. As we pull (or are pulled) on this chain, decisions made today will influence all our tomorrows. While our decisions have this effect, knowing what to choose is not necessarily easy, obvious, or certain, but it is vital, nonetheless.

In a universe so complicated and so intricate we cannot possibly know everything to make perfect decisions. This brings us back to the source of our natural rights and our existence where prayer and quiet contemplation clothed in humility are the only viable options we possess. This is the true nature of faith in our Creator God. This means letting go of the desire to control outcomes and simply lead through virtue, reason, and faith, asking for guidance, and placing all our hopes and aspirations in the hands of our Creator. Nothing in this life will bring about more success, and nothing in the material world is more personally liberating.

CHAPTER 18

The English Civil Wars and the Restoration of the Monarchy

King James I of England, Scotland, and Ireland had approved and issued the English Bibles that carried his name. He had also signed the charter that created Jamestown and later signed other charters that allowed more private British ventures in the Americas. As described earlier, King James I did not recognize Magna Carta as a legitimate document outside of England and his successor Charles I disregarded the document altogether.

This placed the monarchy and the parliament on a collision course that ended with the arrest and execution of King Charles I. Great Britain experienced a tumultuous time known collectively as the English Civil Wars. The execution of King Charles I and the English Civil Wars brought an end to the "divine right of kings." The Long Parliament, as it was called, declared Britain a Commonwealth and claimed to create a republic in January of 1649. Reality was much different, however, as the Parliamentary army that arrested and killed the monarch was run by a military leader named Oliver Cromwell.

Cromwell was a general who wanted to control Great Britain while parading it as a commonwealth republic. Problems occurred immediately, as no written constitution was ready to replace the rule of the monarchy, so Oliver Cromwell used his military to manipulate Parliament when it would not bend to his will. Essentially, Cromwell was a military dictator who did not want to be seen as a dictator or a king, but his attitudes and behaviors were just as much, if not more, despotic than the monarchy they had just overthrown.

Cromwell's purge of the Long Parliament created what is known as the Rump Parliament, and while Cromwell did not attempt to directly control it, he continued to use his generals and soldiers to manipulate and coerce Parliament to follow his will. It may or may not have been Cromwell's original intent to be a despot, but it is difficult for modern American eyes to look at his behaviors and walk away with any other impression.

Until Cromwell's death in 1658, he tried various forms of ruling through Parliament, but he did not appear to understand that if he was going to share power with another institution that he would not always get the results he wanted. Instead of accepting the determinations of the Parliament, he continually tried to influence and even abolish the institution in favor of his desires and the major generals he appointed over Great Britain and Ireland.

Restoration of the British crown came when Cromwell's son was unable to lead the British nation as his father did. He restored the powers of the Parliament, which almost immediately voted to reinstate the monarchy. The Stewart Restoration occurred in May 1660 with the installation of Charles II, son of Charles I. Parliament then declared that Charles II had been the rightful ruler of Britain since the execution of his father. While Charles I believed wholeheartedly in the divine right of kings, his son knew from the past two decades of experience that Britain could not return to such a system.

Instead, it was eventually determined that Britain needed to establish a constitutional monarchy through the Glorious Revolution of 1688, in which the crown can never claim any power without the consent of Parliament. It also was determined that Parliament could not be dissolved without its own consent. This constitutional monarchy has been in place since and was the system whose decisions caused the eventual rift and separation with its American colonies.

Ironically, many of the issues that caused the English Civil War were similar to issues that caused the American Revolutionary War. Some have even argued that one was an extension of the other. In any regard, taxation without representation was a major issue that divided the crown from Parliament, leading to the English Civil Wars, but when the same issue was raised by the American colonists, Parliament claimed that colonists could not have Parliamentary representation because that was reserved for native British subjects.

Furthermore, the elected representatives of the colonists in the colonies did not possess equal sovereignty with the British Parliamentary representatives. Therefore, the crown and Parliament could determine any action toward the colonists and the colonists had no say in the matter. While this had always been the case, events such as the Navigation Acts of 1651, the Molasses Act of 1733, and The Seven Years' War/The French and Indian War (1754-1763) did not push the limits of British American tolerance in their allegiance to the crown. It was really the native British attitude toward the colonists that started the slippery process toward American separation.

The native British mindset toward the British American colonists were a general minimization and disregard for them as British subjects. For example, Benjamin Franklin was a genius in so many areas but was essentially dismissed by the British elite due to his colonial background. This general attitude by most British leaders toward colonists pushed the British American colonists to eventually reject the authority of the crown and Parliament. Before the French and Indian War, it was more of an annoyance that could be ignored, but after the great cost, and ironically, the cost and success of that war, it was only a matter of time before a revolution was kindled.

Americans are somewhat different than their Canadian neighbors because the restrictions and duties required by Great Britain on the British colonists south of Canada simply were not sustainable. After removal of the French threat, there were no real justifications for American colonists to remain subjects of a monarchy 3,000 miles away. While choices on both sides brought a revolution to fruition, it was simply circumstances that made it almost inevitable.

⏤⏤

People of Influence:

The next chapter will focus on individuals whose influences shaped the culture and sensibilities of the United Kingdom and Western Europe during the Age of Enlightenment. Each of the people described is important, but no person stands alone. For every great leader or influencer, there are many more people behind the scenes who have a significant impact without any public recognition.

While the people cited in the next chapter were indispensable for the eventual formation of our Freedom Charters in their current state, there are thousands more who assisted through ideas or physical and moral support. The people I have chosen to mention are not meant to be a complete list, and if I have not included someone of significance it is not a willful act of neglect.

CHAPTER 19

Philosophical Leaders of the United Kingdom and Western Europe

Beginning with ancient concepts attributed to Aristotle and Cicero, preserved by the medieval societies of Islam, Byzantium, and Catholic monasteries, modernized by Renaissance humanism and the Protestant Reformation, and codified in the English legal system, it was only a matter of time before the genius of our Freedom Charters was possible. Before this occurred, however, time required one other essential period now known as the Age of Reason or the Age of Enlightenment, mainly taking place in seventeenth century England, Scotland, and France.

Walter Raleigh (1552–1618)

Walter Raleigh was employed by Queen Elisabeth I. In 1584, he was awarded a royal patent (charter) to explore the lands in America known to the English as Virginia. He was promised one-fifth of all the silver and gold mined from that area if he could establish a colony within seven years of the patent.

His explorations of the Americas make him instrumental in the development of later British colonies, but this was not his primary objective. The true purpose was to establish English bases that could raid Spanish galleons for their treasures. The lost colony of Roanoke was meant to be one of those bases, but conflicts with the native populations exhausted their food supplies, and the venture was an eventual failure.

A second attempt to establish the Roanoke Colony also failed due to more pressing concerns in England's war with Spain. Although Raleigh never actually visited the explored territories of North America, his efforts gave Britain important knowledge and experience in the challenges of colonization.

Edward Coke (1552-1634)

Edward Coke's influence as a lawyer began what is sometimes called a "legal renaissance," as his staunch Protestant sensibilities motivated him to place legal limits on the clergy as well as the royal classes. Edward Coke was not particularly against monarchy, and he endorsed many of the philosophical arguments for retaining the monarchy, but he believed that only a monarchy subject to law was going to carry his nation into a brighter future.

His most notable influence on English law is the establishment and sustainability of a common law system, rather than a system based in civil law. His most tangible contribution to this is the creation of the Petition of Right, which is considered by many scholars to be equivalent in importance to Magna Carta.

His Petition of Right, adopted in 1628, is important to the future formation of our Freedom Charters in that it enhanced property rights through no taxation except through Parliament and no quartering of soldiers during peacetime. It also expanded the freedoms of English subjects by forbidding imprisonment without cause and declarations of martial law during peacetime.

While Coke's work set the premise for change in the laws of England, it was the English Civil Wars from 1642 to 1651 that put most of his ideas into effect by ending Divine Right of Kings.

William Shakespeare (1564–1616)

"I think the King is but a man, as I am. The violet smells to him as it doth to me. The element shows to him as it doth to me. All his senses have but human conditions. His ceremonies laid by; in his nakedness he appears but a man."—*Henry V* (**4.1.105**)

William Shakespeare is perhaps the best-known playwright in history. His plays have been performed around the world for many centuries, and his words still move people in a deep and personal way. He wrote on issues such as king versus civil war, republic versus monarchy, religion in government, and war and peace.

While Shakespeare's contributions can be found through many of his plays, his most notable influence is on the English language itself. Shakespeare was on par with Italian poets such as Dante and Petrarch. The use of his language moved people in waves of emotion. His elegant prose and memorable lines set a level of romance and sophistication in the English language like no other English-speaking person in history.

Our Freedom Charters certainly inherited this gift, which is especially found in parts of the Declaration of Independence and the Preamble to the United States Constitution. Our Freedom Charters are not only intellectually inspiring, but also stimulate the emotions of the soul in patriots for the causes of Liberty.

Rev. John Cotton (1585–1682)

John Cotton was a reverend of the Church of England but later rejected the rigidity of that denomination over the individual freedoms of the Puritans. He was persecuted in England as a nonconformist and eventually fled to the Massachusetts Bay Colony. His teachings in Boston had a major impact on the sensibilities of the people of Massachusetts.

Of all his teachings, the most notable was his fear of power. His distrust of power was well learned in England and through his Calvinist belief system. Both taught him that man cannot be trusted to do what is right, so trust in God and His laws is the only option for humanity.

Rev. Cotton's primary influence on our Freedom Charters was the worldview that human-beings are too sinful by nature to be trusted with the mantles of power, and that the civic system works best when people put their trust in God first, are responsible for self-governing, and the powers of the government are diffused into small segments.

Rev. Samuel Rutherford (1600–1661)

Samuel Rutherford was a Scottish, Presbyterian minister known for his nonconformist views. He wrote many letters and sermons that had a significant impact on people's perception of the role of the monarchy. In 1644, he wrote *Lex Rex* (Law and King) that spelled out his perception of the powers of government through the balancing of the powers of law and man.

Rutherford referenced an abstract understanding called a social contract, in which all people have political and moral obligations to each other in society. This contract is not a human choice but ordained by our Creator God. Kings and queens also are obligated under this contract through natural and human law. This belief eliminated the prospect of a divine right in the royal classes by stating that constitutional laws are supreme to kings and queens.

When the monarchy was restored after the English Civil Wars, Rutherford wrote a sermon in Latin and lectured the new King Charles II in his church. He was later arrested and executed for his audacity, but the words and principles he preached were not forgotten when England finally accepted a constitutional monarchy for its government.

His notable influence on our Freedom Charters are the direct challenges on the rights and actions of the British monarchy. The audacity of the Declaration of Independence, directly and specifically, calling out the sovereign ruler of England, King George III, and all his abuses, were an action that required extreme courage in the face of certain war, persecution, and death if captured.

John Milton (1608–1674)

John Milton was an English poet and writer who championed the ideas of republicanism. "Give me the liberty to know, to utter, and to argue freely according to conscience, above all liberties," is a quote attributed to him. As a Calvinist, he was strict on his beliefs in the powers and responsibilities of the individual.

While he is best known for his book *Paradise Lost*, John Milton's greatest contributions to the principles of our Freedom Charters are his works entitled *Areopagitica*, in which he wrote about the importance of free speech and freedom of the press, *Of Education* that championed educational reform focused more on the individual and less upon conformity to society, *A Treatise of Civil Power* that promoted the rights and powers of individual conscience over external forces, and *The Tenure of Kings and*

Magistrates, which was a pamphlet supporting the people's right to "dispose" of a monarch who does not act for the common good.

Thomas Hobbes (1588-1679)

Although Thomas Hobbes supported a strong monarchy, his book *Leviathan* was instrumental in illustrating the many reasons government is necessary. It sometimes occurs to people, in their spirit for independence and liberty, to believe that a government is not required. This is a fallacy that Hobbs corrects because without government, "Life is nasty, brutish, and short."

The spirit of individual freedom and liberty is an essential ingredient in a free society. Just the same, a strong government is also required as a counterbalance to individual abuses. His writings about the necessity of government helped to properly ground our founders and framers when developing a system that exercises appropriate government powers without trampling the rights and powers of the people as individuals, organizations, and societies.

Algernon Sidney (1622–1683)

Algernon Sidney wrote a book entitled *Discourses Concerning Government,* which is often referred to as a handbook on revolution. He served in the calvary of the Parliament during the English Civil War and was executed many years later for conspiring against the restoration of the English monarchy.

Sidney was considered a radical and became a martyr to other radical revolutionaries in the British Americas. Even so, Algeron Sidney set high standards for the people who do not wish to be ruled by a strong monarch by stating, "If vice and corruption prevail, liberty cannot subsist; but if virtue has the advantage, arbitrary power cannot be established. Liberty cannot be preserved if the manners of the people are corrupted."

Sidney was a reminder to the founders and framers (and us) that simply throwing off the yoke of tyranny is not enough. People must be deserving of freedom and liberty through their abilities to manage their own affairs with integrity and honor. Responsibility for self-governing requires the dignity and discipline of virtue. Allowing human vice to run unchecked will jeopardize liberty, making way for the harsh hand of government.

John Locke (1632–1704)

"The state of nature has a law of nature to govern it, which obliges every one: and reason, which is that law, teaches all mankind, who will but consult it, that being all equal and independent, no one ought to harm another in his life, health, liberty, or possessions . . . when his own preservation comes not in competition, ought he, as much as he can, to preserve the rest of mankind, and may not, unless it be to do justice on an offender, take away, or impair the life, or what tends to the preservation of the life, the liberty, health, limb, or goods of another."

John Locke is perhaps the most influential and referenced philosopher of the British Enlightenment, especially when it comes to the framing of our Freedom Charters. He is the author of works such as: *An Essay Concerning Human Understanding; Two Treaties of Government Books 1 and 2; The Fundamental Constitutions of Carolina; A Letter Concerning Toleration; Some Thoughts Concerning Education; and Some Considerations of the Consequences of the Lowering of Interest and the Raising the Value of Money*. In these writings, Locke sets many premises for the philosophical foundations of the founders and framers of the American republic.

Inspired by the social contract theory in Samuel Rutherford's *Lex Rex*, John Locke was both a political and moral philosopher, creating a unique perspective on the moral obligations of people as political entities. In a time when many philosophers in the Age of Reason pushed an atheist viewpoint, John Locke wrote a book entitled *The Reasonableness of Christianity as Delivered in the Scriptures*. This work demonstrated that faith and reason are very much compatible and can work in tandem to promote justice.

While there are many contributions from John Locke, the one that seems most relevant to the founding premises of our Freedom Charters is its basis in natural law. From ancient to modern times natural law is described as the template for all human laws, and these laws are rooted in never changing principles. While change is certainly an everlasting part of the entities that occupy nature, the laws that govern nature were set from creation forward and have continued unmovable throughout history.

The works of John Locke and his influences on our Freedom Charters is a lengthy study unto itself. So many of his thoughts and philosophies are integrated into the American system, it's almost impossible to separate his thoughts from the charters themselves. While an enticing prospect, this author will leave investigation and the full writings of John Locke to others.

Issac Newton (1642–1727)

Issac Newton is best known for his work in physics, in which his establishment of Newtonian Laws continues to be used today. Before Albert Einstein, Newton's work in physics was the only format humanity had for understanding the basic laws of physical existence. While Einstein's work demonstrated that there is much more to the physics of the universe,

Newtonian Law continues to be the basis of all physics at the everyday human level of reality.

Newton's significance to our Freedom Charters is twofold. First, he demonstrated how science and faith are not natural adversaries. Newton was a man of faith, who also understood that science plays a significant role in human lives, and that conflicts between scientific findings and interpretations in scripture does not automatically negate one or the other. While scripture is a communication of holy laws, the Holy Bible is not a science book, but a testament of faith in the God of Abraham. The Bible's role is not to teach us about the physical realities of the material universe, but moral laws of human behavior and the benefits of eternal and divine love.

Second, Newton's work and belief in the "fixed laws" of nature demonstrate how natural laws do not change at our level of existence. Forces such as motion and gravity are based on rules that were established long ago, and these forces on earth do not change over time. Other forces that we do not understand can confound us, but they also are established and fixed. While beings can change over time, the laws that govern their basic existence do not. In physics, whatever is true now has always been true, even when we don't fully understand it.

Charles de Secondat (Montesquieu) (1689–1755)

"There won't be freedom anyway if the judiciary body is not separated from the legislative and executive authorities."

Montesquieu was a French judge and politician who had a heavy influence on many of the people of the English and American Enlightenment. He was a successful lawyer and author who wrote many books including one about the Roman republic and empire. A very influential book entitled *The Spirit of the Laws* had a great impact on the founders and framers of the American republic.

The Spirit of the Laws was banned by the Roman Catholic Church. He argued for personal freedoms and the separation of powers in government. His focus on liberty was important because he better defined what it is and what it is not. Liberty has nothing to do with democracy and is not permission to behave anyway desired and does not permit slavery.

His most important influence on our Freedom Charters is the separation of powers in government. The powers of the executive, legislative, and judicial were seen by Montesquieu as very different aspects of power that cannot be allowed to work as one entity, if liberty and justice are to be served. Each branch of government has its own significance. Combining them makes a population vulnerable to abuse and subject to tyranny.

Adam Smith (1723–1790)

"It is the great multiplication of the productions of all the different arts, in consequence of the division of labor, which occasions, in a well-governed society, that universal opulence which extends itself to the lowest ranks of the people."

Adam Smith is to the American economic system as John Locke is to the American political system. A moral and thoughtful philosopher on the virtues of capitalism, Adam Smith gives extremely detailed critical analysis of the capitalist system and its propensity for prosperity in society. Two very influential books entitled *Theory of Moral Sentiments* and *An Inquiry into the Nature and Causes of the Wealth of Nations* have been studied by economists for centuries and still rank with the most persuasive books on economics and capitalism.

During his time, the accumulation of gold and silver were viewed as the measure of national wealth. Smith wrote that national wealth was not held so much in precious metals but in trade. He wrote how production of goods at market prices, sold in free markets with fair and equitable competition would provide the best products and labor at the best prices and wages. While Smith's beliefs perhaps placed too much trust in human integrity, his system allowed for later regulation of business by government. Allowing for the balance and counterbalance of commerce through private businesses and public governments, the American economic system through our Freedom Charters eventually evolved from laissez faire capitalism to a free market model.

Charity and natural ethics were also important aspects of Smith's philosophy, as he believed in the goodness of human empathy for others. Adam Smith believed that a significant portion of the population, not being regulated by government entities, will behave in ethical and moral ways on their own. The founders and framers understood that while this can be true in many cases, there needs to be a stop gap force in place to ensure that unscrupulous people do not run rampant. This is checked in our Freedom Charters by government entities and the popular sovereign when the private individuals, organizations, populations or government entities are not following basic ethical standards.

David Hume (1711–1776)

David Hume was a popular philosopher of the Age of Reason. Almost all his writings on various subjects set a standard for the general mindset of the people of Britain, Europe, and America during his lifetime.

His essays entitled *Political Discourses* are particularly relevant to our Freedom Charters because his viewpoints set so many worldviews in economics, commerce, taxation, trade, money, and interest. As mentioned earlier, prosperity is an essential element of a free society, and David Hume's views, as adapted by the founders and framers of the American republic, gave us the "gift of opulence" compared to other nations.

David Hume is also said to have had a direct influence on the wording of the Declaration of Independence. Thomas Jefferson originally wanted it to say, "We hold these truths sacred and undeniable . . . " but Benjamin Franklin, being a student of Hume, thought that the Declaration should be empirically based, reflecting the Age of Reason rather than the age of the church. The words were then changed into that most essential line, "We hold these truths to be self-evident . . . " making it a product of the times, times when faith and reason were overtaking religious dogma in Western worldviews.

Immanuel Kant (1724–1804)

Immanuel Kant is considered one of the masters of Enlightenment thought. His use of reason to buttress the ideas of personal freedoms were defined and supported through the already established ideas of natural law and the social contract. His basic idea is that natural law grants us certain rights and freedoms, while our social contract protects those rights and freedoms. His most relevant writings for our Freedom Charters are called *Metaphysics of Morals,* in which he identifies, defines, and describes all the basic premises of our natural rights.

Part One: The Doctrine of Right conveys his thoughts on the natural rights of the people as individuals and as populations, each as a sovereign entity. *Part Two: The Doctrine of Virtue* makes the distinction between rights and virtue. The former are outer freedoms, and the latter are inner freedoms. Put simply, rights are innate qualities that grant us the power of making personal choices toward others; virtues are innate qualities that grant us the power of making personal choices for self.

This essentially breaks down to the natural rights of beliefs and behaviors. They are the right of conscience and the right to exercise that conscience in actions that promote the general welfare of ourselves and each other. The state has the role of the social contract to protect natural rights of individuals from other individuals, organizations, populations, and government entities who would violate them. This is achieved through the legitimate establishment and enforcement of human laws derived from natural law administered through due process.

Since being bound by the social contract is not based on individual choice or by consent, the state must exercise great care when administering human laws, which have the potential of violating natural rights. The purpose of the state is not to command people into submission, but to rely upon their natural abilities to reason. Rational beings who respect the natural rights of others do not require intervention by the state. People who do not respect the natural rights of others are subjected to consequences of the law, enforced by the government, following a uniform due process.

Part III

CHAPTER 20

Settlers, Pilgrims, Puritans, and the Charters of British America

Initial attempts at colonization in North America east of the Mississippi River began in the 1500s with the Spanish in what is now the state of Florida and small parts of what is now the states of Alabama, Mississippi, and Louisiana. The city of St. Augustine was established on the Atlantic Coast in September 1565 and is currently the oldest continually inhabited Western city in the United States.

The areas west of the Mississippi River were colonized by the French and Spanish in the 1500s. Areas controlled by France were called Louisiana, but it ranged from today's state of Louisiana, up to Quebec, Canada; the state of Minnesota; and across to the states of Colorado, Wyoming, and Utah. Other areas conquered by Spain were from today's Mexico and state of Texas, across to today's state of California and up to today's Canada and part of the state of Alaska. In the latter 1700s, Russia laid claims to what is most of today's state of Alaska.

British colonization in the Americas was explored and attempted in the late 1500s and early 1600s. Newfoundland and Roanoke colonies failed, preceding the first successful attempt in what is now the United States with the establishment of Jamestown in 1607. Jamestown was named in honor of King James I who approved the charter allowing a private British organization called the Virginia Company a chance to settle in the New World. At the time, all the East Coast of North America from what is today the state of South Carolina to what is today the state of New York was called Virginia and open to colonization. North of that to Canada would eventually be called New England.

—◆◆◆—

The 1606 charter called the "First Settlement of Virginia" was given to the Virginia Company of London. This charter established permission from King James I for British subjects to "begin their plantation and habitation in some fit and convenient place, between four and thirty and one and forty degrees of the said latitude, alongst the coasts of Virginia, and the coast of America. . . . "

The charter that led to the establishment of Jamestown is significant to our Freedom Charters because it stopped the Spanish and the French from entirely owning the lands of the New World. Jamestown allowed England to have a base in North America. This foothold also would permit the English legal culture a foundation in the New World.

Most of these settlers represented the Church of England in their religious practice and philosophy. Conversion and the spreading of Western civilization to the native Americans was the primary justification for the venture, but the royal crown, the Virginia company of London, and each settler had their own agendas that the first settlement in Virginia served, few of which were primarily focused on conversion or "civilizing" the native populations.

Jamestown survived up to the end of the 1600s. While it was the first "successful colony" in British America, credit for the beginning of the

British American colonies that revolted against the British crown usually goes to the Plymouth Colony founded in today's state of Massachusetts in late 1620.

❈

The settlement of Pilgrims in Plymouth Colony would later kickstart the Massachusetts Bay Colony in what would continue to the creation of other British colonies, eventually becoming British America and the United States of America. This continuation into the later 1600s of a sustaining presence of British subjects eventually expanded into thirteen British colonies south of Canada.

Many Dutch peoples settled what was called New Netherland in what is today the state of New York and parts of today's New Jersey, Connecticut, Delaware, Rhode Island, and Pennsylvania. New Netherland, established in 1614, surrendered to the United Kingdom in 1664 after three wars with Great Britain. Since that time, the Dutch people have played an interesting internal and external role in the founding of the American republic.

❈

As stated earlier, Puritans are Protestants who broke away from the nationalistic churches founded during the Protestant Reformation. The Roman Catholic Church was international and based on conformity dictated by the papacy, while the Protestant churches were nationalistic and based on independence from the papacy but controlled by the royal class. The Puritans were individual Christians who believed in personalized interpretations of the newly translated Bibles through their different languages. Puritans would not swear loyalty to any sovereign but to the God of Abraham Himself. This brought them much trouble, since the Protestant sovereigns required sworn loyalty by their subjects to maintain the perception of their legitimacy.

Any individual Christian might become a Puritan Christian, but their rejection of the established Roman Catholic and national Protestant churches in places such as Britain, France, Switzerland, Holland, and Germany put them in serious jeopardy. Persecutions caused Puritans to flee their homelands in search of religious freedom.

Persecution from the English crown forced many Puritans to flee the United Kingdom. Puritan Christians of Great Britain fled to Holland to escape these persecutions. Families made their way sporadically and often separately, as they were not given permission to leave the Isle of Britain. Holland was home to many British Puritans for over a decade before it was decided by some to leave Holland for the Americas to establish what they believed would be a Puritan Christian state.

After stopping in England to charter two ships for the Americas, one ship proved unseaworthy and had to be abandoned. In September 1620, 102 British subjects, most of whom were Puritans, set sail in the *Mayflower*. They did not receive a royal charter like those of Jamestown, but by this time, King James was simply glad to be rid of them.

The Mayflower Compact was an agreement between the settlers, and with the sponsors of the Plymouth Colony in America. An interesting aspect of the compact was how it was originally established along collectivist lines but proved unworkable in the reality of remote settled living in the Americas. They later restructured their administration along individualist lines, in turn setting many American political, economic, and religious sensibilities for centuries to come. One of the primary architects of this compact, William Bradford (1590-1657) will be documented further in the next chapter.

—⬦⬦—

As more British subjects began mass migrations to the New World, the royal sovereigns of Great Britain began issuing more formal charters for settlements. This eventually led to the establishment of separate British colonies, thirteen of which would formally separate from the British crown on July 4, 1776, to become the United States of America.

—⬦⬦—

African slaves were not forced into servitude in New England at the same pace as Virginia (the Southern colonies) or of the West Indies (the Caribbean Islands). This was not based on moral objections but rather as a product of lower demand. Most slaves from Africa were sent to the Caribbean, where they were put to work primarily on sugar plantations. Many others were sold to Southern colonies to work mainly on tobacco and cotton plantations.

The New England climate did not permit massive plantations for the most part, but slaves were brought to New England to perform other labor, mostly in household duties. Native Americans and whites from Ireland were also enslaved in New England, but black slaves from the Caribbean were most preferred based on cost and behavior.

Puritan religious sensibilities were very much focused on the Hebrew Old Testament that did not forbid slavery. Even parts of the Christian New Testament that mentioned slavery did not forbid it. Dehumanization, plus a distorted view of salvation of the soul, played a central part in Puritan sensibilities accepting slavery as a legitimate institution, with a few exceptions.

While slavery in New England was much less frequent than in the Southern colonies or the Caribbean, New Englanders were certainly heavily involved in the slave trade, which was extremely lucrative. Yankee traders were New Englanders whose ships became a major part of the Atlantic slave trade.

Following the course from New England to Africa, Yankee traders would load masses of slaves into their cargo ships, setting sail for the islands of the Caribbean. Once there, they would trade the most physically healthy of slaves for other commodities such as sugar, rum, spices, salt, and other slaves who were not wanted. They would then sail to the Southern colonies, where more slaves were sold. The remaining slaves and commodities were then brought to Rhode Island and the Massachusetts Bay Colony for sale.

Most Puritans excused the abhorrent state of slavery by believing that this was the only way slaves could learn the gospels. Europeans thought that Christianizing the slaves would bring them closer to God, salvation, and civilization, but it seems that this distortion continued well after a slave converted to Christianity.

This is one important aspect of slavery and conquest from the Age of Discovery forward. Christian Europeans and colonists needed a justification for this repulsive institution, and it was achieved through the belief that they were introducing "savages" to a superior culture and Christian salvation. Like Alexander the Great spreading civilization in the form of Hellenism, Europeans saw themselves as the heirs of ancient Greece and Rome, emulating this "superiority" in civilization and religion.

212

The next chapter will focus on individuals whose influences shaped the culture and sensibilities of the American Enlightenment and Revolution. As before, each of the people described is important, but no person stands alone. For every great leader or influencer, there are many more people behind the scenes who have a significant impact without any public recognition.

While the people cited in the next chapter were indispensable for the eventual formation of our Freedom Charters in their current state, there are thousands more who assisted through ideas or physical and moral support. The people I have chosen to mention are not meant to be a complete list, and if I have not included someone of significance, it's not a willful act of neglect.

It also must be noted that none of the endeavors of these men would have come to fruition without the dedicated love, support and labor of countless mothers, wives and children who received no official acknowledgment; nor the immense physical labor and suffering of African slaves whose lives and existence were horrific circumstances that can only be described as a holocaust of torture, degradation and dehumanization that lasted from the Age of Discovery in the 1400s through the American Revolutionary War and into the 1860s.

None of these people were officially recognized at the time for their contributions, nor were they afforded respect and recognition of their God given natural rights which were so championed by these men of vision. It would be well beyond their generations and centuries before any semblance of distinction and dignity were given mention and credit.

Not enough can be said or written about this here, but while outrageous to modern sensibilities, these travesties of justice, humanity and Christian teachings gave the founders and framers of the American republic the material production and surplus required to fight and win the war for independence from Great Britian.

Furthermore, after the war for independence, and even after the end of slavery in 1865 and formal recognition of civil rights of women and African Americans in the twentieth century, this country continues to struggle with the effects that these realities have had and still have on American society. It is my desire to one day see universal recognition and respect for the natural rights of every human being conceived into this world, without unjust rationalizations of why this should not be so.

CHAPTER 21

Philosophical Leaders in the American Colonies and the United States of America

The following list of modern people from the British American colonies/ United States have been identified as essential influences in the process of establishing the roots of the American system created by our Freedom Charters. As in Chapter 19, I will not attempt in-depth biographies of these people, as my primary purpose is to describe their ultimate effect on the structure and format of our Freedom Charters. Therefore, I will only write about their direct influence on the development of colonial ideas, culture, and lifestyle. For a more in-depth understanding of each person, there are many biographies and some autobiographies already written for your reading indulgences.

John Carver (1576–1621)

John Carver was instrumental in the financing of the Puritan venture on the *Mayflower*, an important writer and first signer of the Mayflower Compact, the first serving governor on the *Mayflower* and of the Plymouth Colony. He also brokered the first official treaty between the indigenous people and the British crown. Although his time alive in the New World was tragically short, his work was essential in the long processes leading to our Freedom Charters.

William Bradford (1590–1657)

William Bradford was an important leader and the second governor of Plymouth Colony. Recognizing the flaws in the original Mayflower Compact, Bradford was a crucial author of the revised version that abandoned the collectivist foundation and inserted a premise based upon individual merit. His sensibilities and influences set a new tone for the first sustained colony in British America, carrying into future colonies, in and through the American Revolution, the creation of the American republic, and our Freedom Charters.

In his writings entitled *Of Plymouth Plantation,* William Bradford documented the founding and functioning of Plymouth Colony. First was the recognition of private property rights and the right to sell private property, goods, and labor for personal gain. This change in philosophy produced surpluses for the first time. These surpluses were then brought to the market to be sold for profit. This profit was reinvested in the production of goods and labor, producing more surpluses with greater economic and financial security for the colony and its individual residents.

Free-market competition between settlers also ensured the best quality products at the lowest prices. This is how many Pilgrims were able to settle their debts. It also created a new mass migration of more Puritans to New England.

Governor John Winthrop (1588–1649)

Recognizing the success of Plymouth Colony, King Charles I granted a charter to the Massachusetts Bay Company. John Winthrop excitedly joined this organization and was made governor, as his English estates were sold and transferred through this new charter to lands in New England. A master organizer, Governor John Winthrop brought a thousand Puritans to the shores of the Massachusetts Bay Colony to establish this legally recognized private British venture.

John Winthrop wrote a sermon entitled, *A Model of Christian Charity*, in which he spoke of the now famous "city upon a hill." Winthrop believed the settlers were making a covenant with the God of Abraham and each other like the ancient Israelites. So, ten years after the initial voyage of the *Mayflower*, Winthrop's ship the *Arabella* brought and led masses of Puritans into New England, following the same path in his mind as the ancient Jews to their promised land in Caanan. Each step establishing themselves in the Americas was seen through the lens of God's Holy Covenant with ancient Israel. This pattern of belief, paralleling ancient Judaism, has remained part of the American worldview ever since.

Author's Note: Perhaps something of interest, the completion of this book before being sent to editing is occurring now at Logan International Airport in Boston. The part of the airport where I am currently sitting is part of what was called Governors Island in Massachusetts. This was the property of Governor John Winthrop until the building of a fort here in the 1800s. Now it is part of Logan Airport. Just FYI.

William Penn (1644–1718)

William Penn was the son of a knighted British admiral of the same name. While his father fought several of the wars against the Dutch that won New Netherlands for Britain, Penn was the founder and served as the first British governor of the Province of Pennsylvania. Originally Puritan, William Penn was exposed to the teachings of a new religious offshoot called The Quakers. This put considerable strain between him and his famous father.

Quakerism was rooted in Christianity and more of a lifestyle than a religion. Instead of focus on religious dogma, Quakers believe that God can be personally experienced through our personal relationship with Him and other people. Quakers have a very literal moral code based on the teachings of Jesus Christ. This makes Quakerism a beacon of religious tolerance, nonviolence, and fairness.

William Penn put the virtues of Quakerism into the founding philosophy of his newly established colony with great success. Innovations of fairness and religious tolerance had significant impacts on Pennsylvania and other colonies. Some ideas such as a jury of peers was an innovative concept that made its way into our Freedom Charters. Other influences reinforced ideas such as private property rights, the right to political dissent, freedom of the press, and of private businesses. This brought the concept of organizational sovereignty to the forefront. Organizations were legal entities with rights and powers like other legal entities.

In his collaborative efforts with the aged William Bradford entitled *The Excellent Privilege of Liberty and Property,* both men published a reproduction of Magna Carta in English from the time of King Edward I, spelling out the philosophy of personal liberty and property as a birthright of British subjects. This important event took place in 1687, bringing the teachings of Magna Carta to American readers exactly one hundred years before the completion of the U.S. Constitution that would be sent to the various states for ratification. Other aspects of this publication were letters titled "To the Reader" and "Introduction" that spelled out the exact reasons for the efforts to bring Magna Carta to America in English. This was an indispensable moment into the long journey to the American Revolution and our Freedom Charters.

Codified into the Province of Pennsylvania's founding documents were many aspects of Quakerism that eventually made their way into our Freedom Charters. The significance of William Penn and Quakerism in our Freedom Charters cannot be emphasized enough. His life is a fascinating tale of political and religious justice. His influences on the concepts of freedom and liberty on both sides of the Atlantic are in epic proportions and cannot be given their full credit in these limited writings.

Jonathan Edwards (1703–1758)

Jonathan Edwards is our first influencer born in the eighteenth century, and unlike the influencers documented so far, Jonathan Edwards was born, lived, and died all within the boundaries of the British American colonies. He is the first truly American person described in these writings.

Edwards was responsible for what is called The Great Awakening. This was a religious philosophy rooted in the fundamentals of Puritanism. The Great Awakening was necessary because humanity ebbs and flows when it comes to religious and moral fervor. The human flaw of complacency can be very destructive to people and societies. Edwards saw how the British American colonists were wavering in their religious and moral foundations, and this trend left unchecked could lead to complete destruction of society.

Jonathan Edwards was a great fan of Sir Isaac Newton and his blending of science and faith. He saw, as Newton did, that science and faith are not in a state of combat with one another, but partners in a more virtuous endeavor, the pursuit of truth. Whether truth can be found through science or through faith, both are approaches that have their merit depending upon the task at hand. As stated earlier in these writings, science is the pursuit of truth in our physical/material existence where faith is the pursuit of truth in our abstract social/emotional/spiritual plane. Both serve the intellect and are essential aspects of the human condition.

The most important influence from Jonathan Edwards as applied to our Freedom Charters was his belief in the practical uses of science and faith. While scientific knowledge and inner virtues are noble things, they only really matter if they produce an effect on people and our outer environment. Pure science is a grand thing, but unless it can be applied to the lives of people and our world, it serves no advantageous purpose. Great virtues that are trapped inside someone's heart and mind, having no external effects on people and the world, are also inconsequential in the grand scheme of existence. While pure scientific knowledge and inner personal faith are blessings of consciousness, leaving them unapplied to the outer world is akin to precious gems and metals buried deep inside the earth unmined.

Edwards was also a fan of John Locke. Within the principle of the social contract, John Locke describes the beauty of personal virtues as applied to our emulating the Creator God. God's perfection is unattainable for humanity, but as His children in His image, human beings can come as close to perfection as possible through personal virtues. In his book *The Nature of True Virtue*, Edwards puts forth the belief that humanity was created to display the glory of God and not to serve the selfish desires of humanity. Even our love for ourselves, others, country, and nature are not sinful if they serve to glorify God's greatness. By doing God's will, we will access His grace, guidance, and protection through divine providence.

Benjamin Franklin (1706–1790)

Here is another moment when all that came before had a direct effect on the formation and structure of our Freedom Charters. One of the most famous and influential of the American founders, Benjamin Franklin, was a notable writer, inventor, businessman, politician, and scientist long before he ascended to the ranks of a founder and framer of the American republic. Very much influenced by the writings of Jonathan Edwards, Franklin became the model of what a fully realized American can be.

A polymath who approached Leonardo DaVinci in intelligence, Benjamin Franklin was a man of faith, reason, science, writing, journalism, printing, publishing, invention, business, politics, diplomacy, statesmanship, and constitutional republicanism.

One of the eldest of our American founders and framers at the time, Benjamin Franklin brought the wisdom of a long and fruitful life to the collection of people who would design, establish, and begin our great experiment in self-governing. Being of the generation of Jonathan Edwards, Benjamin Franklin was a model influencer from the generation just before the majority generations of the founders and framers of the American republic.

Originally from Boston, at age 15 Benjamin Franklin began working as a printing apprentice for a newspaper that his brother had started. He became politically involved in the ideas of free speech and freedom of the press when his brother was jailed for a few weeks by the governor of Massachusetts for writing some unflattering criticisms.

He became a fugitive by leaving his brother without permission to begin his own life in New York, then Philadelphia at age 17. After a brief stint in London, England, where he learned of Enlightenment ideals, he returned to Philadelphia to start a guild of tradesmen and artisans called

Junto (together). This organization gave rise to other organizations and began the process of bringing the practical application of ideas from the European Age of Enlightenment to British America.

Franklin helped to form the first library in Philadelphia by writing a charter for the Library Company of Philadelphia. Later he became a publisher and columnist for *The Pennsylvania Gazette*, a newspaper he helped start. Franklin saw his efforts through the lens of the Quakers and Jonathan Edwards, as he believed his work should glorify God by teaching moral virtues to the American colonists and be a champion of "useful knowledge."

In 1734, Franklin became a grand master of Freemasonry and reprinted the book *The Constitutions of the Free-Masons*. Just two years earlier, he had started publishing the now famous *Poor Richard's Almanack,* which was a successful and profitable series of stories and sayings. He continued to write and publish more books and letters, usually under pseudonyms, that expressed ideas and proverbs of great wisdom.

Later, he began the first volunteer firefighters' company in Philadelphia. He also fashioned and sold a process to make paper currency for the colonies of New Jersey, Delaware, and eventually Pennsylvania to fight counterfeiting. As postmaster general of Pennsylvania and eventually for all the British colonies, Franklin engaged in product, service, administrative, and logistical improvements, many of which continue to be used today.

In 1751, he started an academy based on a pamphlet he wrote and published called *Proposals Related to the Education of Youth in Pennsylvania*. This set the course of American education away from classical studies and toward practical ones. Two years later, he started the *American Philosophical Society* to help scientists and inventors share ideas and information about discoveries and inventions that can be applied to everyday living. During the Seven Years' War (the French and Indian War), he formed a militia to defend Philadelphia when the politicians charged with the duty refused to act.

Franklin was wealthy and able to retire before age 50 but did not stop being a productive colonial citizen. He was elected a councilman and justice of the peace of Philadelphia and eventually elected to the Pennsylvania Assembly. He continued with many other private and public endeavors in business, science, and politics that 20 years later led to him being selected as a representative of the Province of Pennsylvania for the American Continental Congress. The influence and genius of Benjamin Franklin is far beyond our ability to calculate. It is also much more than described here. A full study of his autobiography and biographies is the only way to do justice to his life and influence.

Samuel Adams (1722–1803)

Samuel Adams was born in Boston. His career began unremarkably as a failed merchant, businessman, maltster/brewer, and tax collector. His career really took off when he entered politics and was a firebrand revolutionary speaker leading up to the American Revolutionary War.

In 1768, he was the leader of an underground organization designed for "noncooperation" with the British government whose actions directly led to British troops occupying Boston. This group of revolutionaries did not remain solely in Boston but networked with others throughout the thirteen colonies. One of his greatest contributions was that of publisher, writing articles against the British government in the Americas. These writings were heavily influenced by the works of John Locke and made their way throughout the thirteen colonies.

Adams was elected to the Massachusetts House of Representatives and became an open critic of the British Parliament for its stand on taxation without representation. Adams became more radical as the British Parliament continued to behave in ways that he saw as "unconstitutional" (referring to the British Constitution).

His radicalism was mainly expressed with involvement in an underground political group called the Sons of Liberty. Adams was a witness to the Boston Massacre in 1770 and likely participated in the Boston Tea Party. He was certainly much more of a hands-on revolutionary, actively engaged in what can easily be called sedition against the British Empire. His writing also became more radicalized as he began publicly criticizing the governor of Massachusetts and even King George III himself.

As the British government continued to pass more restrictions and more taxes on the colonists, Adams became more vociferous for liberty and committed to the cause of noncooperation, eventually culminating in his support for a revolutionary war against Great Britain. He and his second cousin, John Adams, were later chosen members to represent Massachusetts at the Continental Congress.

George Mason (1725–1792)

From the colony of Virginia, George Mason was a big proponent of state rights and individual rights in our Freedom Charters. He was a planter and politician who served many roles in the process of creating the United States Bill of Rights using his drafting of the Virginia Declaration of Rights as a model.

George Mason is considered the father of the Bill of Rights and a champion of liberties for state governments and individual citizens. His writings had a great impact on the views and speeches of another Virginian named Patrick Henry whose oratory brought the written views of George Mason to throngs of people who were unable to read them.

George Mason served as a member of the Constitutional Convention of 1787 in Philadelphia but refused to sign the final draft because it did not contain a Bill of Rights and kept slavery legal. Staunchly antislavery, Mason spent most of his life and career working within the colony and then the state of Virginia for the freedom and liberty of all individuals.

Mason was dedicated to the idea of "small republicanism," as he believed a state republic was better able to respond to the direct needs of their citizens than a large federal republic. The writings and influence of George Mason significantly contributed to the ideas of American Federalism, in which a large federal government did not completely reign over the smaller state governments, but rather worked in tandem with state governments for the security and prosperity of the people and organizations of the entire American system.

John Dickinson (1732–1808)

From Pennsylvania, John Dickinson was a moderate voice of reason when hotter heads seemed to have the advantage. He was a prolific writer whose open letters clearly and concisely made the voices of the colonists heard, not as a mob of rabble rousers, but as intelligent, educated, and dignified British subjects. Dickinson's writings also helped to better define the exact grievances that the colonists expressed as loyal subjects to the crown.

Dickinson was chosen as a Pennsylvania representative to the Continental Congresses and is best known for his extension of the Petition to the King and the Olive Branch Petition to King George III on behalf of the colonists who wanted to avoid war, further bloodshed with England, and separation from the crown. A thoughtful man, his writings earned him the title Penman of the Revolution, as he gave the British authorities opportunities to avoid the upcoming conflicts. His chief rivals in the Continental Congress were the delegates from Massachusetts who were already bloodied and primed for war with Britain.

Of all the members of the Continental Congress, he was the only member to be absent from the vote for independence, did not sign the Declaration of Independence, and never supported separation from England. He was, however, a confirmed supporter of the cause for liberty. He helped to draft the Articles of Confederation and served a noncombat role as an officer in the militia. After the revolution, he supported the Constitutional Convention, ratification of the United States Constitution, and served as the first governor of Delaware, then Pennsylvania. John Dickinson demonstrated how pacifists can also play a role in the defense of American liberty.

John Adams (1735–1826)

Second cousin to Samuel Adams, John Adams was of a milder personality. An educated Massachusetts lawyer working in private practice, John Adams was assigned the defense of the British soldiers who fired on the colonists in the Boston Massacre, gaining them a judgment for acquittal.

John Adams joined the revolutionary cause after experiencing demoralization and oppression from the British occupation of Boston, along with the decree by British Parliament that any future trials concerning British soldiers or administrators would be held in England or another colony, usurping the Massachusetts colonial judiciary. When the British Parliament took over payment of the salary of the governor of Massachusetts, Adams saw this as usurping the Massachusetts colonial legislature.

Although he was a central figure as an American founder and framer, his greatest contributions to our Freedom Charters were accomplished during and after the Revolutionary War. As a member of the Continental Congress, he was an impassioned advocate for separation from Great Britain. He, along with Benjamin Franklin, helped Thomas Jefferson with the drafting of the Declaration of Independence. During the war, he served overseas in the Dutch Republic and eventually gained favor from Dutch investors who provided the new United States of America with its first line of credit.

As a writer of the new *Massachusetts Constitution* in 1780, his ideas concerning presumption of innocence and the right to private counsel for a person accused of a crime made their way into our Freedom Charters. As a diplomat, he was a central figure in the negotiation of the peace treaty between Britain and the United States in Paris, and as the first serving Vice President and the second President of the United States, John Adams continued many precedents set by President George Washington, most notably America's strong desire to stay out of European wars.

Deeper personal insights into the soul of the man can be gathered through the posthumous publication of the letters to and from his wife Abigail, now entitled *My Dearest Friend*, along with other letters written to and from Thomas Jefferson after both men's retirement.

John Hancock (1737–1793)

The famous, uber wealthy man of his day, John Hancock is best known for his large signature and being the first signer of the Declaration of Independence. A mercantilist, John Hancock was involved in the businesses of shipping, shipbuilding, investment banking, real estate development, wholesaling, and import/export trading. Born into wealth, then magnifying that wealth through shrewd business skills, John Hancock was admired and envied throughout his extravagant life.

As a statesman, he served as the first and third governor of Massachusetts and President of the Second Continental Congress. Unlike many of the founders, he did not come from simple beginnings and had much to lose by supporting the revolutionary cause. His course was set into motion very early to become an important colonist in the British hierarchy. Instead, he became a dedicated patriot supporting separation from England, which eventually cost him most of his fortune. This tremendous cost of personal treasure, however, did not deter him from the cause he believed to be righteous and correct in the eyes of God and history, and he was never reported to have regretted his decisions to do so.

After the Revolutionary War, he was instrumental in having Massachusetts adopt the U.S. Constitution for ratification and gave many of his riches to the poor, widows, and orphans. Hancock was a bold, wealthy man with a shrewd personality. Most people who knew him either loved him or hated him; few were indifferent. In the end, most of the animosity toward John Hancock came from fellow citizens of his home state.

Thomas Paine (1737–1809)

Thomas Paine was an American patriot and pamphleteer who is best known as the author of a seditious book entitled *Common Sense*. At a time when the population of the colonies was approximately two and a half million people, over half a million copies of his book were printed and distributed. In it he argued that Great Britain was too small and too distant to be able to rule over vast lands in the Americas. He also argued that while Britain was needed for the initial creation and defense of the American colonies, the colonies of British America had outgrown the need for a ruling foreign monarch, and America was ready for self-rule.

Paine's writings provided a foundation from which the Declaration of Independence was written. Inspired by the need for liberty and independence, Thomas Paine was able to write his arguments in a clear and concise manner, appealing to a great many American colonists. His writings took some focus from the British government as a whole and began what became the argument against King George III personally. While the American Revolutionary War was well underway by the time *Common Sense* was first published, his writings served as a focal point against King George III and for the needed recruitment of revolutionary war soldiers. This earned him the title, Father of the American Revolution. His pamphlet entitled *The American Crisis* published toward the end of 1776 continued to serve in recruitment of soldiers for the revolutionary cause.

In 1780, Paine published a pamphlet entitled *Public Good* arguing that lands west of the original thirteen colonies should belong to the government of the United States and not to individual states that were once colonies. This argument had a major impact on the post war structure of the United States through the Northwest Ordinance, an act of Congress under the Articles of Confederation, that future lands of the United States would be their own states and not extensions of the original thirteen states. This made Thomas Paine several enemies, especially in Virginia, where many wealthy people (including George Washington, James Madison, and Thomas Jefferson) were poised to gain great personal wealth through newly surveyed lands west of Ohio. Paine made other enemies of the founders and framers, including people like John Adams, who saw many of his arguments for democracy dangerously leading toward anarchy.

While during the war Thomas Paine was a great asset to the cause, his words and writings after the revolution were seen by some as a liability to the founders and framers of the new republic. One such incident happened when he wrote a scathing attack on then President George Washington. While Washington was a man with many faults, it was the perspective of most people that Thomas Paine's criticisms were unwarranted, undeserved, and even disrespectful of a hero to the American people and the American Revolution.

Paine saw a need for revolution against all monarchies and was a dedicated supporter of the French Revolution in 1789. In his pamphlets entitled *Rights of Man,* he argued against all monarchial governments. His words, however, caused him turmoil, as he was targeted by the British government and then by the new French government, which was devolving into despotic anarchy. His argument to spare the life of King Louis XVI did not gain him any favors, and he was eventually arrested and held by radical elements of the French Republic, barely escaping execution. He later met and advised Napolean Bonaparte for a brief period but then became a critic as he saw Napolean's rise to dictator of the French.

Paine returned to the United States with his reputation sullied by his previous writings attacking Christianity, republican government, and George Washington. His involvement with the French Revolution was very unpopular at home, and he didn't even retain the right to vote in his adopted state of New York. Of all the founders and framers of the American republic, Thomas Paine was one of the most complicated and controversial personalities of his time.

Thomas Jefferson (1743–1826)

One of the most famous of the founders, Thomas Jefferson, is best known for being the primary writer of the Declaration of Independence. Despite this accomplishment, he has also become a controversial figure due to his words "All men are created equal," while he continued his entire life to own slaves.

Along with Benjamin Franklin and George Washington, Thomas Jefferson is one of the most recognized and discussed founders of the

American republic. He was born and raised in the colony of Virginia as a Southern gentleman. He could read classical literature in its original Greek and Latin and collected a very impressive personal library throughout his genteel and bookish life.

He reported that his earliest memory was being carried by one of his father's slaves nestled with a pillow; while on his deathbed in July 1826, he was attended to by a slave and lover named Sally Hemings. The most significant personal event of his childhood and perhaps his life was the death of his father when he was 14 years old. After this trauma, Jefferson retreated into books and became a scholar of Enlightenment reading, owning many books by Enlightenment authors such as John Locke, David Hume, and John Milton. He also was a great enthusiast of religious literature, having several Bibles and sermons by contemporary religious leaders. He even owned and read an English translation of the Koran for religious comparison to Christianity.

The dichotomy of the man is difficult to ignore. His Enlightenment education, his slave owning culture and lifestyle, his library of religious literature, along with statements critical of the Christian church makes Thomas Jefferson a hard person to pin down with any certainty. If I may try to understand and explain his cognitive dissonance, I believe that while he was an idealist who could see what should have been through Christian teaching and Enlightenment thought, he was also a product of his time and culture where Africans and women were often seen as property rather than people. He was certainly a conflicted character with many inconsistencies between his thoughts and writings compared to his actions and lifestyle.

Regardless, his contributions to the American Revolution, the direction of the American republic, and the first document in our Freedom

Charters are undeniable. As a wealthy plantation owner, Thomas Jefferson came from one of the wealthiest colonies in British America, which meant that he had much more to lose by joining the revolutionary cause than many of his companions. The Stamp Act certainly hit his financial interests harder than most, but it was likely his idealist beliefs in natural rights of the individual, the rights of British subjects through Magna Carta, and the results of the English Civil War that fed his zeal for rebellion against the British crown.

Apart from being the primary author of the Declaration of Independence, Thomas Jefferson also drafted the Virginia Constitution, was ambassador to France, served George Washington as America's first Secretary of State, and became the third President of the United States, expanding its territory exponentially with the Louisiana Purchase. Jefferson was not comfortable speaking in front of large crowds, but his writings essentially became the conscience of the American Revolution, the early American republic, and our Freedom Charters.

Despite empowerment as a writer, statesman, architect, plantation owner, and diplomat, he was not very gifted as a businessman or investor and died in his old age after losing a vast fortune and accumulating enormous, unpayable debts. In many ways, the incongruencies of Thomas Jefferson are imitated by one of his greatest legacies, the American federal government.

Patrick Henry (1736–1799)

Patrick Henry was also from Virginia but was much the opposite of Thomas Jefferson. Known for his great oratory skills, Patrick Henry had little formal education and was far from the elite class of Virginia genteel society. He possessed, however, a very gifted intelligence with keen insights that propelled him to high standings in Virginia society.

Named after a reverend uncle who was known for his gifted sermons, Patrick Henry was also a genius of the spoken word and the art of persuasion. By fifteen years old he was fluent in Greek and Latin, but still retained a colonial Virginia mountain accent in English. As Thomas Jefferson was the primary creator of the Declaration of Independence and James Madison the architect of the U.S. Constitution, Patrick Henry, alongside George Mason, was a primary influence and instigator of the American Bill of Rights. He was instrumental in having those amendments argued and ratified into law.

His verbal skills made him a competent lawyer before he was able to join the Virginia Bar. Since he had very little formal education, it took some unorthodox finagling to get seated and tested for the exam, and his passing of the exam was due more to his personality and verbal skills than his test-taking abilities.

Patrick Henry joined the revolutionary cause early as a great believer in individual liberty. He was well read of the Enlightenment thinkers of Europe, especially Montesquieu. His famous phrase, "Give me liberty or give me death," stirred much emotion in the American colonist cause for liberty and revolution, and even after the American Revolutionary War, he was a great critic of the large federal government that had been created by the U.S. Constitution.

He favored small republicanism, believing that each state should be a semi-independent republic that could respond to the needs of its citizens much better than a large federal republic. Because of his arguments for our Bill of Rights, the natural rights of the citizens and the states as legal entities were not ignored in the federalist model created by our Freedom Charters.

John Jay (1745–1829)

John Jay is best known for the Jay Treaty and his writings in the Federalist Papers, which was a New York publication of letters written by him, Alexander Hamilton, and James Madison, promoting the ideas and passage of the federalist model of the United States Constitution. During the Revolutionary War, Jay served as president of the Second Continental Congress, engaged in counterintelligence operations for the patriot cause and served as the United States Ambassador to Spain. There, he convinced Spain to recognize the United States of America as a separate country from Great Britain, secured some financial assistance for the revolutionary cause, and negotiated trade treaties for his new country. He also was the first Chief Justice of the United States Supreme Court after the ratification of the U.S. Constitution, making several decisions that set the course and meaning of judicial precedent.

Jay was a part of the federalist wing of the early American political structure, favoring the creation of a strong central government. His primary contribution to the young republic was the Jay Treaty with England, which avoided war and helped establish the U.S. precedent of non-involvement in European affairs.

He was against slavery but participated in the system by purchasing and later releasing slaves. This unorthodox process was controversial to the abolitionists, but Jay was also of the opinion that slavery should be phased out of the United States, not abolished in one swoop.

Benjamin Rush (1746–1813)

Dr. Benjamin Rush was a practitioner of the healing arts. As a physician, he assisted many of the founders and framers with their physical health, promoting wellness through a clean environment and personal hygiene. He also worked as an Enlightenment thinker protecting many from the scourges of smallpox through a questionable practice of limited exposure to the disease, which was the forerunner to vaccinations.

As a founder and patriot, he served the Continental Congress as a part of the Pennsylvania delegation and was a signer of the Declaration of Independence. Dr. Rush was active in Pennsylvanian society as a humanitarian and philanthropist. He was also a supporter of Pennsylvania's passage of the new U.S. Constitution. He is less known, but certainly a significant person in the process of making our Freedom Charters come to fruition.

James Madison (1751–1836)

Known as the father of the U.S. Constitution, James Madison is probably the least known of the more significant founders and framers of the American republic and our Freedom Charters. As the creator of the Virginia Declaration of Rights, in June of 1776 his Virginia Plan became the template for the discussions and arguments in the American Constitutional Convention of 1787, which he lobbied to organize. As a writer of the Federalist Papers, James Madison's detailed explanations of the reasonings behind the U.S. Constitution was instrumental in its passage, and for later generations of Americans to better understand this complex document.

James Madison was from the colony of Virginia. He came from a wealthy plantation family with many advantages in education and genteel connections. He served as a prominent leader in the United States Congress and was a close friend and advisor of President George Washington. Madison's research into ancient republics allowed for the unique formation of American Federalism, attempting to implement the virtues and avoid the vices of large and small republican governments. Although a stanch supporter of a strong federal system, James Madison understood the nature of political power very well and made provisions for a U.S. Constitution that protected states' rights, as well as the later passage of the Bill of Rights that protected the natural rights of individual citizens, private organizations, and society as a whole.

One of Madison's greatest contributions to the meaning of the newly ratified U.S. Constitution was a court case called Marbury v. Madison, in which it was determined that the U.S. Constitution was in fact the law of the land and not just a set of principles, as were prior constitutions throughout human history. This decision was known to institute an important aspect of constitutional law called judicial review. What's interesting about this case is that Madison lost the case, and the Supreme Court ruled that his actions were illegal, but it also ruled that the separation of powers prohibits the court from making dictates to the executive branch and so the judgment was invalid due to lack of jurisdiction. Or so this is my understanding of it.

Judicial review is a process that begins with lower courts and ends with the United States Supreme Court in determining the constitutionality of various laws and regulations passed by state and federal legislatures and interpreted by lower courts. Judicial review is a fundamental stopgap measure to ensure the U.S. Constitution is followed consistently throughout all jurisdictions of the United States.

Although Madison created the form of federalism used by the United States of America, he did not support the Federalist Party promoted by Alexander Hamilton, choosing rather to work with Thomas Jefferson to create the Democratic-Republican Party. Madison also served the Jefferson administration as Secretary of State, being instrumental to the

Louisiana Purchase, and when serving as fourth President of the United States, promoting the continued expansion of American lands at the cost of the Spanish empire and native American tribes.

John Marshall (1755–1835)

John Marshall was a lawyer and statesman who had the distinction of serving in all three branches of the United States federal government. He served the executive branch as Secretary of State to President John Adams, served the legislative branch through the United States Congress, representing the State of Virginia, and was appointed the Chief Justice of the United States Supreme Court by President James Madison.

Marshall's primary influence was that of chief justice, where he served longer than any other person in American history and sat in judgment of many important court cases of the new American republic. This includes the Marbury v. Madison case discussed earlier, establishing the judicial branch as an equal co-partner of the United States federal government. Other decisions determined that the U.S. Constitution is supreme to state contract laws, protects organizations as legal entities from usurpation by state governments, forbids state governments from taxing federal organizations within their state's jurisdiction, and established that national treaties are superior to state laws concerning property rights. His rulings also determined the United States Supreme Court can hear appeals from state courts in civil and criminal trials, that freedom of navigation is federally protected within and between states, and final rulings affecting the sovereignty of indigenous tribal lands within states lay within the jurisdiction of the federal government, not state governments.

John Marshall was most important to the Freedom Charters as the readings of these documents played out in post-revolutionary America.

This is especially true with the specific enumerated rights of the federal government and the general reserved rights of the states. This aspect of the Freedom Charters will be described in a future chapter.

Aaron Burr (1756–1836)

Aaron Burr came from the province of New Jersey. He was a patriot officer in the revolutionary war, politician, and businessman. He was also a maternal grandson of the Reverend Johnathan Edwards described earlier. He is best known today as the man who shot Alexander Hamilton in a legally sanctioned duel on July 11, 1804.

During the American Revolutionary War, Burr served under Colonel Benedict Arnold in some Canadian campaigns and distinguished himself as a brave and loyal soldier to the revolution. He was promoted to captain and assigned to the staff of General George Washington in New York but left that post to return to direct combat on the battlefield. Burr felt slighted by General Washington, who never recognized his bravery and service during the retreat from New York City with an accommodation, something that always bothered Burr. He was later responsible for the defense of some of the New Jersey border, fighting British troops who came out of New York. He also led a unit that guarded a pass to the Continental Army's winter camp at Valley Forge, Pennsylvania.

Burr was a distinguished military hero who did not directly influence the creation of our Freedom Charters, but like many others who are not known today, his service in defense of the new United States helped ensure that these documents came to fruition as historically significant and influential.

Although from New Jersey, after the war Burr successfully started practicing law in New York. He was elected and served in the New York

State Assembly, where he unsuccessfully lobbied to have slavery in New York abolished. He was appointed Attorney General of the State of New York and later was elected to become a United States Senator representing New York. Burr was a cunning politician and businessman who made several enemies as he skirted all sides of the state and federal political divide.

His reputation as a war hero served his ambitions well but fell short of making him President of the United States during the election cycle that chose Thomas Jefferson; however, he did serve as Vice President to Thomas Jefferson's first term. He later created the Manhattan Company, which was a venture to break into the monopolized banking world of New York City. Through some clever financial and legal tactics, the Manhattan Company provided fresh water to lower Manhattan in New York City then turned the surplus investment capital into a company bank. This, as well as his involvement in the Democratic-Republican Party, put him at odds with his chief political and financial rival Alexander Hamilton.

Like many people in human history, Burr did not receive the attention and appreciation he deserved. He was always just on the outside of the "in crowd" of the American Revolution. Virtually unknown to most present-day Americans, his contributions and acclaim has been revitalized by a modern Broadway musical named for his chief nemesis.

Alexander Hamilton (1757–1804)

Born fatherless, poor, and orphaned on the obscure Caribbean Island of Nevis, Alexander Hamilton became one of the most influential founders of the American republic. An intellectual genius, Alexander Hamilton foresaw and invented many of the systems Americans understand and use today. From a strong standing military to an economic powerhouse fueled by investment banking, Alexander Hamilton's vision for America is more alive today than it was during his limited lifetime.

Hamilton had no prominent family ties to speak of and little is known about his life before moving to New York for a formal education and a dazzling career. One thing that should be mentioned, however, is that the West Indies of Hamilton's time was not the vacation paradise it is today. Quite the contrary, the islands of the Caribbean were lawless and violent but in fact more lucrative economically than all the British colonies in North America combined because of commerce in sugar, alcohol, and slaves.

Hamilton's experience with the realities of slavery in the Caribbean made him staunchly anti-slavery his entire life. He found the entire institution abhorrent, and while he was one of the greatest supporters of the capitalist economic model, he saw the dehumanization of slavery as a horrific crime that could not be supported or sanctioned on any moral grounds.

After making his way to New York City via Boston, he began classical studies at The Academy in Elizabeth, New Jersey (now Snider Academy), meeting a man named William Livingston, who was a supporter of the revolutionary cause against Great Britain. Many midnight conversations as well as a wealth of reading materials turned the young Hamilton into a supporter of the patriot cause.

A student at King's College (now Columbia University), Hamilton became more involved in the patriot cause by writing concise, intellectual refutations of a loyalist pamphleteer, although his letters were anonymous for his own protection. All this occurred while Hamilton was still in his teens.

During the American Revolutionary War, Hamilton served as an artillery captain and caught the attention of then General George Washington.

Washington convinced Hamilton to accept a promotion to lieutenant colonel and a position on his staff, although Hamilton felt his rightful place was on the battlefield.

Before the end of the war, Hamilton was begrudgingly given a combat command by General Washington, and Hamilton led three divisions of American soldiers at the Battle of Yorktown. The victory of this battle brought the fighting war to an end with the patriots as victors.

After the war, Hamilton settled down to raise a family, passed the New York Bar through self-teaching, served in the Congress of the Confederation, and wrote many of the letters now called The Federalist papers which, as explained earlier, were the primary arguments for the passing and ratification of the new United States Constitution.

Washington never forgot the bright and witty Hamilton and appointed him as the first Secretary of the Treasury for both his terms in office. It was there that his wit and genius had the most impact on American history. Hamilton successfully addressed the concerns of public credit by repaying government bonds to the bond holders as promised, something that many believed would not happen. He then proceeded to invent an entire financial system for the new United States of America and set up the first national bank and the minting of money for the country.

Part of the economy was damaged by smuggling, so to fight that scourge, Hamilton lobbied for the creation of a service called the Revenue Cutter Service that eventually evolved into the United States Coast Guard. Another proposed form of government revenue was a tax on imported and domestic alcohol. This, in turn, created the infamous Whisky Rebellion that needed to be put down by the presence of government troops. Fortunately, it ended without bloodshed but caused people to question the greater powers of the federal government.

Hamilton continued as a leader of the Federalist Party, which was quite offensive to other members of Washington's cabinet like Thomas Jefferson. His Federalist Party affiliation and his national bank dominance in New York also made enemies with other people like Aaron Burr.

Another, less dignified first of Alexander Hamilton's career in the new republic was a sex scandal that called his public honor and integrity into question. While infidelity was far from abnormal by men of his standing, it was suggested that Hamilton had given some money to a third party to invest in land speculation based upon his insider knowledge of future federal policies. To destroy this myth, Hamilton published all the blackmail letters he received from his lover's husband and explained to the American people that while he was guilty of unfaithfulness to his wife, he never behaved unethically in the administration of his office. This cleared his name with the American people but humiliated his loyal wife and children simply to save his political and historical reputation.

This embarrassment took a greater toll when his son was killed in a duel defending his family honor from others who mocked him. This event cemented his wife's resentment for the rest of his life, and she destroyed all their correspondence with each other so no one in the present or in the future could have any insights into the intimate nature of their relationship.

Alexander's tragic end came when his politics became personal to the then Vice President Aaron Burr. Burr felt his honor had been insulted by a letter and remarks that Hamilton was supposed to have made. Burr challenged Hamilton to a duel and shot him in that duel. Hamilton died on July 12, 1804.

Hamilton's widow, Elizabeth, survived another 50 years, making contributions to the new republic by starting the first private orphanage in New York. She was instrumental in keeping her husband's contributions to the

American revolution and the American republic alive and continued to work as a philanthropist until her death on November 9, 1854, less than seven years before the opening of the American Civil War (1861-1865).

James Monroe (1758–1831)

Another prominent Virginian in a line of influencers, James Monroe served the revolutionary war cause as a soldier in Washington's attack on Trenton and even suffered a musket ball wound during the engagement. Monroe was influenced by the politics and ideas of Thomas Jefferson and believed wholeheartedly in a new type of republicanism.

Monroe's contributions to his state of Virginia and the American republic included governor of Virginia, senator in the United States Congress from Virginia, ambassador to France during the initial phases of the French Revolution of 1789, and a major player in the Louisiana and Florida Purchases. Yet James Monroe, like James Madison, is one of the least known founders and framers of the American republic.

Ironically, Monroe was against the classical versions of republicanism and the adoption of our Constitution, yet he proved to be a dedicated visionary for the future direction of our American republic and our Freedom Charters. This legacy is best known in a famous point of view of American presence and future destiny called the Monroe Doctrine. This doctrine has been referenced by Presidents in the nineteenth, twentieth, and twenty-first centuries. It has served as the basis for the American purpose and legacy in the world.

Monroe's primary legacy is ideological, in addition to one of tangible accomplishments. He was the fifth President of the United States and the last of the original founding generation of Americans to serve the role. John Quincy Adams, son of John Adams and a child during the American

Revolutionary War, would lead the nation from our executive branch after Monroe's departure from politics.

Two major influences James Monroe had on our Freedom Charters are in its application. First and foremost, the Monroe Doctrine was essentially a statement of noninterference to and from the powers of Europe. Monroe believed that America should stay out of European politics and affairs in the Eastern hemisphere while stopping any further colonization by European powers in the Western hemisphere. His goal was to see the accomplishment of constitutional republicanism in all the colonies of the Western hemisphere through direct and indirect interventions by the government of the United States.

This, of course, bred resentment from European and colonial powers in both hemispheres as American interference and imperialism became an established goal of the United States in the Americas. While this doctrine was limited in its immediate success, it set a precedent and worldview for our federal government's role in international affairs into the nineteenth and twentieth centuries, through the year 1941 when the United States was finally forced into a dominant global role in the Second World War.

The second of his influences was an unpublished manuscript entitled "The People, the Sovereign." Those writings stated the exact order and purpose for the American constitutional System, which would continue forward from that time. In those writings Monroe explained that the United States of America was not like other republics in history. Earlier republics certainly served as models for ours, but America was different in that the people of the United States were a distinct and separate sovereign power within the constitutional system.

Historically, republics integrated the people as a sovereign entity, but as a segment of the government. The ancient Roman Republic, for example,

244

saw its government as "The Senate and People of Rome." Earlier republics in history also saw the popular sovereign as a component of the government sovereign. The United States was established with the popular sovereign as a separate entity, and Liberty was the core element of this system, not government.

George Washington (1732–1799)

Purposefully saved for last by this author, George Washington is by far the most famous American in history. Washington, D.C., our nation's capital, is named in honor of this man who contributed in so many personal and practical ways to the foundation, establishment, and beginning administration of the early American republic. Born and raised in the colony of Virginia, George Washington lost his father at the age of eleven. While he did receive formal schooling, it was nowhere near as involved or prestigious as his siblings or many of the other founders of the American republic. His high attention to accuracy and detail made him a gifted land surveyor, draftsman, and mapmaker, and his handwriting and sense of precision led him to the successful drafting of some books on courtesy and etiquette.

His brother Lawrence died after a long battle with tuberculosis, but because of Lawrence's prestigious service in the Virginia Militia, George Washington was given a commission as an officer. Washington's reputation and limited military training propelled him very quickly through the ranks of the colonial militia and placed him much too early in positions of command. This would come to haunt him later as the psychological effects of losing the lives of his comrades through tactical errors weighed heavily on him throughout his life.

Washington served the Virginia Militia honorably in the Seven Years' War (the French and Indian War), but his mistakes as a military tactician and quasi-diplomat caused the war itself to be much more volatile and expensive than it would have otherwise been. While his experience and knowledge of the frontier west of the colony of Virginia (the future states of Kentucky and Ohio) helped him immensely in his future roles as General and President, his initial lack of understanding of the native tribes and their French alliances caused much grief for all sides.

In a great historical irony, it was the expense of the war that he escalated that caused the British Parliament to enact heavy taxes on the colonies, leading to the American Revolutionary War and the inevitable break with England. His service in the French and Indian War was honorable and made him widely known. This was essential in preparing him to be the military leader of the patriot cause in the American Revolutionary War.

After his service in the French and Indian War, Washington returned to Virginia, married, raised two stepchildren, and helped to raise his grandchildren. He began plantation life growing wheat and tobacco. Washington continued to seek significance by running for and serving in the Virginia Legislature representing his home county.

Washington had felt slighted and insulted by the British commanders who automatically outranked him because they had commissions from the crown, while he was seen as having only a colonial commission. This feeling of being minimized and ignored continued as the British Parliament continued to pass laws and taxes that benefited the people from England but restricted or punished the colonists. After years of dejection, Washington's loyalty to the crown wavered while the patriot cause became more enticing.

Washington stood much taller than most men of his time, and when he rose up as a representative of the colony of Virginia at the Continental

Congress in full military uniform in 1775, he was all but a shoo-in to be assigned the job and duties of commander in chief of the Continental Army of the United Colonies. This is when his experiences fighting for Britain became a major asset in combating the British army and navy that greatly outmanned and out supplied his forces. He knew British sensibilities and tactics and could predict many of the strategies they would use to suppress the colonial rebellion and bring British America back into compliance with the edicts of Parliament and the British crown.

Washington knew he could never go toe to toe with the military of the British Empire, so he decided to adopt guerilla tactics learned on the frontier. Washington used a "hit and hide" strategy against the British, which caused high enemy casualties and depleted their resources, not allowing their numerical superiority all its advantages. In a war of attrition, the Continental Army wore down the British army, which was used to fighting conventional wars in straight lines and formations, and whose numbers could not be replaced immediately. This strategy, plus extensive help from the French army and navy made it impossible for Britain to continue to justify the expense of the war in men and material.

After a significant British defeat and surrender at Yorktown in Virginia, there was no way King George III and the British Parliament could continue to justify war in the Americas. Washington was not present in Paris, where England finally signed a peace treaty, recognizing the United States of America as a separate and independent country from Great Britain, but his work as commander in chief of the United States armed forces granted him the unofficial title of "First American."

His next contribution was serving at the Constitutional Convention. He initially balked at the idea of serving but later accepted as the leading delegate from Virginia. He was elected to preside over the convention but was very careful to remain a referee and not engage in politics, which were heated and very heavy at times. It was decided that revamping the Articles of Confederation was simply not possible, so the convention began working on the Virginia Plan of James Madison, which Washington supported.

After the convention closed and the proposed final draft of the Constitution was sent to the states for ratification, Washington accepted an offer to be the president of the College of William and Mary and remained in that ceremonial position until his death.

Running for President of the United States under the new U.S. Constitution, George Washington won a majority of votes in every state. John Adams was elected his Vice President because, at that time, the runner up was awarded that position. President Washington then began to assemble his cabinet of administrators and advisors with people like Thomas Jefferson as Secretary of State and Alexander Hamilton as Secretary of the Treasury.

President George Washington immediately began setting Presidential precedents. He knew the importance of every action and how it would reverberate through time. His cabinet was composed from the Federalist Party and Democratic-Republican Party, and much of his time was spent refereeing between the two. Washington saw how both sides had very valid points and how a blend of both philosophies was needed to keep the young republic alive while adhering to its founding values.

Washington was exhausted after his first term and ready to step down but did not do so out of fear that party fighting would tear apart everything he had worked for. By the end of his second term, he congratulated the new President John Adams and left for Mount Vernon almost immediately. Thus, two terms and a quick departure became the precedent that most Presidents followed until the twentieth and twenty-first centuries.

Washington's death in 1799 hit the nation hard, and there were many ceremonies, memorials, and eulogies to honor the man who most people thought was beyond reproach. His legacy continued as a new capital city was established with his name, streets, parks, monuments, and eventually an entire state that touches the Pacific Ocean. The reputation and legacy of the man as an American Cincinnatus has survived the test of time; his name and effect on the American republic and our Freedom Charters reaches across the continent touching the Atlantic and Pacific Oceans, both figuratively and literally.

CHAPTER 22

The British American Colonies and the United States of America

American colonists saw themselves as loyal British subjects and believed in the British system of laws and justice, so their rights and needs being denied was highly offensive to them. Their understanding of Magna Carta, Petition of Right, Enlightenment thinking, the creation of a constitutional monarchy, and classical learning led many of them from righteous indignation to armed rebellion. While gaining representation in Parliament was an option they could have pursued, it's unlikely they would have been given the number of representatives that could have made a difference.

Earlier attempts at colonial unification were proposed before the desire to separate from the crown gained momentum. Benjamin Franklin suggested The Albany Plan of Union to the legislature of New York in 1754. This idea was inspired by his experience with a native American confederation called the Iroquois, but this initial attempt to organize the colonies as a confederation was not taken seriously and dismissed.

It was the actions of the new Parliament and King George III that pushed the colonists to separation and revolution beginning with The Sugar Act of 1764. This was the first direct tax on the American colonies to be forcibly collected by the British Parliament. It was not only a tax on goods coming from England to the colonies, but it also prohibited the colonies from exporting certain products to foreign countries to reduce competition with British exports to those countries. It also restricted colonial trade with other countries so most colonial products could only be shipped to Britain. Britain could then dictate the prices they would pay for the products then resell them to foreign countries at an extreme markup. People accused of violating these laws were considered guilty until they could prove themselves innocent, another violation of Magna Carta and the Petition of Right.

This outrage was quickly followed by the Currency Act, which forbade colonial legislatures from printing their own currency. This required all colonists to only use the British pound sterling in all transactions. Heavy penalties were issued to any colonial governments that violated this law. The American colonists again had no say or recourse to this edict.

Colonial tempers were brewing when, in 1765, the Stamp Act was imposed by Parliament on the colonists without their consent. This act dictated that the colonist could only use paper from Britain that had a special stamp on it that required payment to possess. Anyone carrying a paper document, or any other product made with paper, that did not have this stamp was in violation of the law. While this stamp tax was not hefty, it was instituted without the consent of the colonists. Some met in New York and issued The Declaration of Rights and Grievances, which was 13 resolutions to address the unconstitutional (British constitution) acts of the crown and Parliament toward the colonists who were rightfully British subjects.

At this point, Sons of Liberty went into action and essentially committed acts of terror against British officials who were charged with selling the stamped papers. Throughout the colonies, British officials were threatened, harassed, and their homes were even vandalized by mobs of colonists organized by Sons of Liberty. It went even further as American shippers were fearful of buying the stamped paper, as they might become targets of the mobs. They did not want to risk sailing without the stamped documents, so they simply remained in port and refused to trade with Britain. British shippers were also caught in the middle of this fiasco and were not able to bring products to the colonies and exchange them for colonial products.

While many in Britain pleaded with Parliament to revoke the Stamp Act, Parliament did not want to bend to terror tactics. They ended up repealing the act but also asserted that Parliament had every right to impose taxes on the colonial British subjects and began quartering British soldiers in colonial homes, which was forcing the colonists to house and feed them without the colonists' consent. This was another violation of Magna Carta, but trade between Britain and the colonies returned to normal.

In 1768, Parliament instituted the Townshend Act, which placed a tax on materials shipped from Britain to the colonies, and this material could only be made available to the colonists from Britain. While this tax was very small and would not have been difficult to pay, it was instituted without the consent of the colonists and restricted the ability to pay the fair market value of the products, so the colonists simply boycotted buying British products. At this time, a ship owned by John Hancock was seized at a wharf in Boston Harbor for smuggling these products from elsewhere, but before the inspection could be made, the Sons of Liberty arrived and a fiery speech with threats from Samuel Adams caused the inspectors to flee.

At this point, Benjamin Franklin, who was in England, wrote an open letter showing how the boycott was costing the British much more money than was being brought in by the Townshend tax. Parliament eventually repealed the order but sent British troops into Boston to restore order. It wasn't Franklin's letter that convinced them because, as a colonist, he did not rank high enough for their attention, but the act was withdrawn due to British merchant complaints about the colonial boycotts and what it was costing them and British subjects back in Britain.

The situation was becoming precarious, as many colonists saw the taxes without representation as unfair but thought the use of mobs to intimidate government officials as a prelude to anarchy. Mob rule was a legitimate concern that many colonists began to fear quietly, and forced occupation of Boston by armed troops was reminiscent of Oliver Cromwell's tactics.

On a March morning in 1770, a group of colonists organized in front of a lone British soldier in Boston. As their insults turned into a violent assault, other British troops came to his assistance. As the troops attempted to escort the soldier away from the mob, they were blocked, harassed, and assaulted with garbage and ice. The British soldiers loaded their weapons and aimed them towards the mob. The mob was in a frenzy and began daring the soldiers to fire. Apparently one soldier was struck by an icicle, and his weapon discharged. The other soldiers feeling their lives in danger fired into the crowd, killing several civilians. This event was called the Boston Massacre.

Parliament decided to revoke the Townshend Act with an exception for tea. Tea would continue to be only purchased by the colonists from Britain at dictated prices with a tax. Sons of Liberty then snuck on board British merchant ships docked at Griffin's Wharf in Boston Harbor loosely dressed as Mohawk Indians. They then broke open over 300 crate containers and dumped the tea into the harbor. This event is known to posterity as the Boston Tea Party.

In response, Parliament issued what is called The Intolerable Acts, which were four new laws designed to punish the colony of Massachusetts for their unruly, undignified, and illegal behaviors. First, they suspended the Massachusetts Constitution and closed Boston Harbor, stationing warships there to enforce the closure and to hold people detained by British soldiers for suspicious behaviors. Then they replaced the people's elected governor with an appointed military governor, giving him complete control and discretion in the fulfillment of his duties. Then they ruled that any British official accused of capital crimes would be tried in England or another colony. Finally, they allowed British soldiers to occupy any unoccupied dwelling without having to pay the owner or allowing him or her to inspect their property for damage.

Boston and all of Massachusetts was essentially under arbitrary martial law, and lack of representation in Britain gave the colonists no recourse, which were more violations of the Magna Carta and Petition of Right. This escalation of tensions with Britain alarmed everyone on both sides of the Atlantic, so much so that a congress of representatives from each colony was called to meet in Philadelphia.

The First Continental Congress met in Philadelphia in October 1774. This congress understood that their future was tottering between the two undesirable states of martial law and mob rule. The Pennsylvanian Quaker John Dickinson was a voice of moderation and wrote The Petition to the King, which was ignored by the crown. It was there that Dickinson, and the other members signed the Continental Association, which was an oath of solidarity between all colonies to boycott all trade with England until the Intolerable Acts were repealed. Until that time no colony was to import, consume, or export any products from, with, or to Britain. It was also there that Patrick Henry stood and declared "I am no longer a Virginian; I am an American." The first congress essentially laid the foundation for the Second Continental Congress.

In the time between the two conferences, armed conflict officially took place in Lexington and Concord, Massachusetts on April 19, 1775. It was a brief shootout with militiamen in Lexington by British troops, major combat in Concord, then massive casualties of the British regulars along their retreat to Boston. This "shot heard round the world," was a wakeup call on both sides, with the risks of death and complete destruction for the colonists and the British land forces.

The Second Continental Congress first convened in May 1775. It comprised two main factions, "the conservatives" led by John Jay and John Dickinson, and "the radicals" led by John Adams and Thomas Jefferson. John Dickinson began work on the Olive Branch Petition, declaring that the colonists were still loyal to the British crown. Then it was decided that he and Thomas Jefferson start work on the Declaration of the Causes and Necessity of Taking Up Arms, which was a petition for the rights of colonists to self-defense as loyal British subjects, not as separatists. In August 1775, King George III issued the Proclamation of Rebellion, which ended all attempts by the colonists to follow a non-separatist agenda.

By this time, the American Revolutionary War was well underway with General George Washington as commander in chief of the Continental Army and various state militias fighting a guerrilla war with the British army. The individual battles and war will not be described, as this book's focus is on our Freedom Charters, but it needs to be strongly stated that without the courage and sacrifice of the soldiers and sailors of the Revolutionary War and every American military veteran since, our Freedom Charters would not have been able to exist and survive to today.

Thomas Jefferson wrote the Virginia Declaration of Rights, which was passed in Virginia on June 12, 1776. This served as the template for our first Freedom Charter, The Declaration of Independence, approved by the Second Continental Congress on July 4, 1776, which has since been considered the birthdate of the United States of America. Specifics of this and the other Freedom Charters will be described in greater detail in the final chapters of this book.

—⚬—

The Continental Congress had quite a task in front of them, as they had declared separation with Britain, which was an act of rebellion and war. They needed to help build and supply forces that would be fighting the most powerful empire on earth at the time. They needed to develop and agree on a charter for the operation of the new nation, they needed to keep thirteen different states working on the same goal as a team, and they did all this while knowing that at any moment each of them could be arrested, tried, and executed by the British government. After the Declaration of Independence was approved by the delegates of the new united states, Benjamin Franklin was reported to have said, "Now we must all hang together, or surely we will all hang separately." We can only imagine the weight they felt at this moment in history.

The war was the greatest domestic challenge of that time, but the issues of state sovereignty ran a close second. Sovereignty of the individual, of each state, and of the new nation was a concept that had never been so deliberately thought out. Never in history had such a task been undertaken, and some feared that perhaps they were not up to the challenge. This again is where everything that had come before became a resource to investigate, debate, and decide.

All influences from ancient, medieval, and modern times came together to give direction, and first was faith in God. It involved reflecting on ancient times and recognizing the sovereignty of the God of Abraham, how humanity was made in His image, how creation and imagination were part of our human makeup, how our Creator bestowed upon us natural rights, how human laws needed to mirror natural law, how faith and divine providence can lead us to a greater future, how our God is a God of laws, and how our ancestors' quest for a new godly nation was reflected in God's covenant with ancient Israel. All this was embedded in the conscience and subconscious minds of the founders.

That moment was also a product of medieval and modern ideas, in which church domination was seen as undesirable and that Magna Carta created a sense that no human power should be absolute, and the powers of the individual as a sovereign entity was recognized through Renaissance thought. That was how the Protestant Reformation broke away from the conformity of the Roman Catholic Church, and how the national Protestant churches took on the mantles of power, causing another break called Puritanism. It was how the Puritans came to the Americas looking to build a godly nation and how interactions with native Americans and native Africans caused some to question the rightfulness of what was being done, while others thought this was an example of superior culture and God's will.

It was the address of a broad range of subjects from the beginning of civilization, such as self-preservation, free will, self-determination, family ties, material surplus, personal ownership, trade, taxes, money, economics, slavery, prosperity, rule of law, freedom, liberty, representative government, and so forth. It also was how each founder was a product of his time and place in history and, at that time, their primary concern was fighting the power of the British Empire, a single despotic entity that could dictate to the colonists arbitrarily without recourse.

⸻

The colonists, therefore, in 1777 constructed the Articles of Confederation. These articles were designed to bring cohesion to the separate thirteen American states without infringing on them as sovereign entities. These articles will not be described in detail here, but they were certainly a necessary invention to carry the new nation through the very difficult time of conception, gestation, birth, and survival as an infant entity.

As the war continued, the need for a federal entity was paramount, but it could not come at the expense of state sovereignty. It was a delicate balance of give and take that allowed the new nation to fight its war of independence while remaining respectful of the sovereign states that had recently been created from the former British colonies.

War continued for several years, and when it ended with the surrender of the British and the agreed evacuation of all British troops from the United States of America, it must have been a surreal moment to all who were alive and aware at the time. It took two years to put together a peace treaty in which Britain recognized the United States as a separate and sovereign entity. The Articles of Confederation worked very well during the war, but peacetime is a completely different reality, and that document had many flaws that made it impractical to continue in its current form and in the long term.

A Constitutional Convention was called by many of the founders. That council became the framers of the new nation. The main issue was the rights of the states versus the rights of the federal government. Many others were concerned that the rights of the individual and society as a whole were being forgotten. So, before the U.S. Constitution was voted on and sent to the states for ratification, it was James Madison who promised Patrick Henry that a Bill of Rights would be directly following. On September 17, 1787, the new Constitution was sent to every state for ratification. Delaware was first to ratify the document and is now considered the first state of the new union, and on June 21, 1788, New Hampshire became the ninth state to ratify the document, giving it a supermajority of votes. The remaining states approved and accepted the document before it took effect, except for North Carolina and Rhode Island, which eventually did.

This Constitution prescribed enumerated rights with limitations of the new federal structure.

A Bill of Rights became the first duty of the new government. Twelve Constitutional amendments were discussed, debated, and sent to the states for ratification. The first two were not ratified at that time, so the new Bill of Rights for the United States of America consisted of ten new Constitutional amendments. The Bill of Rights ended with the statement that any rights not covered in constitutional law were reserved for the state governments or for the people of the United States of America. Since that time, many more amendments have been debated and voted on. Some have become constitutional law, and some have not.

The American Revolution:

The next and final chapters will attempt to define, describe, and comment on the Freedom Charters in their entirety. These are products and continuations of the American Revolution.

The American Revolution is often confused with the American Revolutionary War, and while the war for independence (from 1775 to 1783) is certainly part of this revolution, the American Revolution itself started much earlier and is ongoing. This is because the American Revolution is a full experiment in national self-government.

American Exceptionalism:

The term American exceptionalism is used to describe this experiment, but it is often misunderstood. Terms such as American exceptionalism, American idealism, and Americanism are incorrectly compared to an "old world" concept called nationalism. The difference is important because old world nationalism is based upon ethnic bloodlines, whereas Americanism is based on ideas. The American ideals cover a broad range of subjects such as freedom, liberty, economics, prosperity, rule of law, representative government, uniformed military controlled by civilian government, civilian law enforcement, and much more.

This work is not meant to be a complete or final word on any of this, as it is not in my purview or within the range of any individual. It is simply a mental exercise in which the principles and foundations of the American republic can be defined, discussed, and understood by anyone with interest in the subject.

Part IV

CHAPTER 23

Our Freedom Charters
(with author's commentary)

In Congress, July 4, 1776

    The unanimous Declaration of the thirteen united States of America, When in the Course of human events, it becomes necessary for one people to dissolve the political bands which have connected them with another, and to assume among the powers of the earth, the separate and equal station to which the Laws of Nature and of Nature's God entitle them, a decent respect to the opinions of mankind requires that they should declare the causes which impel them to the separation.

One vital aspect of being human is our ability to form relationships with others. Forming healthy relationship bonds is essential to our happiness, safety, and wellbeing. Sometimes we must dissolve those bonds because the relationship becomes toxic and detrimental to one or more of the people in that relationship. As rational beings, our thoughts and feelings can be expressed in many ways, and we owe it to ourselves and to most others to think and verbalize exactly why separation is necessary.

We hold these truths to be self-evident, that all men are created equal, that they are endowed by their Creator with certain unalienable Rights, that among these are Life, Liberty and the pursuit of Happiness.—That to secure these rights, Governments are instituted among Men, deriving their just powers from the consent of the governed,—That whenever any Form of Government becomes destructive of these ends, it is the Right of the People to alter or to abolish it, and to institute new Government, laying its foundation on such principles and organizing its powers in such form, as to them shall seem most likely to effect their Safety and Happiness. Prudence, indeed, will dictate that Governments long established should not be changed for light and transient causes; and accordingly all experience hath shewn, that mankind are more disposed to suffer, while evils are sufferable, than to right themselves by abolishing the forms to which they are accustomed. But when a long train of abuses and usurpations, pursuing invariably the same Object evinces a design to reduce them under absolute Despotism, it is their right, it is their duty, to throw off such Government, and to provide new Guards for their future security.—Such has been the patient sufferance of these Colonies; and such is now the necessity which constrains them to alter their former Systems of Government. The history of the present King of Great Britain is a history of repeated injuries and usurpations, all having in direct object the establishment of an absolute Tyranny over these States.

Belief is a human virtue of faith: faith in self, faith in others, and faith in a Creator God. We also believe certain realities are demonstrated true through their own virtues. One of these is that the universe is far too complicated and sophisticated to have occurred by random chance or by accident. Intelligence is certainly behind every level of existence from quantum mechanics to super galactic structures. The level of life on earth is one such level of existence, and it makes sense to believe that an intelligent creator, our Creator God, created human beings for some great purpose and that each human being comes into this world the same way.

This Creator God made humanity in His own image, and as the first sovereign of power in the universe, He has also granted us sovereignty over our own lives. As self-aware beings, we are charged with rights and responsibilities from our Creator God. Some of those natural rights are the right to exist (self-preservation), the right to make choices (self-determination), and the right to find what brings us peace in body and mind (pursuit of our own desires.) This is individual sovereignty. It is a natural right granted by the Creator God, and no entity in this world has the right to arbitrarily violate or deny this gift.

Governments are also sovereign entities but must be derived through the consent of the people who are served. This consent is expressed through free and independent elections of representatives who are charged with limited powers to provide the services that fall within the duties of the government entities. These duties are not arbitrary but derived through written laws based on a certain set of premises.

When a government stops providing the services that are within their purview or begins taking actions and responsibilities that are outside of its purview, it is the right of the citizens to act in a way that will alter or abolish that government.

Such was the case of the British American colonists of the late eighteenth century. It was not appropriate to simply discard the British system that had a long and noble history. That would have been an act of arrogance. Rather it was the objective to change these circumstances through the forces of faith, free will, reason, and imagination for the benefit of those alive at that time and for their posterity.

Unfortunately, British injustices and colonial grievances became so numerous and so severe that it was no longer possible to find justice for the American colonists as British subjects. This required a separation from the British crown and the taking up of a mantle of new power, sovereign and equal to the power from which the colonists were separating.

To prove this let the facts be presented to a candid world.

He has refused his Assent to Laws, the most wholesome and necessary for the public good.

He has forbidden his Governors to pass Laws of immediate and pressing importance, unless suspended in their operation till his Assent should be obtained; and when so suspended, he has utterly neglected to attend to them.

He has refused to pass other Laws for the accommodation of large districts of people, unless those people would relinquish the right of Representation in the Legislature, a right inestimable to them and formidable to tyrants only.

He has called together legislative bodies at places unusual, uncomfortable, and distant from the depository of their public Records, for the sole purpose of fatiguing them into compliance with his measures.

He has dissolved Representative Houses repeatedly, for opposing with manly firmness his invasions on the rights of the people.

He has refused for a long time, after such dissolutions, to cause others to be elected; whereby the Legislative powers, incapable of Annihilation, have returned to the People at large for their exercise; the State remaining in the mean time exposed to all the dangers of invasion from without, and convulsions within.

He has endeavoured to prevent the population of these States; for that purpose obstructing the Laws for Naturalization of Foreigners; refusing to pass others to encourage their migrations hither, and raising the conditions of new Appropriations of Lands.

He has obstructed the Administration of Justice, by refusing his Assent to Laws for establishing Judiciary powers.

He has made Judges dependent on his Will alone, for the tenure of their offices, and the amount and payment of their salaries.

He has erected a multitude of New Offices, and sent hither swarms of Officers to harrass our people, and eat out their substance.

He has kept among us, in times of peace, Standing Armies without the Consent of our legislatures.

He has affected to render the Military independent of and superior to the Civil power.

He has combined with others to subject us to a jurisdiction foreign to our constitution, and unacknowledged by our laws; giving his Assent to their Acts of pretended Legislation:

For Quartering large bodies of armed troops among us:

For protecting them, by a mock Trial, from punishment for any Murders which they should commit on the Inhabitants of these States:

For cutting off our Trade with all parts of the world:

For imposing Taxes on us without our Consent:

For depriving us in many cases, of the benefits of Trial by Jury:

For transporting us beyond Seas to be tried for pretended offences

For abolishing the free System of English Laws in a neighbouring Province, establishing therein an Arbitrary government, and enlarging its Boundaries so as to render it at once an example and fit instrument for introducing the same absolute rule into these Colonies:

For taking away our Charters, abolishing our most valuable Laws, and altering fundamentally the Forms of our Governments:

For suspending our own Legislatures, and declaring themselves invested with power to legislate for us in all cases whatsoever.

He has abdicated Government here, by declaring us out of his Protection and waging War against us.

He has plundered our seas, ravaged our Coasts, burnt our towns, and destroyed the lives of our people.

He is at this time transporting large Armies of foreign Mercenaries to compleat the works of death, desolation and tyranny, already begun with circumstances of Cruelty & perfidy scarcely paralleled in the most barbarous ages, and totally unworthy the Head of a civilized nation.

He has constrained our fellow Citizens taken Captive on the high Seas to bear Arms against their Country, to become the executioners of their friends and Brethren, or to fall themselves by their Hands.

He has excited domestic insurrections amongst us, and has endeavoured to bring on the inhabitants of our frontiers, the merciless Indian Savages, whose known rule of warfare, is an undistinguished destruction of all ages, sexes and conditions.

In every stage of these Oppressions We have Petitioned for Redress in the most humble terms: Our repeated Petitions have been answered only by repeated injury. A Prince whose character is thus marked by every act which may define a Tyrant, is unfit to be the ruler of a free people.

The King had behaved in a lawless manner that was in violation of the rights of all British subjects. He had not fulfilled his duties as prescribed by law and disregarded the right of others to the fulfillment of their duties or to act in his stead when he failed to act. He had violated the rights of the people (a popular sovereign entity) by failing to act and had behaved as a tyrant in preventing the people's representatives (a sovereign government entity) from acting for the benefit of the population that the King was legally bound to serve through the social contract.

The King had made it difficult or impossible for others charged with duties of public service to complete their jobs and did not keep open records of meetings and decisions for the viewing and understanding of the public. This prevented analysis from outside entities and the people who were directly affected by these processes.

When representatives of the people brought this to his attention in open discourse, he dissolved those legal entities to silence their statements and prevent the people from having legal avenues to address their grievances. While the peoples' representatives have been silenced, the duties and obligations of their services have not been fulfilled, leaving the individual, private and public organizations, the people, and the state vulnerable to misfortune and attack.

He had also violated property rights and the rights of the people to freely navigate to their desired location. This included those who wanted to come to the country in a legal and organized manner.

He had obstructed the rights of individuals, organizations, and the people to a legal system of justice that served their needs, and he disregarded their natural and legal rights. He had done this by making the judicial process a part of his own making, while using his influence, force, and threat of force to obtain his will without regard to the needs or wills of his subjects.

He created new offices without the people's consent and had used those offices to harass and restrict the people who they should have been designated to serve and protect. He kept standing armies in the streets and in people's homes without their consent and in violation of Magna Carta and the Petition of Right. This military was not under the control of the people's representatives, or any other legal entity prescribed by law, making them illegal and immune from justice or being held responsible for criminal acts toward the people of the colonies.

He invented crimes and denied the people and the people's representatives from having legal control and sovereignty over trade, taxes, trial by jury, security in their homes from foreign summary justice. His behaviors were arbitrary and oppressive, not rooted in any legal code or tradition guaranteed to rightful British subjects. He arbitrarily altered and abolished the traditional legal system that had been in place for centuries to avoid these types of offenses, including legal charters, laws, and the cherished form of government guaranteed to British subjects wherever Britain had jurisdiction. He also had assaulted the people individually and as a population, killing, burning, and destroying their cherished lives, liberties, and properties. This was the very opposite of his prescribed duties in a constitutional monarchy.

He waged war, plundered land and sea, and destroyed lives and properties without regard for natural rights granted by the Creator God and legal rights granted by sovereign and approved human law. He also brought foreign mercenaries to sovereign British territories to assault and murder his own subjects, which was an ultimate act of barbarism and unworthy of a civilized potentate.

He captured and executed subjects who were rightfully exercising their right to navigation and self-preservation, as well as friends and family members of the same, simply due to innocent affiliation. He also encouraged others to engage in acts of barbarism toward his own subjects.

During all this, his subjects remained loyal to the sovereign legal authority of the crown, petitioning to address grievances, which was discounted and ignored. This made him unfit as a sovereign authority over his subjects and required separation, even armed resistance, when necessary, to secure the natural and legal rights of individuals, organizations, populations, and legal government entities.

Nor have We been wanting in attentions to our British brethren. We have warned them from time to time of attempts by their legislature to extend an unwarrantable jurisdiction over us. We have reminded them of the circumstances of our emigration and settlement here. We have appealed to their native justice and magnanimity, and we have conjured them by the ties of our common kindred to disavow these usurpations, which, would inevitably interrupt our connections and correspondence. They too have been deaf to the voice of justice and of consanguinity. We must, therefore, acquiesce in the necessity, which denounces our Separation, and hold them, as we hold the rest of mankind, Enemies in War, in Peace Friends.

The people continued to see the crown, Parliament, and other British subjects as kin and had given ample warning that these circumstances were taking place, but never were their concerns addressed or even validated. The private charters that brought them to their land were never designed or intended to make them servants or slaves to the government of Great Britain, and the government was not acting in accordance with its range of duties and responsibilities.

The colonists continued to warn the crown and Parliament of Great Britain about what was happening, but they never responded in a way that demonstrated any care, concern, or effort to understand and reverse their course. Even native-born British subjects did not heed their requests nor support their cause in significant numbers to any logical end, which, like all other human beings made them our enemies in war, while we desired their peaceful friendship.

We, therefore, the Representatives of the united States of America, in General Congress, Assembled, appealing to the Supreme Judge of the world for the rectitude of our intentions, do, in the Name, and by Authority of the good People of these Colonies, solemnly publish and declare, That these United Colonies are, and of Right ought to be Free and Independent States; that they are Absolved from all Allegiance to the British Crown, and that all political connection between them and the State of Great Britain, is and ought to be totally dissolved; and that as Free and Independent States, they have full Power to levy War, conclude Peace, contract Alliances, establish Commerce, and to do all other Acts and Things which Independent States may of right do. And for the support of this Declaration, with a firm reliance on the protection of divine Providence, we mutually pledge to each other our Lives, our Fortunes and our sacred Honor.

Therefore, the peoples' representatives of the United States of America as a legal and sovereign body proclaimed in public and in the presence of our Creator God that the British American colonies from that moment in history forward, were rightfully free and independent states, that they no longer had any obligations to the British government, and their new government was then a legal and equal sovereign to all other nations of the earth, granting them all sovereign rights and responsibilities to exercise those duties. This was declared and sworn by the legal representatives of the people in the presence and providence of our Creator God to be protected and secured by an oath of their lives to each other, their material fortunes on this earth, and their sacred honor as free, independent, and sovereign entities.

The United States Constitution

We the People of the United States, in Order to form a more perfect Union, establish Justice, insure domestic Tranquility, provide for the common defence, promote the general Welfare, and secure the Blessings of Liberty to ourselves and our Posterity, do ordain and establish this Constitution for the United States of America.

With much concern about rights comes equal concern for responsibilities. Natural rights create a natural responsibility to safeguard those rights. This document called the United States Constitution was a thoughtful and deliberate attempt to secure natural rights of all sovereign entities through a system of law and justice.

Human beings are fallible; therefore, the virtues of people cannot be the only safeguard against tyranny as it was in ancient Athens and ancient Rome. So, a system was created to purposefully limit the powers of government by diffusing it many times in many areas. This distribution of power is called American federalism. It creates a federal entity with specifically numbered (enumerated) rights, but then breaks up those responsibilities and powers into smaller, diverse parts.

Article. I.

Section. 1.

All legislative Powers herein granted shall be vested in a Congress of the United States, which shall consist of a Senate and House of Representatives.

Section. 2.

The House of Representatives shall be composed of Members chosen every second Year by the People of the several States, and the Electors in each State shall have the Qualifications requisite for Electors of the most numerous Branch of the State Legislature.

No Person shall be a Representative who shall not have attained to the Age of twenty five Years, and been seven Years a Citizen of the United States, and who shall not, when elected, be an Inhabitant of that State in which he shall be chosen.

Representatives and direct Taxes shall be apportioned among the several States which may be included within this Union, according to their respective Numbers, which shall be determined by adding to the whole Number of free Persons, including those bound to Service for a Term of Years, and excluding Indians not taxed, three fifths of all other Persons. The actual Enumeration shall be made within three Years after the first Meeting of the Congress of the United States, and within every subsequent Term of ten Years, in such Manner as they shall by Law direct. The Number of Representatives shall not exceed one for every thirty Thousand, but each State shall have at Least one Representative; and until such enumeration shall be made, the State of New Hampshire shall be entitled to chuse three, Massachusetts eight, Rhode-Island and Providence Plantations one, Connecticut five, New-York six, New Jersey four, Pennsylvania eight, Delaware one, Maryland six, Virginia ten, North Carolina five, South Carolina five, and Georgia three.

When vacancies happen in the Representation from any State, the Executive Authority thereof shall issue Writs of Election to fill such Vacancies.

The House of Representatives shall chuse their Speaker and other Officers; and shall have the sole Power of Impeachment.

Section. 3.

The Senate of the United States shall be composed of two Senators from each State, chosen by the Legislature thereof, for six Years; and each Senator shall have one Vote.

Immediately after they shall be assembled in Consequence of the first Election, they shall be divided as equally as may be into three Classes. The Seats of the Senators of the first Class shall be vacated at the Expiration of the second Year, of the second Class at the Expiration of the fourth Year, and of the third Class at the Expiration of the sixth Year, so that one third may be chosen every second Year; and if Vacancies happen by Resignation, or otherwise, during the Recess of the Legislature of any State, the Executive thereof may make temporary Appointments until the next Meeting of the Legislature, which shall then fill such Vacancies.

No Person shall be a Senator who shall not have attained to the Age of thirty Years, and been nine Years a Citizen of the United States, and who shall not, when elected, be an Inhabitant of that State for which he shall be chosen.

The Vice President of the United States shall be President of the Senate, but shall have no Vote, unless they be equally divided.

The Senate shall chuse their other Officers, and also a President pro tempore, in the Absence of the Vice President, or when he shall exercise the Office of President of the United States.

The Senate shall have the sole Power to try all Impeachments. When sitting for that Purpose, they shall be on Oath or Affirmation. When the President of the United States is tried, the Chief Justice shall preside: And no Person shall be convicted without the Concurrence of two thirds of the Members present.

Judgment in Cases of Impeachment shall not extend further than to removal from Office, and disqualification to hold and enjoy any Office of honor, Trust or Profit under the United States: but the Party convicted shall nevertheless be liable and subject to Indictment, Trial, Judgment and Punishment, according to Law.

Section. 4.

The Times, Places and Manner of holding Elections for Senators and Representatives, shall be prescribed in each State by the Legislature thereof; but the Congress may at any time by Law make or alter such Regulations, except as to the Places of chusing Senators.

The Congress shall assemble at least once in every Year, and such Meeting shall be on the first Monday in December, unless they shall by Law appoint a different Day.

Section. 5.

Each House shall be the Judge of the Elections, Returns and Qualifications of its own Members, and a Majority of each shall constitute a Quorum to do Business; but a smaller Number may adjourn from day to day, and may be authorized to compel the Attendance of absent Members, in such Manner, and under such Penalties as each House may provide.

Each House may determine the Rules of its Proceedings, punish its Members for disorderly Behaviour, and, with the Concurrence of two thirds, expel a Member.

Each House shall keep a Journal of its Proceedings, and from time to time publish the same, excepting such Parts as may in their Judgment require Secrecy; and the Yeas and Nays of the Members of either House on any question shall, at the Desire of one fifth of those Present, be entered on the Journal.

Neither House, during the Session of Congress, shall, without the Consent of the other, adjourn for more than three days, nor to any other Place than that in which the two Houses shall be sitting.

Section. 6.

The Senators and Representatives shall receive a Compensation for their Services, to be ascertained by Law, and paid out of the Treasury of the United States. They shall in all Cases, except Treason, Felony and Breach of the Peace, be privileged from Arrest during their Attendance at the Session of their respective Houses, and in going to and returning from the same; and for any Speech or Debate in either House, they shall not be questioned in any other Place.

No Senator or Representative shall, during the Time for which he was elected, be appointed to any civil Office under the Authority of the United States, which shall have been created, or the Emoluments whereof shall have been encreased during such time; and no Person holding any Office under the United States, shall be a Member of either House during his Continuance in Office.

Section. 7.

All Bills for raising Revenue shall originate in the House of Representatives; but the Senate may propose or concur with Amendments as on other Bills.

Every Bill which shall have passed the House of Representatives and the Senate, shall, before it become a Law, be presented to the President of the United States; If he approve he shall sign it, but if not he shall return it, with his Objections to that House in which it shall have originated, who shall enter the Objections at large on their Journal, and proceed to reconsider it. If after such Reconsideration two thirds of that House shall agree to pass the Bill, it shall be sent, together with the Objections, to the other House, by which it shall likewise be reconsidered, and if approved by two thirds of that House, it shall become a Law. But in all such Cases the Votes of both Houses shall be determined by yeas and Nays, and the Names of the Persons voting for and against the Bill shall be entered on the Journal of each House respectively. If any Bill shall not be returned by the President within ten Days (Sundays excepted) after it shall have been presented to him, the Same shall be a Law, in like Manner as if he had signed it, unless the

Congress by their Adjournment prevent its Return, in which Case it shall not be a Law.

Every Order, Resolution, or Vote to which the Concurrence of the Senate and House of Representatives may be necessary (except on a question of Adjournment) shall be presented to the President of the United States; and before the Same shall take Effect, shall be approved by him, or being disapproved by him, shall be repassed by two thirds of the Senate and House of Representatives, according to the Rules and Limitations prescribed in the Case of a Bill.

Section. 8.

The Congress shall have Power To lay and collect Taxes, Duties, Imposts and Excises, to pay the Debts and provide for the common Defence and general Welfare of the United States; but all Duties, Imposts and Excises shall be uniform throughout the United States;

To borrow Money on the credit of the United States;

To regulate Commerce with foreign Nations, and among the several States, and with the Indian Tribes;

To establish an uniform Rule of Naturalization, and uniform Laws on the subject of Bankruptcies throughout the United States;

To coin Money, regulate the Value thereof, and of foreign Coin, and fix the Standard of Weights and Measures;

To provide for the Punishment of counterfeiting the Securities and current Coin of the United States;

To establish Post Offices and post Roads;

To promote the Progress of Science and useful Arts, by securing for limited Times to Authors and Inventors the exclusive Right to their respective Writings and Discoveries;

To constitute Tribunals inferior to the supreme Court;

To define and punish Piracies and Felonies committed on the high Seas, and Offences against the Law of Nations;

To declare War, grant Letters of Marque and Reprisal, and make Rules concerning Captures on Land and Water;

To raise and support Armies, but no Appropriation of Money to that Use shall be for a longer Term than two Years;

To provide and maintain a Navy;

To make Rules for the Government and Regulation of the land and naval Forces;

To provide for calling forth the Militia to execute the Laws of the Union, suppress Insurrections and repel Invasions;

To provide for organizing, arming, and disciplining, the Militia, and for governing such Part of them as may be employed in the Service of the United States, reserving to the States respectively, the Appointment of the Officers, and the Authority of training the Militia according to the discipline prescribed by Congress;

To exercise exclusive Legislation in all Cases whatsoever, over such District (not exceeding ten Miles square) as may, by Cession of particular States, and the Acceptance of Congress, become the Seat of the Government of the United States, and to exercise like Authority over all Places purchased by the Consent of the Legislature of the State in which the Same shall be, for the Erection of Forts, Magazines, Arsenals, dock-Yards, and other needful Buildings;—And

To make all Laws which shall be necessary and proper for carrying into Execution the foregoing Powers, and all other Powers vested by this Constitution in the Government of the United States, or in any Department or Officer thereof.

Section. 9.

The Migration or Importation of such Persons as any of the States now existing shall think proper to admit, shall not be prohibited by the Congress prior to the Year one thousand eight hundred and eight, but a Tax or duty may be imposed on such Importation, not exceeding ten dollars for each Person.

The Privilege of the Writ of Habeas Corpus shall not be suspended, unless when in Cases of Rebellion or Invasion the public Safety may require it.

No Bill of Attainder or ex post facto Law shall be passed.

No Capitation, or other direct, Tax shall be laid, unless in Proportion to the Census or enumeration herein before directed to be taken.

No Tax or Duty shall be laid on Articles exported from any State.

No Preference shall be given by any Regulation of Commerce or Revenue to the Ports of one State over those of another: nor shall Vessels bound to, or from, one State, be obliged to enter, clear, or pay Duties in another.

No Money shall be drawn from the Treasury, but in Consequence of Appropriations made by Law; and a regular

Statement and Account of the Receipts and Expenditures of all public Money shall be published from time to time.

No Title of Nobility shall be granted by the United States: And no Person holding any Office of Profit or Trust under them, shall, without the Consent of the Congress, accept of any present, Emolument, Office, or Title, of any kind whatever, from any King, Prince, or foreign State.

Section. 10.

No State shall enter into any Treaty, Alliance, or Confederation; grant Letters of Marque and Reprisal; coin Money; emit Bills of Credit; make any Thing but gold and silver Coin a Tender in Payment of Debts; pass any Bill of Attainder, ex post facto Law, or Law impairing the Obligation of Contracts, or grant any Title of Nobility.

No State shall, without the Consent of the Congress, lay any Imposts or Duties on Imports or Exports, except what may be absolutely necessary for executing it's inspection Laws: and the net Produce of all Duties and Imposts, laid by any State on Imports or Exports, shall be for the Use of the Treasury of the United States; and all such Laws shall be subject to the Revision and Controul of the Congress.

No State shall, without the Consent of Congress, lay any Duty of Tonnage, keep Troops, or Ships of War in time of Peace, enter into any Agreement or Compact with another State, or with a foreign Power, or engage in War, unless actually invaded, or in such imminent Danger as will not admit of delay.

Article I of the United States Constitution created the Legislative Branch of the federal government, which is charged with the most enumerated responsibilities to the nation. These numerous but limited responsibilities are presented to this branch because it is the most diverse and most representative of the people of the United States. Different members come from different states, being elected from their respective state or state district. They are the most accountable to the people because each one has a constituency that is limited to the state or district from where they were elected. They must be elected to office, not appointed, unless it's to fill a temporary vacancy.

Other than congresspeople, only the President in the Executive Branch is elected and that is a national election determined by an electoral college, not a popular vote. Every other official who serves in one of the other branches is hired or appointed. Congresspeople are the most democratic of the branches, but they are not a democracy because they are not representing themselves alone but every person in their constituency (whether or not that person voted for them.)

They are also responsible for setting up our system of federal courts, except the Supreme Court of the United States, and monitoring their progress in the pursuit of justice, but they are not responsible for duties within their respective state, as those positions are fulfilled by state representatives and governors who operate independently with reserved rights, implied by the United States Constitution.

Article. II.

Section. 1.

The executive Power shall be vested in a President of the United States of America. He shall hold his Office during the

Term of four Years, and, together with the Vice President, chosen for the same Term, be elected, as follows

Each State shall appoint, in such Manner as the Legislature thereof may direct, a Number of Electors, equal to the whole Number of Senators and Representatives to which the State may be entitled in the Congress: but no Senator or Representative, or Person holding an Office of Trust or Profit under the United States, shall be appointed an Elector.

The Electors shall meet in their respective States, and vote by Ballot for two Persons, of whom one at least shall not be an Inhabitant of the same State with themselves. And they shall make a List of all the Persons voted for, and of the Number of Votes for each; which List they shall sign and certify, and transmit sealed to the Seat of the Government of the United States, directed to the President of the Senate. The President of the Senate shall, in the Presence of the Senate and House of Representatives, open all the Certificates, and the Votes shall then be counted. The Person having the greatest Number of Votes shall be the President, if such Number be a Majority of the whole Number of Electors appointed; and if there be more than one who have such Majority, and have an equal Number of Votes, then the House of Representatives shall immediately chuse by Ballot one of them for President; and if no Person have a Majority, then from the five highest on the List the said House shall in like Manner chuse the President. But in chusing the President, the Votes shall be taken by States, the Representation from each State having one Vote; A quorum for this Purpose shall consist of a Member or Members from two thirds of the

States, and a Majority of all the States shall be necessary to a Choice. In every Case, after the Choice of the President, the Person having the greatest Number of Votes of the Electors shall be the Vice President. But if there should remain two or more who have equal Votes, the Senate shall chuse from them by Ballot the Vice President.

The Congress may determine the Time of chusing the Electors, and the Day on which they shall give their Votes; which Day shall be the same throughout the United States.

No Person except a natural born Citizen, or a Citizen of the United States, at the time of the Adoption of this Constitution, shall be eligible to the Office of President; neither shall any Person be eligible to that Office who shall not have attained to the Age of thirty five Years, and been fourteen Years a Resident within the United States.

In Case of the Removal of the President from Office, or of his Death, Resignation, or Inability to discharge the Powers and Duties of the said Office, the Same shall devolve on the Vice President, and the Congress may by Law provide for the Case of Removal, Death, Resignation or Inability, both of the President and Vice President, declaring what Officer shall then act as President, and such Officer shall act accordingly, until the Disability be removed, or a President shall be elected.

The President shall, at stated Times, receive for his Services, a Compensation, which shall neither be encreased nor diminished during the Period for which he shall have been elected, and he shall not receive within that Period any other Emolument from the United States, or any of them.

Before he enter on the Execution of his Office, he shall take the following Oath or Affirmation:—"I do solemnly swear (or affirm) that I will faithfully execute the Office of President of the United States, and will to the best of my Ability, preserve, protect and defend the Constitution of the United States."

Section. 2.

The President shall be Commander in Chief of the Army and Navy of the United States, and of the Militia of the several States, when called into the actual Service of the United States; he may require the Opinion, in writing, of the principal Officer in each of the executive Departments, upon any Subject relating to the Duties of their respective Offices, and he shall have Power to grant Reprieves and Pardons for Offences against the United States, except in Cases of Impeachment.

He shall have Power, by and with the Advice and Consent of the Senate, to make Treaties, provided two thirds of the Senators present concur; and he shall nominate, and by and with the Advice and Consent of the Senate, shall appoint Ambassadors, other public Ministers and Consuls, Judges of the supreme Court, and all other Officers of the United States, whose Appointments are not herein otherwise provided for, and which shall be established by Law: but the Congress may by Law vest the Appointment of such inferior Officers, as they think proper, in the President alone, in the Courts of Law, or in the Heads of Departments.

The President shall have Power to fill up all Vacancies that may happen during the Recess of the Senate, by granting Commissions which shall expire at the End of their next Session.

Section. 3.

He shall from time to time give to the Congress Information of the State of the Union, and recommend to their Consideration such Measures as he shall judge necessary and expedient; he may, on extraordinary Occasions, convene both Houses, or either of them, and in Case of Disagreement between them, with Respect to the Time of Adjournment, he may adjourn them to such Time as he shall think proper; he shall receive Ambassadors and other public Ministers; he shall take Care that the Laws be faithfully executed, and shall Commission all the Officers of the United States.

Section. 4.

The President, Vice President and all civil Officers of the United States, shall be removed from Office on Impeachment for, and Conviction of, Treason, Bribery, or other high Crimes and Misdemeanors.

Article II of the United States Constitution created the executive branch, which also has enumerated responsibilities and duties. This is very different from the legislative branch because it is much smaller and much less diverse. As chief executive, the President of the United States sets domestic and foreign policies that need to be uniform and consistent. The President is also commander-in-chief of the United States armed forces, which means the position gives that office great latitude in the deployment of troops and ships of war.

The President's cabinet is a group of advisors who are handpicked but also require approval of the Senate. The President also nominates federal judges to serve in the judicial branch, but those officials must also be approved by members of the United States Senate. The office of the President has taken on many more responsibilities since its creation. This was caused by domestic and foreign strife that required the rapid and uniform decisions of an executive officer, not a segmented and diverse legislative body.

Since the American Civil War (1861-1865) the office of the President has had to adapt to a large range of factors such as war between the states, westward expansion, world wars, as well as all the technologies that have made the pace of life on earth much faster than it once was. This rapid pace often does not give time for noble debates but executive decisions that are rapid and complete. Because of this, the legislative branch has attempted to expand its role of oversight in many national affairs, as well as expanding regulations on technologies and institutions that did not exist when the Constitution was written.

Article. III.

Section. 1.

The judicial Power of the United States, shall be vested in one supreme Court, and in such inferior Courts as the Congress may from time to time ordain and establish. The Judges, both of the supreme and inferior Courts, shall hold their Offices during good Behaviour, and shall, at stated Times, receive for their Services, a Compensation, which shall not be diminished during their Continuance in Office.

Section. 2.

The judicial Power shall extend to all Cases, in Law and Equity, arising under this Constitution, the Laws of the United States, and Treaties made, or which shall be made, under their Authority;—to all Cases affecting Ambassadors, other public Ministers and Consuls;—to all Cases of admiralty and maritime Jurisdiction;—to Controversies to which the United States shall be a Party;—to Controversies between two or more States;— between a State and Citizens of another State,— between Citizens of different States,—between Citizens of the same State claiming Lands under Grants of different States, and between a State, or the Citizens thereof, and foreign States, Citizens or Subjects.

In all Cases affecting Ambassadors, other public Ministers and Consuls, and those in which a State shall be Party, the supreme Court shall have original Jurisdiction. In all the other Cases before mentioned, the supreme Court shall have appellate Jurisdiction, both as to Law and Fact, with such Exceptions, and under such Regulations as the Congress shall make.

The Trial of all Crimes, except in Cases of Impeachment, shall be by Jury; and such Trial shall be held in the State where the said Crimes shall have been committed; but when not committed within any State, the Trial shall be at such Place or Places as the Congress may by Law have directed.

Section. 3.

Treason against the United States, shall consist only in levying War against them, or in adhering to their Enemies, giving them Aid and Comfort. No Person shall be convicted of Treason unless on the Testimony of two Witnesses to the same overt Act, or on Confession in open Court.

The Congress shall have Power to declare the Punishment of Treason, but no Attainder of Treason shall work Corruption of Blood, or Forfeiture except during the Life of the Person attainted.

Article III created the judicial branch, which has several responsibilities. First was to establish a Supreme Court for the administration of justice. Another was to determine the constitutionality of new laws. Yet another responsibility that evolved over time was to be the referee of squabbles between the legislative and executive branches. The judicial branch ideally is nonpolitical, only reading laws. Humans are flawed, however, making this a relative truth.

Federal justices are appointed and do not need to run in elections. Of the three branches, this makes them the most removed from the citizens, ideally, because it should make them detached from the changing whims and winds of political culture. This has several benefits and drawbacks.

Human laws, as a reflection of natural law, should make them slow to change. The enduring consistency of laws makes them less susceptible to arbitrary changes, but this has not always been the case. Creation of laws is not part of the purview of the judicial branch, but interpretation of what is read can be a tricky thing, and there is a very short distance between reading of laws, interpretation of laws, and creation of laws.

This reality places the judicial branch in competition with the legislative branch, especially when the speed of a judicial decision can be much more rapid and uniform than the speed of a deliberating body. Faster is not always better, however, and when any branch reaches outside its assigned scope it is in violation of its constitutional duties and sacred oaths.

Article. IV.

Section. 1.

Full Faith and Credit shall be given in each State to the public Acts, Records, and judicial Proceedings of every other State. And the Congress may by general Laws prescribe the

Manner in which such Acts, Records and Proceedings shall be proved, and the Effect thereof.

Section. 2.

The Citizens of each State shall be entitled to all Privileges and Immunities of Citizens in the several States.

A Person charged in any State with Treason, Felony, or other Crime, who shall flee from Justice, and be found in another State, shall on Demand of the executive Authority of the State from which he fled, be delivered up, to be removed to the State having Jurisdiction of the Crime.

No Person held to Service or Labour in one State, under the Laws thereof, escaping into another, shall, in Consequence of any Law or Regulation therein, be discharged from such Service or Labour, but shall be delivered up on Claim of the Party to whom such Service or Labour may be due.

Section. 3.

New States may be admitted by the Congress into this Union; but no new State shall be formed or erected within the Jurisdiction of any other State; nor any State be formed by the Junction of two or more States, or Parts of States, without the Consent of the Legislatures of the States concerned as well as of the Congress.

The Congress shall have Power to dispose of and make all needful Rules and Regulations respecting the Territory or other Property belonging to the United States; and nothing in this Constitution shall be so construed as to Prejudice any Claims of the United States, or of any particular State.

Section. 4.

The United States shall guarantee to every State in this Union a Republican Form of Government, and shall protect each of them against Invasion; and on Application of the Legislature, or of the Executive (when the Legislature cannot be convened) against domestic Violence.

Article IV makes every state a smaller constitutional republic, legally equal to other states and supposedly more in tune with the needs of their citizens. The state governments have their own system of laws and justice, but they must remain in line with the premises and laws of the federal constitution. The U.S. Constitution grants states reserved rights that are essentially anything outside the enumerated rights of the federal government.

The people are sovereign entities as individuals, organizations, and populations. They have certain rights and responsibilities prescribed by their status as citizens of the United States and residents of their state. The individual is the first rung of a long ladder that reaches next to family and friends, neighbors and neighborhoods, cities and townships, counties or parishes, and congressional districts.

States and the federal government are the top two rungs in place to serve the people, not to rule over them or be their masters. The people also have reserved rights that are essentially anything outside the enumerated rights of the federal government or the reserved rights of their state.

Article. V.

The Congress, whenever two thirds of both Houses shall deem it necessary, shall propose Amendments to this

Constitution, or, on the Application of the Legislatures of two
thirds of the several States, shall call a Convention for proposing Amendments, which, in either Case, shall be valid to all
Intents and Purposes, as Part of this Constitution, when ratified by the Legislatures of three fourths of the several States,
or by Conventions in three fourths thereof, as the one or the
other Mode of Ratification may be proposed by the Congress;
Provided that no Amendment which may be made prior
to the Year One thousand eight hundred and eight shall in
any Manner affect the first and fourth Clauses in the Ninth
Section of the first Article; and that no State, without its
Consent, shall be deprived of its equal Suffrage in the Senate.

Constitutional laws are in place to protect the states and the people
from arbitrary rule. Constitutional amendments keep the document
relevant. So, the United States Constitution can be altered, but changing constitutional law is a slow and difficult process required to balance
both realities.

Technically, executive orders and court rulings are not new laws,
but some can have that effect, and since all laws are supposed to begin
in the legislative branch, executive orders and court rulings that effectively create new law are usurpations of the divided powers of the federal government. While an executive order or a court ruling is much
faster, they ignore the safeguards that are in place to protect the states
and the people from arbitrary rule. This has been an ongoing problem
since the founding, and it will likely continue as an issue while the
United States Constitution is the supreme law of the land.

This brings us to another part of **Article V**, which is potential constitutional conventions. These conventions are ways in which many legal issues could be addressed in one swoop. The constitutional convention of 1787 was originally presented as a revamping of the Articles of Confederation, but when it was determined that it was not possible, the Virginia Plan was introduced and the current U.S. Constitution was debated, passed, sent to the states, and ratified. One interesting aspect of the Constitutional Convention of 1787 was that the representatives of the people elected by the Articles of Confederation were not involved with that process.

While the frustrations with our modern government are felt by almost everyone, no matter their politics, I believe it would be an extremely risky and tragic event if another constitutional convention ever took place. With the polarization of various parts of the American population and culture, I believe that a future convention would not only be a completely outrageous and dangerous event, but it would also destroy the concept of natural rights and many other premises of our current system that have been its justification since inception.

Article. VI.

All Debts contracted and Engagements entered into, before the Adoption of this Constitution, shall be as valid against the United States under this Constitution, as under the Confederation.

This Constitution, and the Laws of the United States which shall be made in Pursuance thereof; and all Treaties made, or which shall be made, under the Authority of the United States, shall be the supreme Law of the Land; and the Judges in every

State shall be bound thereby, any Thing in the Constitution or Laws of any State to the Contrary notwithstanding.

The Senators and Representatives before mentioned, and the Members of the several State Legislatures, and all executive and judicial Officers, both of the United States and of the several States, shall be bound by Oath or Affirmation, to support this Constitution; but no religious Test shall ever be required as a Qualification to any Office or public Trust under the United States.

The transfer of systems from the Articles of Confederation to the United States Constitution needed to be as seamless as possible. The Articles of Confederation had been in place for over a decade and many agreements had been made with that system in mind. Simply changing the system did not automatically negate previous agreements and treaties.

The greatest fear that many had during that transition was the issue of state governments becoming irrelevant or disappearing all together. Like Article IV, **Article VI** was an important part of reassuring the states and the people that their state governments were not going to be discarded, and that the federal government was not going to take over all roles and responsibilities of the state governments.

As mentioned in "Chapter 2: Ancient Egypt," provincialism, or people seeing themselves as part of a local group rather than a nation, was an issue in ancient Egypt and with the new United States of America. With the new federal constitution, people needed reassurance that their state identity was not going to be replaced by a national identity. Even by the time of the American Civil War over 80 years later, many Americans saw themselves as citizens of their states first and their nation second. The preservation of the Union did a lot to change that perception in the north and the south.

Today, it's much different, as modern Americans tend to not see a conflict between their U.S. citizenship and their state of residence. Events such as the Spanish American War, the First World War, and the Second World War not only elevated the perception of American citizenry in the eyes of the people, but inventions giving us rapid travel and rapid communication have closed both literal and figurative distances among Americans, creating greater unity. From a societal perspective, the world is a much smaller place than it once was.

Article. VII.

The Ratification of the Conventions of nine States, shall be sufficient for the Establishment of this Constitution between the States so ratifying the Same.

To offset the fear that a simple majority would rule over a minority, **Article VII** set the standard for ratification to the level of supermajority. Modern sensibilities tend to look for simple majority rule, but simple majorities are not always best when it comes to large or highly emotional issues. There are several instances where supermajorities are required for the changing of laws, rules, or procedures. This prevents 50.1 percent of the people from dictating to 49.9 percent of the others.

It's also important to remember that like natural rights, many of our constitutional rights are not subject to a majority vote. The Thirteenth Amendment forbids slavery. That cannot be overturned by a simple majority, and as part of the natural right to self-preservation and self-determination, issues like slavery should never have been determined by human votes, but by self-evident principles that the sovereignty of the individual is a direct gift from our Creator God. If something is self-evident and correct, it's correct whether it's recognized by a majority or not.

The United States Bill of Rights
Amendment I:

"Congress shall make no law respecting an establishment of religion or prohibiting the free exercise thereof; or abridging the freedom of speech, or of the press; or the right of the people peaceably to assemble, and to petition the Government for a redress of grievances."

As stated earlier, religion, faith, and God are three completely different things. The founders knew this well, but modern people who are not people of faith or not educated in their faith generally do not know this. Freedom of religion is an integral part of the founding of the American republic and the framing of our Freedom Charters. It's important to understand, however, that phrases such as "freedom of religion" and "separation of church and state" are not meant to separate our nation from faith in our Creator God. Faith in our Creator God is the most basic premise of Americanism, as without this sovereign entity, natural rights do not exist.

Many modern definitions and sensibilities do not necessarily distinguish between "religion" and "God," and many present-day people do not make the distinction. Modern distortions of these realities have obfuscated many of the issues related to this essential aspect of our modern free society.

To a person of the eighteenth century, religion is a manmade structure and organization administered by people. Judaism, Islam, and the various Christian denominations are a few examples of religion to an eighteenth-century person. Faith, on the other hand, is a very personal relationship between the Creator God and the individual. This Puritan concept of our Creator God is not seen through the eyes of an organized religion with leaders and followers, rather it's a very specific, special, and unique relationship between two entities.

Freedom of speech is the right to express one's conscience, but there are limits to this concept. People have the right to express their conscience, and others have the right to listen if they choose. No one has the right to silence a speaker, and no listener is obligated to pay attention. People who shut down or interrupt other people speaking are violating a person's right to free speech; they are not exercising it. Voices who are attempting to start an immediate panic without cause are not exercising free speech; they are simply endangering others. Noise ordinances are not necessarily violations of free speech, as the level of sounds, measured in decibels, should not be beyond what is generally acceptable and necessary to be heard by those who choose to listen.

Freedom of the press is another issue obfuscated in modern times. Today "the press" is seen as organizations whose profession is to uncover and report news. While this is certainly a part of the press, there are many others that meet the definition. Originally, "the press," meant those who used the printing press to communicate information. Anyone with a printing press was considered a part of it, such as pamphleteers. Today, we don't necessarily have printing presses for the dissemination of information. New technologies such as radio, television, and the internet make it possible for almost anyone to be considered exercising freedom of the press. All should be respected, and none should be silenced.

The right to peacefully assemble is certainly protected, but this also has limits, as no one has the right to block public access to a street or building. People or organizations that do so are violating other people's right to move freely. Peacefully assembling also means being nonviolent. People who are violent while assembling, or towards nonviolent assemblers, are violating the rights of others to peacefully assemble.

The redress of grievances is an ongoing process because, as one group gets its desired results, there will be others that did not. Everyone has grievances, since we all live in an imperfect world. As anyone who has worked for the public or in any office or work environment knows, grievances are never ending. It's simply part of the human condition.

Amendment II:

"A well-regulated Militia, being necessary to the security of a free State, the right of the people to keep and bear Arms, shall not be infringed."

The right to bear arms is the last line of defense against government tyranny. This individual sovereign and popular sovereign right of the eighteenth century has become muddied and confused in our twenty-first century sensibilities and interpretations. To understand it, however, we must first look to the sensibilities of the people who wrote the Second Amendment to the United States Constitution.

Like the ancient Romans (during the republican era), the founders and framers of our Freedom Charters were fearful of government tyranny. They were fixated on the ideas of liberty and fearful of the powers that strong central governments could be used against the states or the people, but state governments could also misuse their powers against the people. The British Empire attempted to control the colonies and the people through a large standing army, some quartered in people's homes, that was used to spy, intimidate, and enforce the King's will.

Americans did not want to have a large standing United States military for fear that it would be used in the same manner. With a small federal force, each state was charged with maintaining a state militia necessary to maintain internal order and protection from external threats (mobs, other states, the federal government, Indian tribes, or other countries). States do not have the funding sources of the federal government, so many state militias were voluntary and fully supplied by the militiamen themselves.

Although a state militia was not a standing army, the founders knew that it, too, could be used to infringe on the rights of citizens. To counterbalance the need for state militias, the founders wrote that individual citizens had the right to keep and bear arms. This would allow for militiamen to have quick and easy access to their firearms and give individuals or groups of individuals an opportunity to defend themselves from the state militias that could be used to intimidate or control the population. The founders had an intense distrust of powerful governments, and they figured that at some point a President might use the federal army against a state(s), or a state governor could use a state militia against the people. Both events have occurred in the past 250 years.

So, if we understand the mindsets of the people who wrote the second amendment, it is not a mystery at all. "A well-regulated Militia" (which is a state-sponsored military rather than a large national military), "being necessary to the security of a free State" (the militias have to exist in order to protect the state from internal disorder or foreign invasion), "the right of the people to keep and bear Arms, shall not be infringed" (the people have the right to possess private firearms for use in the militia and in order to ensure that militias are not used against the people (as individuals or as a population).

Present sensibilities confuse this amendment for several reasons. First, many people are not educated about American history and do not understand the evolution of American thought and culture. Second, hunting and personal self-defense are two added bonuses to having privately owned firearms. Because this is how they are most often used, people tend toward the idea that the right to keep and bear arms was only meant for those purposes. Third, many people believe that the only reason for the people to keep and bear arms was for serving in the militias. Since 1916, the federal government has taken partial control of the state militias for training and quick access to reserve units. State militias were replaced with National Guard units who are completely supplied by the federal government.

So, if people wrongly believe the right to keep and bear arms was only to serve in the state militia, then there is no reason for private individuals to possess firearms? No! A little understood purpose of the right to bear arms is that the people are the last line of defense against government tyranny. Police forces and standing armies can be misused against the people because lawmakers and their laws can ignore their constitutional roles to serve the interests of the people. Governments have vast resources, and an unarmed population could not possibly resist a tyrannical government. This has been proven time and again in countries run by dictators. Therefore, it comes down to the citizens, acting as individuals and in groups to protect their natural rights to life, liberty, and property by any legal means, and through armed force if necessary. This is not only a right in American society but also a responsibility and duty of every citizen to secure all natural rights for us and our posterity.

The first and second amendments to the U. S. Constitution are undoubtedly the most volatile and debated aspects of the Bill of Rights. This is because the rights they grant are used actively on a daily basis by many Americans rather than generally exist to passively protect the populace from unfair treatment.

Amendment III:

"No Soldier shall, in time of peace be quartered in any house, without the consent of the Owner, nor in time of war, but in a manner to be prescribed by law."

Coming directly from revolutionary war experiences, King George III quartered soldiers in private homes to supply his troops for free and to spy on and intimidate his subjects. This was specifically outlawed by the third amendment and has seemed to be a nonissue since. Time will tell, however.

Amendment IV:

"The right of the people to be secure in their persons, houses, papers, and effects, against unreasonable searches and seizures, shall not be violated, and no Warrants shall issue, but upon probable cause, supported by Oath or affirmation, and particularly describing the place to be searched, and the persons or things to be seized."

To be secure in our persons and personal belongings is a right of individual sovereignty. Privacy and private property are essential in a free society.

This amendment protects people from random and arbitrary intrusions and violations of their personal sovereignty.

Collectivists confiscate private properties and proclaim, "To each according to his needs and from each according to his abilities." This Marxist idea is greatly flawed, as is all of Marxism, because it does not recognize the inherent rights of the individual.

Marxism has been an ongoing threat to Americanism since the nineteenth century. Marxism has changed its name many times to hide its presence, as this philosophy has been discredited time and again for centuries. One tactic of Marxism, and any collectivist philosophy, is to hijack words that mean something benign and use them as cover in propagating their agenda of ultimate control of all entities.

Amendment V:

"No person shall be held to answer for a capital, or otherwise infamous crime, unless on a presentment or indictment of a Grand Jury, except in cases arising in the land or naval forces, or in the Militia, when in actual service in time of War or public danger; nor shall any person be subject for the same offence to be twice put in jeopardy of life or limb; nor shall be compelled in any criminal case to be a witness against himself, nor be deprived of life, liberty, or property, without due process of law; nor shall private property be taken for public use, without just compensation."

This famous amendment is often used in crime and court shows to illustrate how the accused has the right to be silent and not answer questions. This is because the evidence presented should be sufficient for a conviction and the trickiness of language can be used by trained lawyers to outwit regular citizens who do not possess the same verbal skills or training. While this is certainly an essential right to anyone accused of a crime, it is just one aspect of a much more intricate constitutional law.

Capital crimes usually have very heavy sentences. Indictments from a grand jury are much more involved than an indictment from a single prosecutor. Grand juries are citizens held in reserve just to hear evidence presented by the prosecutor, and they must be convinced by evidence that a trial is warranted.

People serving in the military are in special circumstances that require a Uniform Code of Military Justice. Military people have their own system of justice that is appropriate for them because the nature of military life is very different than civilian life. Ironically, military court martials are much less frequent than one might think. While military life is much more severe and restrictive than civilian living, members of the military are much less eager to inflict judgments on other service people because of the harshness of that profession. Also, military people already get a bad rap for being more extreme in their personalities, so court martials are more of an embarrassment for the military who would rather not have the negative press.

Double jeopardy is a term used to describe the right to not be tried for the same crime twice, but this applies to a specific instance of crime and not the crime in general. For example, if someone has been found not guilty of murder in a specific instance, this does not mean they cannot be tried for a different murder if one is accused. Also, the court system does not allow courts to manipulate people's futures by putting them on trial for the same offence until they get a conviction.

Life, liberty, and property are natural rights of the highest order. Therefore, people can only be deprived of these essential aspects of existence through due process of law. This means that the law must already exist before the act is committed or supposedly committed. Due process means that the process of justice has also already been established before the crime was supposed to have been committed and everyone is entitled to the same processes involved in the defense of an accused person.

The government taking private land for public use happens often for the building of roads, military use, expansion of government projects and government services, or environmental preservation. Seizing private property is something that should not be taken lightly, but if all other possibilities have been reasonably exhausted, it is the right of the owner(s) to be fairly compensated by the government before they take possession. Private property is a sacred right in American culture and each time a government entity seizes some, personal sovereignty and freedom are eroded.

Amendment VI:

"In all criminal prosecutions, the accused shall enjoy the right to a speedy and public trial, by an impartial jury of the State and district wherein the crime shall have been committed, which district shall have been previously ascertained by law, and to be informed of the nature and cause of the accusation; to be confronted with the witnesses against him; to have compulsory process for obtaining witnesses in his favor, and to have the Assistance of Counsel for his defence."

Tactics of tyranny often take the form of criminal accusations. If a government entity is abusing its power, it tends to try certain strategies. One is to have a closed trial in which the public is not able to witness the processes. Another is to prolong a trial so it takes years to complete. This harasses the defendant and drains the limited resources of an individual or organization, whereas the government has comparatively unlimited resources.

Another tactic of tyrants is not sharing with the accused exactly what charges they are facing. This vagueness is called "privileged information," and when the accused does not know the crime of accusation, there is no possibility of providing a competent defense. Also, the accused has the right to face the accuser; otherwise, accusations can be hidden behind a veil of uncertainty or even invented by the prosecution.

The assistance of counsel is another right because everyone has the right to a legal defense, and most people are not familiar enough with laws and court proceedings to protect themselves properly. Even if a person is blatantly guilty of a crime, the sentence needs to be in proper proportion to the offense. A competent legal defense can provide this.

Unfortunately, people with fewer financial resources tend to have a defense attorney assigned by the state. While these attorneys are mostly capable, they do not have the staff or the resources that are provided to prosecuting attorneys. The assignment of legal defense from the state is often considered a benefit rather than a right. It's my humble thinking that public defenders should have at least the same support from the state as the public prosecutors.

Amendment VII:

"In Suits at common law, where the value in controversy shall exceed twenty dollars, the right of trial by jury shall be preserved, and no fact tried by a jury, shall be otherwise re-examined in any Court of the United States, than according to the rules of the common law."

Trial by jury is an ancient right that has come down to us through many channels. The need for a jury of peers is important but sometimes difficult to define. There are plenty of people in this world who many of us would not consider our peers, but ordinary people in society tend to fit the bill.

The jury selection process requires both legal sides to examine potential jurors, and there are certain standards that must be followed to obtain a jury free of prejudice. This is a tall order in any human society because prejudice and bias are always found in people due to various personality types, experiences, heritages, education levels, incomes, and many other factors.

What's important is to find people who believe in fairness and justice based on the evidence presented and not on preconceived notions, another challenging task.

Amendment VIII:

"Excessive bail shall not be required, nor excessive fines imposed, nor cruel and unusual punishments inflicted."

This amendment is extremely subjective as to what constitutes excessive, cruel, and unusual. Generally, however, people can discern this based on common sensibilities, and fair-minded people tend to use themselves as a mode of comparison in an empathetic approach to what they think others are or would be experiencing. This can be helpful, but not always.

It seems that, as time has passed, punishments tend to be much less harsh than they once were. There is a balancing point where the punishment should fit the crime. This is true in both directions. The prospect of an open and public trial, as well as judicial review, can help achieve and maintain a balance in this process.

Amendment IX:

"The enumeration in the Constitution, of certain rights, shall not be construed to deny or disparage others retained by the people."

The enumerated rights in the United States Constitution are the rights specified to the federal government. Those rights are limited in scope and number. The rights of the people in the constitution are reserved rights. This means there is no numerical restriction. If the rights of the people were enumerated, then they would only be limited to what is written in the constitution. There is no possible way for a document to list every single individual right that exists or could exist in the future due to societal or technological change.

Amendment X:

"The powers not delegated to the United States by the Constitution, nor prohibited by it to the States, are reserved to the States respectively, or to the people."

This constitutional amendment confirms that rights not enumerated to the federal government or reserved by the states are for the people.

It protects the state entities by granting them reserved rights that are implied from the limitedly defined rights of the federal government.

The entire Bill of Rights is designed to protect certain natural rights of populations and individuals. Additional rights are reserved and can be determined by present and future generations. This is yet another example of how our Freedom Charters are not meant for one or for several generations, but for *all* present and future generations.

CHAPTER 24

We the Sovereigns and Our Freedom Charters

Throughout human history, sovereignty was associated with royalty. It was believed that God or the gods ordained an individual or a group of individuals as sovereign rulers over the people. In the eighteenth century after Christ, the United States of America declared that the people are the sovereign rulers of a country, and this follows a clear and deliberate process beginning with our Creator God.

God is the first sovereign. He created humans in His image and placed them on earth. This gave humanity, sovereignty over the earth. Each person is an individual and begins as an individual sovereign. Individuals form society. Society consists of all individual people living in our communities, and all our communities form populations of "We the people."

In the United States, "We the People" are the first sovereigns. Power is first distributed to every individual person, but full power is not instituted to an individual until the age of consent, which is 18 years of age. From birth to 18 years, a person is legally classified as a minor and has certain rights but is still the responsibility of their parents or an assigned legal guardian.

"We the People" formed our government through the Constitution of the United States of America. In our constitutional republic, it was written that each state of the United States would also form a constitutional republican government, but its constitutions cannot conflict with the federal constitution. The United States Constitution establishes the divisions and roles of our federal government. Anything not written in the constitution for our federal government becomes the responsibility and right of the individual state or the people of that state.

Within a state, people can form legally recognized organizations. These organizations have legal protections and are also considered sovereign. So, the four sovereign classifications are: the population, every individual in that population, private and public organizations, and all elements of our local, state, and federal governments.

In the United States of America, division of power is an essential aspect for its sustainability and success. It's the proper role, distribution, and balancing of these responsibilities and rights, along with their rational implementation, that promote stability and the general welfare of all involved. Through my studies on this topic, I believe I have identified five rights essential to any sovereign entity. This is not to say there aren't more, but this is what I believe I have found.

They are: 1. The Right to Exist, 2. The Right to Defense, 3. The Right to Own Property, 4. The Right to Navigate Freely, 5. The Right to Communicate Freely. It is important to note that no entity can take away these rights from others except through due process of human laws, which are rooted in natural laws and derived from divine laws.

1. The Right to Exist is the right to being. This includes the physical being and the being of conscience.
2. The Right to Defense is the right to self-preservation. All sovereign entities have a right to defend themselves from any others who would attack, damage, or kill them or others.

3. The Right to Own Property is the right to have one's own private and public land, money, objects, documents, and so forth.
4. The Right to Navigate Freely is the right of movement. All sovereign entities have a right to move about freely in communities, the states, and the nation.
5. The Right to Communicate Freely is the right to conscience and the right to communicate any thoughts and feelings of that conscience to others.

While every sovereign entity needs the others to perform certain duties, these sovereigns sometimes have conflicting interests or desires. The legal process established by our Constitution was designed to create laws to address and resolve conflicts when they arise.

I have identified 16 scenarios in which sovereign entities would require a resolution to conflicting interests. While some resolutions may be self-evident, others are not. The first entity is the claimant, and the second entity is the respondent. They are:

1. Individual v. Individual
2. Individual v. People
3. Individual v. Organization
4. Individual v. Government
5. People v. Individual
6. People v. People
7. People v. Organization
8. People v. Government
9. Organization v. Individual
10. Organization v. People
11. Organization v. Organization

12. Organization v. Government
13. Government v. Individual
14. Government v. People
15. Government v. Organization
16. Government v. Government

My next book will define a systematic process, reasoned through the premises of our Freedom Charters and based on each of the sixteen scenarios. It will address general and specific issues facing our nation today. It will not attempt to dictate or impose any predetermined outcomes but how each entity can have their issues addressed and resolved with regard to their status and role as a sovereign entity. The ultimate purpose of this process will be the satisfaction and general welfare of all legal entities within the premises of *OUR FREEDOM CHARTERS*.

About the Author:

John Pitkethly earned a bachelor's degree in Sociology and a master's degree in Counselor Education from the University of Central Florida. He lives with his wife and two children in north central Florida.

Made in United States
Orlando, FL
27 June 2025

62424802R00184